Madame Chiang Kai-shek
and Miss Emma Mills

Madame Chiang Kai-shek and Miss Emma Mills

*China's First Lady
and Her American Friend*

Thomas A. DeLong

McFarland & Company, Inc., Publishers
Jefferson, North Carolina, and London

Thomas A. DeLong is also the author of *Radio Stars: An Illustrated Biographical Dictionary of 953 Performers, 1920 through 1960* (McFarland, 1996; softcover 2006)

LIBRARY OF CONGRESS CATALOGUING-IN-PUBLICATION DATA

DeLong, Thomas A.
  Madame Chiang Kai-shek and Miss Emma Mills : China's first lady and her American friend / Thomas A. DeLong.
    p.   cm.
  Includes bibliographical references and index.

  ISBN-13: 978-0-7864-2980-6
  (softcover : 50# alkaline paper) ∞

  1. Chiang, May-ling Soong, 1897–2003. 2. Presidents' spouses—China—Biography. 3. Presidents' spouses—Taiwan—Biography. 4. Mills, Emma, 1894–1987. 5. United States—Biography. I. Title. II. Title: China's first lady and her American friend.
  DS777.488.C515D45   2007
  951.24'905092—dc22   2006103266

British Library cataloguing data are available

©2007 Thomas A. DeLong. All rights reserved

No part of this book may be reproduced or transmitted in any form or by any means, electronic or mechanical, including photocopying or recording, or by any information storage and retrieval system, without permission in writing from the publisher.

On the cover: background frames and flowers by Kate Irwin; from left (detail) Madame Chiang, February 1943 (Copyright Washington Post, reprinted by permission of the DC Public Library); Emma, 1924, while living in Peking (Mills–DeLong collection)

Manufactured in the United States of America

McFarland & Company, Inc., Publishers
  Box 611, Jefferson, North Carolina 28640
  www.mcfarlandpub.com

To the memory of my late sister
Nancy DeLong Whiteford:
Ultimate Caregiver

Acknowledgments

When Madame Chiang Kai-shek died in October 2003 at age 106, many were surprised to learn that this world-renowned figure had been living quietly, not in Nationalist China, but in Manhattan for several decades. An icon from mid–20th century history, Madame Chiang, in the words of that old military barracks ballad, had faded away like an old soldier. Yet to longtime friends and their offspring, this First Lady of China remained a vivid memory and commanding presence of the global war years and mainland civil war struggle, and later with General Chiang Kai-shek and his government on the island outpost once known as Formosa.

This is the first full and close up biography of Madame Chiang—a subject overlooked for decades. When General Chiang's long tenure as president of Free China ended at his death in 1975, it was thought his widow, a well educated and prolific writer-speechmaker, would pen an autobiography.

On the other hand, her Wellesley College classmate and closest American friend and confidante was well qualified to write her life story. Emma De Long Mills, however, kept to a long set rule: no writing nor interviews during the lifetime of the former Mayling Soong. Since Mills died in 1987, 16 years before Mayling, I, as one of her heirs, was left a treasure trove, along with Wellesley College, of letters, journals, photographs, and various papers on the lives of Mayling and my cousin Emma.

I am grateful to their alma mater for preserving correspondence between the two women covering the period 1917 to the 1970s, and incorporating these letters into the file of Emma Mills. College Archivist Wilma R. Slaight and her assistant Jean N. Berry provided gracious access and fielded numerous questions and requests. Professor Jing-heng Ma of the Department of East Asian Languages and Literatures and Chinese Program encouraged me to complete my task.

Columbia University's East Asian collections, a venerable source of information, opened their doors. Emma studied at Columbia as a graduate student in the 1930s, and Butler Library's Special Collections encompass the records of the American Bureau for Medical Aid to China (ABMAC), a China relief group where she served as both volunteer and staff member. Once again, Columbia Oral History Research Office and its director, May Marshall Clark, served me well, as did Curator of Manuscripts Bernard R. Crystal and his staff.

The sections on Mayling's earliest days in America were written with the help of Summit (N.J.) Free Public Library and Head of Adult Services Robin Carroll-Mann, and the nearby Summit Historical Society and President Sheila Duetsch. Librarian John Strakosch Walz of Summit's Kent Place School shed light on that community's private schools. The Soong sisters' school days in Macon, Georgia, have been well documented by aid of the Washington Memorial Library's Christopher Stokes of its genealogical and historical section. Piedmont College's off-campus library services coordinator, Jennifer R. Inglis, provided material on Mayling's year in Demorest, and an inventory of her files. Lois Morris of the Meredith (N.H.) Public Library helped fill in a biographical gap, namely young Mayling's summer camp days, and family ties, in the Lake Winnipesaukee region.

The daughters of ABMAC longtime executive Allen Lau—Shirley Mow and Katherine Chann—shared their recollections. Shirley opened doors to key sources, and secured a copy of the insightful 1967 thesis of Peggy Ann Blumenthal at Radcliffe College titled "Philanthrophy and Politics: A Study of the American Bureau for Medical Aid to China." Wellesley '15 Dickey Griffin Lightner's three daughters, Dickey Billings, Jane Meads and Shirley Paxton, spoke of the campus of their mother's day and later as undergraduates themselves from the late 1930s to early 1950s.

Long-standing family friends Marylin Chu Chou and Dr. Kitty Chen Dean brought a great measure of Chinese life and culture into my life. Helen Ericson recounted her close association with Emma, beginning at the China Institute circa 1950. Sydney Greenberg, once a GI in China, vividly recalled his encounter with General Chiang. Allen B. Cohen, executive director of the Chinatown Planning Council from 1968 to 1978, and later senior advisor under the retitled Chinese-American Planning Council, spoke of the agency's beginnings in New York. Anna Chennault, widow of General Claire Chennault, shared memories of her friendship with Mme Chiang, godmother of her two daughters. Rita Ferris Briggs, Ursula Van Arnam, Sally Sells Bryan, Robert B. Oxnam, Michele Oka Doner, Rev. Loring Ensign, Joseph Kissane, and architectural historian Christopher Gray kindly contributed various items of knowledge to the text.

The UCLA Film and Television Archives, Los Angeles, provided newsreel clips, and the Museum of Television and Radio, New York, broadcast material. The Franklin D. Roosevelt Library at Hyde Park, N.Y.; Lilly Library of Indiana University; the Washingtoniana Division and the *Washington Star* Collection, District of Columbia Public Library, and Margaret Appleman; the China Institute, and the Pequot Library, Southport, Conn., provided significant assistance. Three other Connecticut libraries were of tremendous help with vintage periodicals, microfilm material, and interlibrary book loans: Westport Public Library, Fairfield Public Library, and Dimenna-Nyselius Library at Fairfield University. To the West, the Hoover Institution at Stanford University opened the Papers of T.V. Soong. Carol A. Leadenham, assistant archivist, as in the past, guided me to key documents. Professor Cornelius C. Kubler, chair of the Department of Asian Studies, and Chinese historian Annie Reinhardt at Williams College responded to my request for background reading on modern China. Keith Gallinelli, former Fairfield resident in Nanking, provided information on the Soongs' Shanghai home.

Interest, encouragement and support came from many directions, especially from Professor Thomas Curran of Sacred Heart University, Fairfield, Conn.; Andrea Azarm; Fred Edmiston; Joan Vanderpoel Gayley; Sheila Simon, and Susan Olsen, executive director of Woodlawn Cemetery.

Andrew L.Y. Hsia, director-general of the Taipei Economic and Cultural Office, New York, graciously responded, forwarding information from the Kuomintang in Taiwan.

Of all the people who have helped with the book, Professor Emeritus Richard C. DeAngelis of Fairfield University Department of History stands out. With a depth of knowledge of Chinese history, he was kind enough to read the text and offer suggestions. His insight and comments were invaluable.

I am grateful to Madame Chiang's secretary, Pearl Chen, for her part in arranging my 1972 visit with Mayling at the presidential residence, Taipei. To Jean and John Childs, special thanks for hospitality at their commodious home in Wellesley Hills during several research trips to the nearby college.

When the intricacies of word processing seemed insurmountable, my daughter Elizabeth D. Delvin never failed to come to my rescue, as did my sons-in-law Hank Delvin and Roy Ingerson, and daughter Sarah Ingerson. Proficient master of the computer and generous friend Denise Woods obligingly polished the copy into publisher-ready form. Zoltan Eszlari of Southport Computer Associates provided hard copy pages. And, above all, my never-ending thanks to my wife Katharine, who encouraged me to write this story of a long and unusual friendship between two remarkable women.

Southport, Connecticut
January 2007

Table of Contents

Acknowledgments   vii
Introduction   1

1. Shanghai   5
2. Nomads   16
3. Wellesley   23
4. Empathy   28
5. New Callings   36
6. West to East   40
7. Among Movers and Shakers   46
8. Sisterhood   55
9. In the Thick of Things   62
10. Sun's Successor   68
11. First Lady   78
12. Trouble Spots   87
13. Pen and Sword   97
14. A Tightening Grip   116
15. Agitation and Angst   127
16. Committed to Victory   138
17. The Common Battle and High Ideals   148
18. Homecoming   157
19. Table Talk   177

20. Victory Without Peace	193
21. Frequent Flyers	207
22. Milestones	221
Epilogue	232
Chapter Notes	235
Bibliography	245
Index	249

Introduction

Two very visible artifacts in the home where Emma De Long Mills grew up influenced the future path of her endeavors. Living with her parents in the New York townhouse of the maternal grandmother she called Ma, Mills frequently passed by the glass case containing the fragile, weather-beaten journal of grandfather George Washington De Long, a naval officer and commander of the long-ago Jeannette Arctic Expedition. For two and a half exasperating years he had entered a daily account of a quest for the North Pole, a voyage which ended in tragedy and his death in 1881. Inspired by his writing—edited and published by his widow Emma Wotton De Long soon after—young Emma at age 15 began her own journal. For the next seven and a half decades she periodically wrote of activities and milestones, travels and friends, observations and opinions.

As a toddler, she took a fancy to the decorative chinoiserie footboard of her mother's bed. It depicted a scene of an Oriental village with pagoda and plum trees, a steep, half-circle bridge crossing a placid pond, and figures busily engaged in life in a foreign and fascinating setting, not unlike the scene painted on blue Canton willowware. Ma and her generation often talked about growing up in France and Germany to such an extent that Emma sought another, and certainly more exotic, part of the world on which to focus and investigate. And so it was that as she grew up she turned to China.

A bright and eager student, she opted to continue her education at a four-year women's college. When the overbearing Ma, who held the purse strings for virtually her entire family, heard of Emma's plans to enroll at Wellesley, she caustically—and prophetically—remarked that a college degree pigeonholed a woman as a schoolmistress or an old maid, probably both. The daughter of a physician, Emma also developed an interest in medicine as well as literature and writing.

The future Madame Chiang Kai-shek came to America at age ten. Her father, Charlie Soong, poor yet ambitious, had left China at an early age to better himself. Soon steeped in American ways, he attracted the attention of missionary-minded Southerners who urged conversion to Christianity and supported his schooling to become a preacher. Returning to his homeland, Soong prospered as a printer of Bibles and a multi-faceted businessman. A foresighted patriot, he backed Sun Yat-sen as he endeavored to bring China out of its feudal existence. Above all, Soong was determined to send each of his six children to America for a Western education.

Mayling Soong, the youngest of his three daughters, grew up Americanized, far away from Shanghai and her parents. In 1913 at age 16, following schooling in New Jersey and Georgia, she entered Wellesley—one of the very few Oriental students then on campus.

A year later Mayling and Emma Mills were living in the same dormitory, where a close friendship unfolded and continued after graduation in 1917. At the former's urging—and the promise of a newspaper job—Emma soon traveled to Shanghai. Part of Mayling's extended family, she stayed in China as a tutor, librarian and journalist for three years, returning to New York for what she thought would be a short family visit. But it proved otherwise. She ended up again living with her aging grandmother, whom she viewed as a hopeless Victorian relic, a professional old lady—indeed, in 30-year-old Emma's eyes, a stumbling block to genuine independence and happiness.

Correspondence with Mayling continued until Mayling's marriage in December 1927 to General Chiang Kai-shek, an emerging leader of a turbulent country of some 450 million people. In 1927 Chiang's position was rather tenuous, as he faced a rising challenge from warlords and China's communist party. Yet with his military and political breakthrough, Mayling became First Lady of China.

In the 1930s Emma fitfully pursued a career as a writer with little success. A perennial student, she took university courses in composition, and studies related to the Far East. Above all, she enjoyed a large circle of friends, and the New York milieu of diverse lectures, concerts, plays and restaurants.

By 1937 Emma began to be caught up in the frequent discussion in newspapers, from lecture platforms and over the radio on developments in China. China was "talking" to Emma as it had again and again ever since her childhood. "I have felt, very definitely a drawing back to China. I suppose it started with my summer visits to Chinese museum collections, and my class talk on Chinese short stories, and then word from Mayling in China after so long an interval."

That year Japan invaded her Asian neighbor, marking the beginning of the undeclared Sino-Japanese War. Mayling called out for aid from American friends, particularly her Wellesley classmates. And she nurtured good will and alliances with Americans in high places: industrialist and presidential candidate Wendell Willkie, publisher Henry Luce, his wife Clare Boothe Luce, and President and Mrs. Franklin D. Roosevelt. But it was Emma who not only raised money to aid Chinese refugees and orphans but began a series of letters to Mayling describing the direction and attitudes of the isolationist United States government vis-à-vis China and the feelings of the man on the street in the struggle between Tokyo and Nanking.

In 1938 Mme Chiang acknowledged the letters' value: "From them I get a very clear and comprehensive insight into the situation in America. I do not have any illusions about the attitude of mind there, because I know that a country where big minorities exist cannot, in international matters, carry on a definite and determined policy when the policy may affect other nations. I know that America is tired of being bled in war, or by wars. However, it is difficult to abandon one's old belief that Americans are inspired by ideals connected with the well-being of the distressed and the underdog."

Moreover, Emma was devoting several dozen hours a week as a volunteer at the newly organized American Bureau for Medical Aid to China. Encouraged by Mme Chiang, Emma helped to set up programs to secure and ship desperately needed medical supplies and equipment for China's beleaguered people, many homeless and faced with famine and disease.

The Pacific war changed the ostensibly rudderless life of Emma, and truly reconnected her to Mayling and China. Emma Mills became a leader of Chinese medical and educational panels and surveys, and in the 1960s, a founder of the Chinatown Planning Council, a multi-service agency assisting New York's growing Chinese immigrant community. At age 74 in 1968 this "old China hand" was elected the first Westerner—and woman—to serve as that group's president. When she died nearly two decades later, Chinese in the United States and overseas had few non–Chinese friends more loyal, resourceful and hardworking.

At middle age during World War II she looked back—and ahead—with the observation, "I was never made for a life of inactivity or solitude or routine."

A friendship that began on a New England college campus grew in strength. Emma became the First Lady of China's closest American confidante, their friendship solidified by the charismatic Mayling's extended visits to New York and Emma's ready availability for assistance, accommodation, and companionship.

Although the Allies expelled the Japanese invaders in 1945, the Generalissimo and Mayling faced Chinese communist forces in a civil war. The Nationalist government fell, then fled from the mainland to offshore Formosa in 1949–50. Chiang and his Lady, reduced in power and scope, nonetheless remained as presidential leaders, ever hopeful of returning to Nanking.

Goaded and encouraged by many to utilize her recollections of China, Emma gave serious thought to a book. Yet she felt uncomfortable about borrowing or extracting material from her very own journal when so much of it focused on the enticing yet controversial Mayling and her family, and on her friends, both Chinese and non–Chinese. She decided not to capitalize or profit from this intimacy with one of the most celebrated and powerful figures of the 20th century. For posterity, their correspondence and Emma's journals record moments and experiences, often close up, and document contemporary issues and results, be it in China or America.

Mayling—her husband's interpreter and adviser and her country's propagandist and heroine—likewise never wrote an autobiography of her long and momentous life in two contrasting worlds.

A record of the unparalleled lives of Mayling and Emma, as I viewed it, need not be lost to posterity. I gathered the pieces—excerpts from countless letters and a bookshelf of journals, segments from published recollections and histories, and insights from interviews of those who knew Mme Chiang and my cousin Emma De Long Mills*—to present this well-documented narrative.

The resulting book on Mayling and Emma spans most of the 20th century. It uses the Wade-Giles system's geographical designations (e.g., Peking rather than Beijing; Canton rather than Guangzhou) then in place. It is not a political or military account of modern China, yet aspects of both influence the narrative of this intimate, sisterly camaraderie of Mayling Chiang and Emma Mills.

---

*DeLong, a compact version of the family name, came into use in the mid–1900s.

1

Shanghai

The first leg of the long journey home ended in Vancouver. A week's train ride across miles and miles of scorched Canadian plains and dizzying mountains left 20-year-old Mayling Soong tired and nervous. There were reminders of the Great War as they traveled West: a whole trainful of returning Canadian soldiers and a trainload of Chinese laborers on their way to France to work as road crews, stevedores and coal miners. "If ever I have any influence, I shall see to it that no coolies are shipped out," Mayling wrote to college classmate Emma Mills from Hotel Vancouver, "for China needs all her own men to develop the mines."[1]

Within a day, she boarded a Canadian Pacific steamship for China, accompanied by her older brother, and guardian-chaperone, Tse-vung (T.V.) Soong, who had taken a job at New York's International Banking Corporation and extended his education at Columbia graduate school to be near Wellesley College in New England. In July 1917 both returning students, Mayling and T.V., anxiously looked ahead to a reunion with their parents in Shanghai, Mayling Olive Soong's birthplace in 1897.

The Soong children were raised as practicing Christians and disciplined students. At an early age they attended Sunday school and were tutored in Chinese language characters and traditional culture. Above all, basic English. The three Soong daughters at age five started their education at Huchun Girls' School, a U.S. missionary–run school, followed by McTyeire, an upper-class Methodist boarding school for girls in Shanghai. Chubby Mayling with pigtails and outfitted in bulky cotton-padded clothes made few friends. Tense and frightened in unfamiliar surroundings, she complained of lack of sleep. Mrs. Soong quickly withdrew her, hiring a private tutor at home. She returned to McTyeire a year or so later, and fared well.

In 1907, ten-year-old Mayling begged her parents to allow her to go to the United States to school with her next-to-oldest sister, Chingling. They agreed, albeit reluctantly, and Chingling and Mayling left China, accompanied by a maternal uncle, Wan Bing Chung, who as a governmental commissioner had been sent by the dowager empress (Tzu Hsi) to study economics. The first-

Wellesley senior—and thoroughly Americanized—Mayling Soong commented as she prepared to return to Shanghai, "The only thing Chinese about me is my face." (Mills–DeLong collection.)

born Soong, Ailing, was already attending college in the States. Her well-to-do parents had programmed all their children to enroll in American schools. "My parents seemingly broke every Chinese tradition in sending me as a child America-ward to study instead of accumulating money for an ample dowry," Mayling later explained. "They were but fulfilling their vision of what educated women could contribute toward a strong revitalized modern China. My mother particularly personified the inner urge to seek intellectual truths."[2]

Years later Mayling explained to Emma Mills how her schooling in America came about. Three days before Chingling sailed, this younger sibling protested over being left out—more so because a cousin, too, prepared for the journey to America and would "get ahead" of her if sent there. Chingling, however, complained that Mayling was always tagging after her and disgracing her at school by her lack of tact. The Soongs laughed at the idea of their youngest daughter leaving home, but she pleaded and pleaded. Mayling had just gotten a new batch of summer clothes, so there was not that excuse. After it was decided in her favor, she fell ill, but wouldn't admit it for fear the Soongs wouldn't let her go.[3]

Their two youngest daughters, and a cousin, all shepherded by their uncle, sailed aboard the *Manchuria* for San Francisco.

Mayling, age 10, and Chingling, 15, were enrolled at Miss Potwin's School in Summit, New Jersey, a small co-ed school. Its headmistress had close family contacts with overseas Chinese who wished to have their children come to the United States, and she periodically had them boarding with her. Although Mayling endured bouts of homesickness, she kept pace with her schoolmates, and outside the classroom joined in to skate, picnic and cut paper dolls. A favorite retreat, the nearby town library, led her to books ranging from Peter Rabbit to Dickens. She developed a system of watching outside the library until she was sure that she would have the librarian and library entirely to herself.[4]

The school year in New Jersey passed quickly. Mayling and Chingling spent the first of a number of summers at camp in Fairmont, North Carolina, and on New Hampshire's Lake Winnipesaukee. Run by Harriet Moses in picturesque Meredith, the lakeside camp gave Mayling her initial exposure to New England, and an opportunity to play tennis. Years later, nephew Louis Kung and his wife, movie actress Debra Paget, came to nearby Wolfeboro Neck, where their quarters became known as the Chiang Kai-shek estate. Mayling visited there on several occasions, and a caretaker recalled soldiers with rifles guarding the roads and gatehouse, and boats and helicopters arriving at night. In September 1908 the two Soong sisters joined their older sister Ailing at a Methodist school in Macon, Georgia. Ailing, an 18-year-old senior at Wesleyan, had entered that women's institution four years earlier. The quiet and mature Chingling was readily accepted. But what to do with little "May," who, of course, was far from the college level, even high school. Nonetheless, she insisted on accompanying Chingling.

The youngest pupil at Wesleyan, and not a bona fide student, she was privately tutored by a college teacher, Margie Burke, whose mother, also a professor there, assumed the role of foster mother. Burke guided Mayling's education, and disciplined her when needed, shopped with her, and made her dresses. A strong influence on the youngster, much of Mayling's future idealism could be traced to Burke's teachings.

A precocious, high-spirited child, Mayling fell into mischief easily, for which she could usually be forgiven because of her quick and clever wit. Once, when lipstick and rouge were considered brazen, an older student said accusingly to her, "Why Mayling, I believe your face is painted!" to which she replied without hesitation, "Yes, China-painted!"[5]

Apparently Mayling needed closer supervision and schooling not available at Wesleyan. Her eighth-grade studies were completed at the Methodist-founded Jesse S. Green Institute, affiliated with Piedmont College in nearby Demorest, Georgia. During the academic year 1909-10 she excelled there in all of her courses except arithmetic. Mayling later wrote that at Piedmont she learned English grammar and rhetoric to the degree that "sessions of wrestling with rambling phrases and split infinitives" had honed her ability to speak and write well. Piedmont's students were largely young adults who had taught in rural primary schools to get the funds necessary to enroll there for further education. "All these people were greatly interested in me," she wrote some 20 years later, "and, for my part, I began to get an insight into the lives of those who had to struggle for a living."[6] (In 1968 Piedmont's president James Walter, while on a world tour with history professor Arthur Rinden, Congregational minister Loring Ensign, and 12 undergraduates, conferred an honorary degree on Mayling at a brief ceremony at the Presidential Residence, Taipei.)

Back in Macon for high school, Mayling moved into a dormitory, sharing quarters with two other specially chosen youngsters—Eloise Ainsworth, daughter of Wesleyan's president, and Marjorie Gugel, niece of a college official. Beginning the study of Latin, Mayling coined a name for this inseparable trio—the tri-puellate. These three frivolous juveniles often raced through the corridors of the main building, kept up with everybody's business and had a finger in many pies. Nonetheless, they sometimes quarreled. Mrs. Ainsworth once lectured Mayling about losing her temper. "Aren't you ashamed?" she admonished. The reply came back accompanied by a sly twinkle in her dark eyes. "No, Mrs. Ainsworth. I rather enjoy it."

In the fall of 1912 Chingling, who had distinguished herself by writing a perceptive college paper titled "The Influence of Foreign Educated Students in China," began her final year in Macon, and Mayling, her college freshman term. Mayling's class elected her sergeant-at-arms, and she proudly carried its banner and led the cheering at special gatherings. She also joined the tennis club.

The young Soong sisters—part of the new emerging China that pushed aside the centuries-old practice of bound feet to restrain movement as well as attract the opposite sex—transformed their demeanor, slang and appearance into American ways as much as possible. Their clothes were made in American fashion, but quite often were of Chinese fabric sent from Shanghai. In the years ahead Mayling kept in touch with her Wesleyan friends. "What of the old maids in our class?" she once wrote to a classmate several decades after leaving Macon at the end of her freshman year. "What are they doing — 'waiting or baiting'?"

An American education remained a priority for the Soong family, yet none had left home at such an early age as Mayling.

Her father, Soong Yao-ju, as a young Chinese with few opportunities in his native Hainan, had been sent to the States and adopted by a sonless uncle in Boston. There, he worked as an apprentice in a family shop selling silk and tea. But the restless and unschooled Soong, Westernized with the name Charlie, sought an education, and in frustration over his menial work and lack of opportunity, stowed aboard a U.S. revenue cutter. The captain, upon discovery of Charlie, assigned him to the crew as a cabin boy. The ship docked in Wilmington, North Carolina, where Captain Jones, a zealous leader in a community of Southern Methodists, oversaw Soong's conversion to Christianity. (Thereupon, Soong added "Jones" as his middle Westernized name.) A local benefactor, ex–Confederate general Julian Carr, took him in as a member of his household and sent Charlie to a small college then known as Trinity, which later became Duke University. The school's president and his wife helped with preparatory studies, even individually tutoring him in English grammar. In 1882 he shifted to Vanderbilt University, whose president, Bishop Holland McTyeire, also had charge of Southern Methodist missionary work in China. Soong returned to China as an itinerant preacher and teacher in Shanghai. He soon turned to business pursuits, including the publishing of Bibles and, secretly, revolutionary pamphlets, and eventually the running of cotton and flour mills. In 1887, age 21, he married Ni Kwei-tseng, a well-to-do and well-connected young woman but above all, a devout Christian, who shared his commitment to religion, education and business. There would be six Soong children—three daughters and three sons—and all were schooled in America over a span of some 25 years, beginning in the early 1900s.

When Chingling graduated from Wesleyan in 1913, Mayling moved on, with a very definite Southern accent and outlook, to Wellesley College near Boston and T.V., then a Harvard upperclassman.

Both brother and sister were exceptional students—part of a new wave of Chinese students in America who would return to their homeland to lead their people in the fields of government, education, medicine and engineering. By 1917 T.V. and Mayling knew the school days with their high measure of independence and indulgence were quickly coming to an end. Within the disciplined and devout household of the Soongs, American and Chinese ways and bearing often would be in conflict.

Aboard ship as the Canadian shoreline passed from view, Mayling felt pangs of homesickness for the United States and her school friends. They had predicted such nostalgia at her send-off from New York's Grand Central Station. "The only thing Chinese about me," remarked Mayling, "is my face."[7]

Of her classmates gathered at the departing train, Emma Mills would miss her Asian school pal the most. She claimed a strong interest in the Far East before ever meeting her and sharing a dormitory. Nonetheless, their friendship fueled Emma's engrossing fascination with China.

Prior to college, Emma had seen little of her own native land, let alone a foreign country. Born in Stamford, Connecticut, on September 16, 1894, the daughter of Walter and Sylvie De Long Mills, she grew up in New York City, living in an upper West Side townhouse designed by well-known architect Clarence True at 324 West 89th Street, near Riverside Drive. The home of her widowed maternal grandmother, the dwelling had ample space for her mother and father — a noted homeopathic physician — a younger brother, several cousins, and occasionally an aunt and uncle, plus a cook and a maid.

A governess-teacher joined the household when Emma reached age four. She and her brother, De Long Mills, received virtually all their primary education at the side of this woman. At age 15 she enrolled at nearby St. Agatha's, a private Episcopal Church–sponsored girls' school from which she graduated in 1913. An above-average student, she set a lifetime goal of reading 10,000 books — a passion that never dimmed. And her letters and journals reveal an erudite and keenly observant writer. Her vivid recollections of 89th Street at the turn of the century include the building of the grandiose 20-room Isaac Rice Mansion and the dedication of the stately Soldiers and Sailors Monument. In the middle of the block between West End Avenue and 89th Street, in a shrubby lot, remained an old and abandoned wooden farm dwelling — a remnant of mid–19th century West Side rural living. In Emma's leisure, she took piano lessons and birdwatching walks along the Hudson in Riverside Park and on elegant Riverside Drive, and spent summers on a family farm in New Market, New Jersey. She had more than her share of childhood illnesses, including a near-fatal case of typhoid fever. (The infamous carrier of the disease, Typhoid Mary, once worked as a domestic in a neighboring brownstone.)[8]

In early August 1917 Mayling mailed a seven-page letter to Emma in New York — the first of many from Shanghai. Men, she noted, had already started to call on her, coming from as far as Peking. There had been no lack of suitors at Wellesley or en route to China. Aboard ship, an architect of Dutch-French background on his way to Sumatra proposed marriage, and, she exclaimed, "I lost my head.... The family here is greatly wrought up!" They were equally alarmed when as an undergraduate she had announced her engagement to a young Chinese at Harvard named Peter Li. A scion of a wealthy family in Kiangsui province, he explained they'd not wed without their parents' approval. Mayling agreed. Luckily for all parties, the unofficial engagement ended in a matter of weeks.

An unhindered, vivacious free spirit, who for nearly ten years had lived without parental supervision in America, now faced family restrictions. "Mother and Father object to my seeing men ... as they don't want me to get

Emma Mills graduated Wellesley shortly after the United States declared war on Germany in 1917. On the homefront she served as a Farmerette and army nurse. (Mills–DeLong collection.)

married for the next three years. As I am quite contented at home, I do not want to marry either—especially as I told you that I met 'my fate' on the boat. Since I cannot marry someone I really care for, I shall not marry for anything else except fame or money. All men are alike to me. I know I sound world-weary; but isn't [it] my luck though not to meet him until on my way home! The way the family scorns him because he is a foreigner would make you think that he is a Barbarian!"[9]

Other callers struck Mayling as immature or opportunistic. At dinners, she met mostly married—and prominent—older men. "And as I am still a 'jeune fille,' and have two married sisters, all I do is sit still and try to look pleasant. My sisters are planning to give me a large reception this fall—sort of a coming out party."

The spacious Soong residence served the needs of a large family. Located in the French Concession of the International Settlement at 491 Avenue Joffre, the European-style three-story dwelling contained 16 large rooms, not counting a big kitchen, plus verandahs and sleeping porches. Outside, amid the gardens, were a lawn tennis court and a croquet court. The servants' quarters, noted Mayling, outshone the drab dorm rooms at Wellesley.

The staff, consisting of five maids, seven men servants, a Chinese and a foreign cook, two coachmen and a handful of gardeners, now came partly under the supervision of newly returned Mayling. Mrs. Soong, however, continued to handle the bookkeeping end of the large household; low wages for domestic help allowed even the most modest of incomes a half-dozen servants. "It is very annoying sometimes, as I forget myself and speak in English to the servants. I forget that I am not speaking in Chinese. At times I cannot express myself in Chinese; then I ring for the butler who acts as interpreter. Of course ordinarily I can express my wishes. But at times, when I am displeased, all power of speaking in Chinese flies."[10]

Her mother also dropped in Mayling's lap the discipline of her two younger brothers, Tse-liang (T.L.) and Tse-an (T.A.). "I have complete control over the two boys, as Mother is so disgusted that she handed them over to me bodily. They are hard to manage, because they are decidedly clever and lazy at the same time. I have whipped the younger one several times, and they both are afraid of me. You don't know what a good disciplinarian I can be!"

Few letters to Emma Mills failed to ask her to arrange magazine subscriptions to such learned publications as *Scribners, Literary Digest, Atlantic Monthly*, and *New Republic*. For the latest in Western fashions, Mayling added to the list *Ladies' Home Journal*. Although she had reverted to traditional Chinese dress—especially the figure-clinging *chi-pao*—she often added Western touches. Shoes were important; she wrote Mills to send a dozen pair of shoe trees.

Mayling, once a late sleeper, no longer could bear to stay in bed late each morning. She began to rise at five-thirty to watch the sunrise and its fascinating mixture of colors, and to listen to the droning sing-song voices of laborers working in the fields. Coolies passing through the streets also sang "Hai Ho" and "Hi Ho" to each other. Her consciousness of outdoor sounds extended to an awareness of the growing plight of peasants. "There has been so much sickness in China. And with the awful, awful Tientsin flood, so much misery is everywhere. Sometimes when I look at the dirty, ragged swarming humanity in our slums, I feel the sense of utter futility in hoping for a great and new China, and the sense of my own smallness. You can not conceive how useless one feels in such surroundings. The percentage of poor here is greater then any you could conceive of in America."[11]

The devout Mrs. Soong actively gave time, energy and money to local charities. "All that is Western is not Christian," she reminded her daughter. Mayling soon agreed to teach Sunday school and assist charitable organizations two or three afternoons a week. Her mother was happy beyond words with these activities. Mayling stood out as the only female Sunday school teacher of boys, particularly as in their Methodist church the men and women sat in separate pews. Her students included a bright fellow of 14, who when eager to answer all the instructional questions, addressed her as "Sir."

Mayling augmented her volunteer work by serving on committees of the Shanghai YWCA and starting a conversational club in English for members. With the Social Committee she planned programs for the monthly meetings. "I rather like the work, for it makes me more interested in all sorts of people, and in a way forces me out of my natural tendency of indifference towards people in general." And participation on the National Film Censorship Committee of China required many hours of movie scrutiny. "Fancy a young, pure, and unsophisticated being censoring what should be instructive for the public!" She found most imported films on the whole very good, readily passing them in spite of "too much mushy love-making, and rolling around of eyes."

Mayling avoided discussion of Chinese political matters in her letters. She believed they would be censored—as occasionally were Emma's letters from the United States. Actually, none of the correspondence from Shanghai revealed any governmental editing. But for political news Mayling thought it wise to send copies of the *China Press*, an American-edited English language newspaper.

In December 1917, however, she wrote of tragedy close to home: the killing of the nephew of her brother-in-law (and husband of sister Chingling) Dr. Sun Yat-sen, looked up as the founder of modern China. The young nephew died from wounds suffered from a bomb by political agitators. In the years ahead Mayling would come to live with such violence close at hand. "Chinese politics is impossible; one never knows what next is going to happen, and one never knows when one's head is going to be the next chopped off."

Mayling celebrated her first Chinese independence day that year, on October 10, a national holiday. Mrs. Soong gave the servants the day off; the rest of the family took a drive by horse carriage, followed briefly by one in an automobile (that summer Mayling had insisted that her parents buy their first car to get about American-style). At the city's large markets on Nanking Road, the young Soongs bought vegetables and sweets from food stands. At home each member of the family prepared a dish. Mayling made fudge, apparently at age 20 her only culinary accomplishment. Father cooked fried chicken. Later, the Soong boys wanted to go to the horse races. Mother and Father, however, as pillars of the church, decided against attending such a sporting event. They settled on a ride to the Bund, the main thoroughfare along the riverfront, and on the way home bought hot, freshly roasted chestnuts. That evening some of the servants ended the holiday by sleeping in the stable. Although they were given the daytime off, several extended their celebration into the evening at a theatre. "Dad was furious, so he ordered all the doors locked. The poor knaves therefore had to spend the cold night out in the stable. I guess they won't steal out again."

The first of Mayling's persistent—and life-long—skin ailments flared up that fall. Called a severe case of acne, it led to hypodermic needle injections that continued for weeks, necessitating the wearing of a veil over her face whenever she ventured outside the house. "I am almost crazy. Finally I am trying some Chinese medicine which I hope will be effective." In desperation, she only went out at night, and with a heavily powdered face.

Weeks of shopping for family and servants preceded Mayling's first Christmas back in China. For staff, she bought handkerchiefs, socks, stockings, candy, oranges and cakes. The stockings, in turn, had to be filled with small gifts. Larger items were wrapped into colorful packages. And there were purchases of playthings for her 11-year-old brother and many young cousins, and of tree decorations. Christmas Day festivities began with firecrackers before everyone gathered around the table for a turkey dinner, American-style.

Among Mayling's gifts—brocades, silks and paintings—there arrived a veritable cartload of flowers, from a persistent suitor. Yet he followed up his largesse with an accusation: she had faked her facial illness in order to refuse his visits. He spread gossip that he had been treated not only without consideration but with actual contempt. His words left Mayling perplexed and furious, and she dropped this suitor, whose name was not revealed in her letters to Emma.

She gradually had become somewhat comfortable with being closely chaperoned and cloistered. "I never go anywhere without either a married sister or my mother," she reported to Emma, "and in fact never during my whole life have I known such strict chaperoning. And the curious part is that I am not resentful in the least; I am just passively acquiescing. You cannot believe this of the little vehement spitfire, can you? Yet it is true.

"And what is worse—I dislike seeing people, men especially. I hate to go down to the parlor. I prefer staying upstairs reading. I just feel my mental powers getting more and more dulled every day. I must make an effort to be intelligent and keep up interest, and not be worried because I see a speck of dust on the mantle piece."[12]

Mayling's calendar in the first months back in Shanghai was filled with notations on varied activities: tutoring her brothers, teaching Sunday school, volunteering at the Y, studying classic Chinese, attending lectures and teas, and planning dinner parties. Nevertheless, she fretted that her life lacked direction and purpose. The years of schooling in America seemed to bring no clear focal point or touchstone. Her siblings pointed her towards a proper marriage. Yet Mayling looked for something else. To Emma, she expressed a hunger for a pattern, a standard, a job.

"If I had a profession I could force myself to work, and work hard. I am not doing anything, and in all probability my brothers will be married within the next few years; naturally I would not care to be a burden to them. They would, of course, be good to me.... I can feel that my two married sisters are putting their heads together for me to make a 'grande alliance,' and brother is more or less acquiescent. You may rest assured that if they talk marriage to me any more, I am coming back to the States. At present, I am in disgrace in the family, because when one of my sisters suggested something to me about marriage, I shut up like a clam, and left the dinner table without a word. Today I refused to go down for meals, and am having my food sent up. Of course, I know that they mean to be kind, but I hate to be tampered with."[13]

Thoughts of an unpleasant marriage and meaningful occupation only made Mayling more "homesick" for America—and the relative freedom at college and the carefree camaraderie among classmates. If Emma only came to China, pleaded Mayling, things then would be clearer and more sorted out. For both of them.

2

Nomads

Mayling missed the urbanity of Emma Mills—her companionship and those of the old college crowd, their discussions and discourse. "You remember my saying that the average conversation between an average man and his wife would drive me to distraction. At present, I am wondering whether I could sustain even a semi-intelligent discussion. My brains seem terribly full of cobwebs."[1]

Pessimism and weariness became a frequent theme in her musings, at least to Emma. These early post-college letters addressed her as "Dada" and were signed "Daughter." During their senior year the word "Dada" was picked up from an avant-garde protest against war that spread from Europe to New York. It soon focused chiefly on a nihilistic approach to art and literature based upon spontaneity and nonsense without intervention of logic or speculative ideas. Provocative and sexually modern women led this movement against prejudice in the art world and feminine docility; this was something the nonconformist Emma connected to, perhaps as early as 1913, from several visits to the salient International Exhibition of Modern Art (the Armory Show), a progenitor of Dadaism. Hence, Emma chose "dada" as her tagline, and Mayling being two and a half years younger adopted the "daughter" appellative. Post-academe isolation entered into most daughter-to-dada letters. "I am feeling more than ever the futility of living, and oh, the eternal emptiness of life! And also the awful, awful loneliness of existence. I recall a quotation which goes something like this: 'Each of us is a nomad, separate, different and alone, each in its separate cell utterly unique, and cannot neither experience nor feel the experience of other nomads.'[2]

"Just think what life means, Dada. If one does not marry, then think of the long stretch of life ahead that has to be lived by oneself alone, for, of course, within a few years the other members of the family will have interests of their own. Again, if one does marry, then think of the awful, awful responsibilities of bringing up children—especially if one should happen to marry a man without great resources. At the same time if one married for wealth and ambition, think what it would amount to if after a short time, the man should lose his fortune. Such accidents often happen, and then there would not even be a particle of affection to keep up one's courage."[3]

There were, in fact, numerous men about, putting forth a case for her to settle down. But Mrs. Soong wanted Mayling to stay single for a few more years, and she acquiesced. "By the way," she informed Emma, "I told you about the millionaire here who wants to marry me, haven't I? Well, my relatives think I am a fool not to take him; however, I am such a fool that I can't realize I am a fool! One thing, though, these last six months out of college have opened my eyes to the value of money; at the same time they also have opened my eyes to the value of Self Respect. I shall never marry without money; at the same time equally certain am I that I shall never marry for money."[4]

Mayling was always eager to share an anecdote. One day she met a foreign missionary—a woman who asked her what she was doing for China. She replied that the hot climate that summer had drained her energy. The conversation turned to moving pictures, and the woman remarked that she had once gone to a movie. When she got up to leave the theatre, she felt spiritually grimy. No one could make her go again. Mayling replied that she thought movies were all right. The missionary then asked, "Would you like to be found there if Christ were to come back to the world?"

Mrs. Soong was considered one of the most upright and prominent Christians in Shanghai, so Mayling kept her silence. But she felt like saying, "Sure, provided that the movie was a screamingly funny one!"[5]

Mayling learned to keep certain opinions and pert remarks to herself, and pass them along in letters to Mills. "I suppose every one feels like a boiler waiting, or rather swelling, to burst at times. When things get too thick, I go to the piano and practice arpeggios; they are really quite effective to relieve 'over-timed' self-expressions!"[6]

China, Mayling recognized, still observed and conformed to conventions, manners and ideas that restricted women. Those who flouted them were called "the New Women"—a somewhat unsavory title, used in a derogatory sense. Mayling was anxious that the "Returned Student" group should not be confused with "the New Woman," who "is really quite shocking in her inability to distinguish and differentiate license from liberty. I am bound to observe and to respect the old conventions which, irritating as they are, at least, bar women from actions questionable not only in themselves but in their influence."[7]

Mayling broke a barrier for her gender when she undertook fundraising for the YWCA among Shanghai bankers. She called on these businessmen, bringing along as chaperone an older YW secretary. At a bank, she first sized up the banker, then spoke about the Y's plans for the development of social service, or perhaps presented a strictly commercial need for money (and the idea that it was in his interest to help the young women of China). A direct appeal from a young Chinese lady rather than a man or foreigner opened wallets.

"I always put on my best clothes (suitable for street). Nothing gives one more confidence than the feeling that she has on a becoming hat, plenty of powder to keep the shine off the nose, and sumptuous furs. To the well dressed, that means a larger contribution will be assured, for the man would be ashamed to give any sum too small to buy my shoes, at least. And then again, I always give the men the privilege of contributing to something which could in time benefit them, for a better China socially means a greater China commercially."[8] Her fundraising skill was put to far greater use later when she effectively raised millions of dollars for Chinese war relief from individuals, companies and government agencies, chiefly in the United States.

But in 1918 she looked directly to the social needs of Shanghai and remedies for its worst evils, such as poor living conditions. She talked of work with a public charity organization—a hands-on task with "nasty smells and dirty sights." Somebody had to do it, she thought, if the city was ever going to be cleaned up. "When you see this mass of humanity, it seems impossible to ever stir them up to any sense of consciousness of living; yet just see the revolutions which have brought the realization of democracy into a country primarily monarchical and aristocratic!"[9]

Ideas and words and hopes didn't bring Mayling out of a self-questioning, unfulfilled state. She considered pursuing physical activities, but in truth remained largely cloistered and sedentary. She manifested a peculiar intertwining of community betterment and individual fulfillment. "I have an active mind, and since I have returned home, I am surrounded with every deadening force possible, deadening actively speaking. What about the various committees I belong to? They are nihil! They are superficial, and the members meet more to observe each other's clothes than to discuss means of improvement. The futility of it all!"[10]

Emma Mills' letters to China shared her own experiences as a recent liberal arts graduate, similarly seeking a meaningful occupation, perhaps marriage—at least a mission in life. She enrolled in a chemistry course at Columbia University and worked part-time at a laboratory at New York's Presbyterian Hospital. Emma also volunteered at a wartime Red Cross center to wrap surgical dressings. She seemed headed for a career in health care or medicine, her father's profession. In the late spring of 1918, with the country fighting in Europe and many young men away from nearby farms, she joined a corps of ladies organized to fill in to cultivate and harvest crops. As a Farmerette, she was chiefly assigned to pick apples in the Hudson Valley, most often with a new friend, the free-spirited and adventurous Agnes (Mandy) Mandeville, whose future would intertwine with Emma's. When the global influenza epidemic suddenly hit rural New York, Mandy and Emma turned, by necessity, to caring for sick townsfolk in Kinderhook, many of whom died as summer turned to fall. Although constantly exposed to the flu, Emma avoided contracting the contagious disease. When the war ended in November, her duty ceased. With that peripheral nursing experience, she then entered training as a recruit in the U.S. Army Nurse Corps. Perhaps that field of endeavor, she thought, would fill the void of any empty life.

The first 18 or so months out of college, indeed, had been a difficult period for Emma. She wrote in her journal that she didn't seem to be going anywhere in particular, was not making new friends, or learning anything academic, or of life. Through serious, ongoing reading, she experienced more of life in books than through reality. "It's a little awesome to be able to taste the whole experience of human kind vicariously," this life-long bibliophile recorded. "I wonder what use the gift was given me for?"[11]

A rush of school friends announced engagements and marriages throughout 1917 and 1918. One day Emma visited Wellesley dorm "big sister" of 1914–15 and newlywed Margaret Dickey Lightner in her cramped Manhattan apartment—and was disturbed by its smallness and darkness. "I'm afraid these two qualities will prove wearing and depressing ... though Dickey seems content enough.... Housekeeping ought not to be her sole occupation. Her hands are rough and stained. Here I am sputtering when probably she never was happier or learning more of real permanent value."[12]

Mayling responded in a similarly odd mood. "I am glad you wrote how you felt, for I am beginning to think that I alone get disgusted with the world in general and myself in particular."

In that letter she reported sad news within her family. Her father had become seriously ill and was slowly losing weight and strength. Every night Mayling gave him a massage with olive oil to soothe his dry, parchment-like skin. His condition was diagnosed as Bright's disease. After a brief hospital stay, Charles Soong came home at the insistence of his wife. "Mother says she does not believe in doctors, and that no one could cure him but God. Hence, she refuses to let him be sweated to throw off the poison. I am frantic ... as his kidneys are not working. I am almost going crazy with the tension and Mother's refusal to follow the doctors' direction. He sleeps most of the time, and his face is swollen. I believe in prayer, but I also believe in medicine."[13]

The progenitor of the Soong family of Shanghai died of cancer at home on May 4, 1918. A quiet and simple funeral followed, with only close friends and relatives in attendance. Although his family had been buried in Canton and Mrs. Soong's relatives locally in West Gate Cemetery, 52-year-old Charles Soong was interred in the International Cemetery, a new burial ground in Shanghai for well-to-do Chinese and foreigners. "Father was the very first person to be buried in that cemetery. He liked being the first in any kind of competition; he would be awfully pleased.

"Father left everything in order, and as Mother knew all about his affairs, we have had no trouble. Speculations by people outside as to whether Father died a millionaire or only mediumly well off would be amusing at any other time. As for the past seven years Father has been 'a gentleman of leisure,' no one outside the family knows how he stands regarding property."[14]

His real estate interests included a house at 30 Seymour Road, a bit smaller and more homey than Avenue Joffre. The family anticipated running it with a reduced staff of seven. To house them, construction began on a garage with upstairs living quarters. Mrs. Soong also started to sell pieces of furniture too large to fit comfortably in the new dwelling, which featured a cement-floor basement—a rarity for Shanghai—a third-floor trunk room and roof garden, a greenhouse, and a garden pavilion for palm trees.

Mayling took charge of all food bills. Servants' meals, she decided, would be brought in to their own quarters from food shops three times a day to simplify kitchen operations and cut down their being around the food supplies and pantry. She heard that foreign friends kept eggs, butter, flour and other staples under lock and key, thus reducing consumption and waste. She installed the locks, and secreted the keys. "You can't imagine how I hate housework. Of course, I don't do anything except direct the servants, but heavens I wish I could live in an apartment all by myself and not have to look after dirt and dust, but just let everything go to the dogs."

Before moving to Seymour Road, several rooms needed refurbishing. A coat of Ningpo varnish used on the walls brought on an outbreak of "paint poison," as Mayling called it. She developed small blisters that swelled and itched, not unlike poison ivy. "Mother said it was because I refused to go to Revival meetings with her that it was a case of Retribution." That year she also fell victim to influenza, and her weight dropped some 20 pounds to 107.

Physically run down, she also suffered mental anguish when, riding with the chauffeur in the family automobile, they hit a young boy who darted in front of the vehicle. With the youngster's mother, they bundled him up into the car and sped off to a hospital. But in less than a minute, the auto ran out of gas. Mayling jumped out and hailed rickshaws: one for the dazed boy and his crying mother; the other for herself. As the rickshaws proved too slow, she stopped, then begged the owner of a parked Ford to take all three to St. Luke's emergency room.

Once doctors began to care for the injured youngster, Mayling left to retrieve her car. She found the car but not Soongs' chauffeur. Unable to drive, she stopped a passing car. Its owner agreed to drive her and the family car home. Upon learning of the accident, Mrs. Soong panicked. The house would be surrounded by police and detectives, she exclaimed, and poor Mayling would probably have to appear in court. A bundle of nerves, Mayling collapsed in bed.

The next morning Mrs. Soong found her delirious with a fever of 105 degrees and wildly yelling not to let the automobile run over her. Two days later, while still bedridden and under the care of two doctors, a police officer came to interrogate her. "I was so feverish that he could not make sense of what I said, especially as from weakness I would drop off to sleep in the middle of a remark." The missing chauffeur, who had no driver's license, never returned. The boy, only slightly injured, quickly recovered. Mayling's recovery, however, dragged on for several weeks.[15]

In late October Mrs. Soong sent her daughter and son T.A. on a holiday to northeastern China to visit sister Ailing, her husband H.H. (Chauncey) Kung, and their two young children, Pauline and David. The Kungs lived at Taku in Shansi province where H.H., a banker, had business interests. A 40-hour train ride from Shanghai to the mountains gave welcomed time to rest and read. En route, she and T.A. stopped for several hours in Nanking, the old capital, where they crossed the Yangtze River to change trains at another railroad station. On the way, they saw many soldiers, both Northern and Southern Chinese troops. Though well-equipped, this army, noted Mayling, lacked the military swagger of foreign soldiers. The Chinese needed only experience and rigorous discipline to measure up, she concluded.

Their itinerary included Tientsin, a less populated city than Shanghai with more residential areas, and similarly divided into foreign concessions for the English, French, Germans, Italians, Austrians and Japanese. Each maintained a municipal governing body. Here, the Kungs joined Mayling and T.A. at a French-style hotel, settling into a wing all to themselves. The change of climate invigorated Mayling, as did the French cuisine, the chance to speak French, and the opportunity to buy "rush-order" custom-made French clothes.

From Tientsin, Mayling and T.A. journeyed some 50 miles north to Peking, where foreign influence seemed much less than in Shanghai and Tientsin. All street names were written in Chinese, and the telephone operators understood only Chinese. Narrow, bumpy streets, often covered with dust and crowded with mule carts, wound around courtyard walls that hid from view most dwellings, large and small. A trip to the Great Wall—wide enough, Mayling wrote, to let three carriages pass in parallel—and to the walls of the old Forbidden City in the heart of Peking led her to observe that "as far as architectural beauty and stability the Chinese are not backward."

Her activities in Shanghai moved in a new direction in her second year back from the United States. Writing now occupied a bit of her time, and a short article about women's colleges in America was published by the local university club—a 500-word piece intended for the Chinese student going to the States. It made quite a stir, and was the only such writing reprinted by the *Shanghai Gazette.*

"I am deliberating over some article in the nature of special reforms for certain evils in Shanghai," she told Emma. "I wish you were here to help me sort out the essentials from the rest of my thoughts. I am also deliberating on writing on American women as college students. I think I ought to do best in matters I know first hand. It is easier for me to write narratives than formal articles and for this reason, I am starting a course in Macaulay for my sole benefit. I want to get the swing and rhythm of analytical writing. I wish you were here to help me get started. I feel so brimful of ideas."[16]

3

Wellesley

Mayling Soong ached with what she called "college sickness," an obsession with memories of all aspects of Wellesley—the bucolic campus, caring faculty, amicable companions, even ardent suitors. All in all, it had been an irretrievable youthful period to which she longed to return but could only relive through reminiscence and reunion.

Her schooling in New England, however, had commenced on a shaky footing. Mayling, after five sunny years in Georgia, had become a dyed-in-the-wool Southerner. She had acquired the Confederate view of the Civil War and the North, particularly Union general Sherman's unconscionable path of destruction in Georgia. On the very first day in Massachusetts, it is told, she did not like the more structured and less friendly Wellesley College. She wasted no time in walking into the office of Edith Tufts, Dean of Residence, and announcing in her soft languid Southern accent, "Well, I reckon I shan't stay around here much longer."

At 16 she was a rather short—5 feet, 4 inches—and plump with closely trimmed dark hair, often embellished with bright ribbons. Her face was round with dark eyes. Her wardrobe reflected the tastes of a typical American college girl.

She arrived with a solid educational background at this prestigious 43-year-old New England women's institution with its demanding curriculum and some 12 miles from Boston—and Harvard. That included a splendid speaking and writing knowledge of English. She decided to major in English literature and composition, chiefly taught by Katherine Lee Bates,[1] and to minor in philosophy, under the tutelage of Mary Whiton Calkins. She relished the exhilaration of discussing into the wee hours neoplatonism and metaphysics ... less so the perplexities of freshman math. She read voraciously, and studied both piano and violin. She also took courses in astronomy, French, history, botany, elocution, and Biblical history. Mayling particularly loved the fiery conflicts of Arthurian romance, a course taught by the English department. Although brought up in a strict religious atmosphere in China, she talked little about religion. Her extra-curricular activities chiefly centered around Tau Zeta

Epsilon, a campus sorority that emphasized the study of fine arts and art appreciation.

A classmate once confessed that Mayling was responsible for getting her through Wellesley. Mayling took her in hand. "Buy Miss Calkins' book—'Persistent Problems of Philosophy'—study it, and come to me every night with what you do not understand."[2] The friend did so and passed her course. Classmates described Mayling as vivacious, sometimes serious and always an individualist. And she had gained a keen social insight into American life from spending most school vacations with classmates.

Helen Hull, her freshman instructor in English composition, later made note of the reminiscences of members of her class who recalled her spells of great activity, alternating with spells of lethargy and idleness that still made the rhythm by which she lived years later. "She would work good and hard for awhile, and then suddenly she would refuse to do anything, work or play. No one could budge her. We thought she was lazy or sulking, but she just brushed us off. Then suddenly she was flying around again."[3]

Mayling came close to making Phi Beta Kappa. The grades of her last semester, senior year—four A's (Philosophy 9 and 16, international politics, literature) and two B's (English history, French)—however, did bring a BA degree with honors. And Wellesley named her a Durant Scholar, the highest undergraduate distinction conferred by the college.

Virtually all of 324 freshmen of the class of '17 lived in houses in Wellesley village. The college assigned Mayling to 6 Cross Street. Emma Mills lived with ten other freshmen, who shared one bathroom, at 603 Washington Street. She wrote home that she seemed "older" and more mature than her classmates. "Wellesley is lots easier then St. Agatha's, and I haven't the proper freshman awe of the place or the people here. I'm called The Village High Brow." In addition to duties as head of a dining table, dishing out food onto plates, she was appointed 2nd floor proctor, as no one else in that job "could keep me still." After a month at Wellesley, she boasted of counting 100 freshman as friends. "I don't know from which side of the family," she wrote her father, "I inherited my spirit of adventure!" Nonetheless, she expressed boredom at times—a trait brought from home. Unlimited class cuts and no required religious services pleased her.[4]

As sophomores, in the fall of 1914, the class moved onto the 300-acre campus. Mayling was assigned to Wood Cottage, a rambling late Victorian-style dormitory. On her room wall she hung an ancient Chinese scimitar, which sometimes frightened students passing by her open door. The 14 residents, including Emma Mills in a nearby room, formed a tight-knit group; many remained close long after graduation. Emma shared quarters with Betty Nicholson, daughter of a Cleveland, Ohio, minister. Their room often filled with dorm-mates, who brought all sorts of things to eat. Emma and Betty were constantly sweeping up crumbs and nut shells. So much noise emanated from there

Wood Cottage residents gather as seniors prepare for Wellesley graduation in 1916. Mayling, in back row, third from left. Emma stands in fourth row, second from right. Mayling called her days on campus the happiest time of her early life. (Mills–DeLong collection.)

in the evenings that the house president living across the corridor often came in to keep them quiet—and usually stayed an hour or two herself! The sanguine Emma acquired a reputation as a good-natured cynic who'd rather go walking than study. She had few if any extracurricular activities—no club, sports, music or drama participation. Time spent with Mayling and various classmates filled the hours apart from studies.

Mayling participated in tennis and swimming, and in winter occasionally joined her housemates in sledding on College Hill or Wood Hill. Used to mild winters in the South, she loathed getting up on early frosty mornings, particularly when an open window fed cold air into her bedroom. She was a notorious and self-admitted sleepyhead in any climate. Emma could always tell if Mayling had been in her room during her absences because her hand mirror would be out of place. Years later, she noted Mayling's occasional childlike vanity as sometimes touching, sometimes exasperating. It often wore Emma out when they were together.

"During our four years together she always seemed to be enjoying life, and imparting her joy to others," remembered classmate Alice DeLisle Kirkham. "Mayling never intruded her own personal affairs on any of us, in fact she was so keen in learning our ideas, and studying our lives that it was difficult to learn much about her and her family."[5] Indeed, she had an eagerness to be Occidental in every way possible. And she was always thoughtful in making the two or three less outgoing Chinese students on campus feel at home. Chinese undergraduates from Harvard came by, sometimes with her brother and guardian T.V. Increasingly, there seemed to be an unaccompanied Chinese boy on the doorstep of Wood Cottage.

Latin, geometry and German proved the hardest first-year courses for Emma; English composition, with B's, the easiest. By her second year, her grades fell to D's, except for English. They improved to three C's (Biblical history, economics, English composition) except for a D (philosophy) by graduation. To follow in the footsteps of her physician father, Emma needed science courses; however, she lacked solid overall liberal arts grades for medical school, few of which welcomed women into their classes.

Above all, Emma's fascination with China from early childhood attracted her to the extroverted and outspoken Chinese classmate living under the same roof. Over the years Emma often reminded others that "she didn't become interest in that land because I knew Mayling, but rather the other way around. And oddly enough, not one of my many other Chinese friendships stems from my knowing her."[6]

The close camaraderie led to Mayling's school-break visits to the Mills household. One summer she stayed at the New Market, New Jersey, country place of Emma's grandmother, where she plunged with vigor into all farm activities.

When some pigs were being brought to the barn, she volunteered to help Emma pick them up in town. They hitched up a horse to a wagon and removed the backseat to transport the animals. Mayling drove, but did not realize the wagon had no cut underneath to change direction easily and nearly overturned. At the depot she and Emma put the pigs in burlap bags and placed them in the wagon. On the trip back, an amused Mayling sat on several bags to keep the squeaking, wiggly pigs from falling out of the wagon. Most of the neighborhood could see that the De Long family had a young Chinese girl visiting.[7]

Mayling and the class of '17 long remembered two momentous events that framed their four years on campus. The first occurred in their freshman term; the second, in the last months of senior year. On the morning of March 17, 1914, the ringing of the Wellesley village fire bell woke students in various dormitories and residences spread about the campus and town. It was the glare of flames reflected in the transom over a bedroom door in College Hall that had initially stirred two upperclassmen from sleep. They sounded the fire alarm on their floor and quickly pounded on doors, commanding everyone to leave the large building. Five-story College Hall housed not only 350 students, faculty and staff but also classrooms, lecture halls, science laboratories, and deans' offices. The well-trained fire brigade leaders rounded up all residents and marched them out to safety. Everyone escaped without injury. The cause, it was thought, was a faulty electrical apparatus in a science lab or the spontaneous combustion of chemicals.[8]

The largest and oldest college building was left a blackened shell. Only two fireproof walls had been part of the structure, and inadequate water pressure added to the disaster. On account of the staggering loss, President Ellen Pendleton immediately ordered the school closed for three weeks, and until the end of the regular upcoming spring recess. Some 1,300 students immediately left the campus. During their absence, a makeshift temporary classroom and administration building—soon tagged the Hen Coop—was built. Burned-out College Hall women residents doubled up with undergrads in other dorms.

Then, three years later, in April 1917, America declared war on Germany, just days before spring break ended. Emma on a walk along New York's Fifth Avenue observed newsboys hawking extra editions. People turned from them as something not quite nice, a disagreeableness to avoid. "The flags are all out, splashes of color in the long gray vista. My heart aches over the future, and yet this crisis does not seem a part of real life. Planning is out of the question; only staring into the dark, and waiting."[9]

Wellesley students returned to campus, talking of war for hours each day and questioning each other as to what they could do for the war effort and what part their communities back home might play in the conflict. The war was remote, but it soon made a greater and greater impact as accounts from the European front dominated the front page of newspapers. Many of Emma's friends accused her of indifference and provincialism when they talked about the war; her feelings cut her off from the seniors in the dorm, except for Mayling, on any but the most trivial topics of conversation. As graduation approached, the class held a meeting. It decided to simplify commencement events, retaining just the baccalaureate, class supper and presentation of diplomas. Emma decided to skip the entire celebration, getting her degree in absentia. Before she left the campus, she bought a graduation present for Mayling—a book that left her "wild with delight."

The young teenager who had wanted to leave Wellesley and the North that first day came to look upon the college as the most influential force in her early years. A crowning, translucent legacy, Mayling recalled later, was her "New England conscience" which did not permit her to rest until her many duties and tasks, especially in wartime, were completed. Having gone to school there, she claimed to have developed "a pseudo New England conscience which does not allow me to flop on my downy couch until the day's work is done."[10]

Back in 1917 and so enamored of learning and education and a sense of duty, she told her American friends that she would go home to China and teach. Wellesley's motto, "Non ministrari, sed ministrare" (Not to be administered unto, but to administer) surely had planted a seed on fertile ground.

4

Empathy

Teaching the youth of China proved not to be the key to happiness, the "touchstone of life," for Mayling.[1] She continued to cling to a sort of sequestered mode of living, with the privilege of withdrawing to a private world at will. Her idea of utopia was a place where as few people as possible ever stepped in, and those few would have to disappear from time to time so she could be alone. Admittedly stubborn and defiant, she often rejected the advice of others. "I despise people who are always trying to make me think as they do. I prefer to be myself and not someone else's idea of myself." Privacy of the mind always persisted as a priority within an often feisty temperament.[2]

And that privacy usually focused on reading. She delighted in receiving a box of school books from Wellesley in March 1919 — nearly two years after it had been shipped. "I have not felt so like my old self since my return home as I did since my books came. Now I feel that some of my old theories and ideas are almost back again. College days do seem so far gone, and life sometimes, especially now, seems rather uncertain, in the sense opposite stability." A scholar at heart, she spoke of her idea of happiness as a life of uninterrupted reading, studying and writing.[3]

Her private time also embraced music lessons. She studied with a Russian music teacher on a German-made piano newly acquired from a European family who was moving from Shanghai. She began to practice three hours a day, and soon noted a marked improvement working with "the very best teacher I have ever had."

Progress and reform in China remained an area of concern and activity for the Methodist-reared Mayling. She worked with the Returned Students' Bible Conference, pointing out its responsibility in being back of every push towards social advancement, and to clarify individual obligations towards their respective churches, which were in a bad state. "For instance, my own pastor is not a bit what he should be as a leader of the flock.... He preaches the rottenest sermons and is most unsanctimoniously lazy.... I am going to try to reform him by giving him some books to read which might give new ideas for his sermons, for as matters now stand I always know what he is going to say before he says it, and I guess everyone else does too."[4]

After graduation from Wesleyan in 1913, Chingling joined her family in Tokyo, where they and Sun Yat-sen had fled after the failure of a coup against the new republic's president Yuan Shih-kai, in whose favor Sun Yat-sen had resigned the presidency the previous year. She became Dr. Sun's secretary, a position Ailing briefly held. He asked the Soongs' permission to wed Chingling, but was refused. Against Chinese tradition Chingling eloped with Dr. Sun, who had divorced his first wife. With her sister married to this revolutionary who worked tirelessly to unite the country, Mayling increasingly paid attention to modern China's political and economic developments. In World War I Japan had declared war on Germany, and Japanese troops occupied Germany's concession-acquired, mineral-rich territory in Shantung peninsula. Japan demanded new rights there — the spoils of war — upon German's defeat. The peace treaty negotiations at war's end leaned toward giving Shantung to Japan. Resentful Chinese delegates built a strong case to end foreign inroads. It led to a anti-imperialist movement by angry Peking university students and young returned students against the old ruling forces and to a boycott of Japanese goods as well as to protests to their government to not sign the Treaty of Versailles. Student-led street demonstrations and anti–Japanese outrage spread to other cities, in what became known as the May Fourth Movement. Chinese merchants closed their shops. Restaurants and theatres locked their doors. Laborers on the railroads walked off their jobs. Vegetable hawkers disappeared. Telephone and other utility workmen struck. Even prostitutes quit their trade. Mayling approved of the boycott in so far as it led to constructive ends. In particular, she applauded the disgruntled students in Shanghai, who believed they were fighting for democracy and self-determination, the very same principles that the Allies in Europe fought for. The May 1919 Movement was the real birth of Chinese nationalism to resist all foreign encroachment, and a significant student crusade. This new spirit of Chinese agitation and nationalism also went on to play a part in forming a communist party in China. Japan won out temporarily. Three years later, in 1922, the Washington naval disarmament conference persuaded Japan to agree to a settlement under which China assumed authority in Shantung.

Mayling urged the teaching of contemporary history in every school, and the fostering of patriotic sentiments. "It is really discouraging," she wrote Emma Mills, "when one thinks of the amount of history the students study, but not one jot of it is about China since the Revolution [in 1911 with Dr. Sun as president]. Our Oriental mind seems to be steeped in the glories and conquests of the past, and if something is not done to change this, we shall be a second Korea."[5]

Appointed a member of Shanghai's Child Labor Commission, Mayling proposed trade schools for "the children of the streets" to counteract the import from Japan of such everyday goods as woven mats. The children would also receive two or three hours a day of instruction in arithmetic and Chinese so that in time they would be able to read newspapers, and thus be informed of the state of affairs in the country.

Mayling sympathized with what France had gone through when Germany took over Alsace-Lorraine in 1871. "With Tsingtau, it is worse for I feel that it is the first echo of the knell to China's integrity and solidarity. Yet if there be a God, I can not help thinking that China will be avenged; yet how hard to wait until that day."[6]

She observed that the Japanese were not afraid of the Chinese government, weak and largely composed of self-interested men. The Japanese, however, were afraid of the Chinese people themselves, "for in spite of what they say about our lack of patriotic feeling, they know only too well that when roused we are a terrible people to deal with. They have had a taste of what length we might be driven to as evinced in the fact that a few days ago several Japanese settlements were destroyed by fire."[7]

Under growing pressure, the dissolute government in Peking secured the resignations of the three key officials favoring the turning over of Tsingtau to Japan. "The Chinese now realize their strength in Union, and so in spite of a rotten Government, there is not going to be any obstacle too difficult to overcome. ... once the Japanese have tasted what we can do, they will be a bit more wary in treading on our toes."[8]

Halfway around the world from China, Emma Mills had entered army nursing school at Camp Meade, Maryland, near Baltimore. Within a month or two of training, she had realized that she had probably made a mistake in pursuing a medical career. Situated in a dreary, isolated backwater of rundown and neglected barracks and medical wards, the base both taught nursing recruits and treated the wounded and shell-shocked from the recently ended war. The flu epidemic of 1918 now spread to this outpost, striking soldier and nurse, and depleting their ranks. Moans, coughs and retchings interrupted sleep, as did nurses' comings and goings to administer medicines and change bedding. But more than physical discomfort, Emma was bored and restless.

Nursing seemed too narrow and unchallenging—a vestige of an old apprentice system. Making beds, dusting floors, dishing out meals, cataloging surgical supplies—this was a wasted life in contrast to the mental stimulation at college. "I am feeling very bitter," she wrote in her journal on January 8. "Must I make every effort, every decision myself or will Fate sometime bring me what I want without my seeking? If I am to have to go hunting for every fragment of adventure, I had best get out at once & not waste two years in this queer prison. What am I talking of? I hardly know."[9]

Her state of mind evidenced a degree of bipolar disorder. She fancied the accustomed comfort and security within her sheltered urbane family environment. Yet she relished free-spirited intellectualism and adventure. Conflicting impulses led to emotional vulnerability, restlessness, frustration, even physical ailments. Surges ranging from aroused highs to depression characterized her life well into middle age.

Emma's frustration over work and relationships filled her letters to Mayling that winter and spring. Empathy—and understanding—between them had not lessened with the passage of nearly two years at opposite ends of the world. Mayling analyzed Emma's mental state as bordering on the hysterical, largely caused by the flu ravaging among trainees, staff and soldiers. "The same conventional 'every dayness' of life, I know, seems almost too oppressive to be borne," Mayling pointed out. "And it's all very well for people to say that if one had an intense and vital 'interest' in life, life becomes transfigured. I say, all this is pure sentimental bosh.... It is silly to talk about feeling old, but I fancy that most of us who have been out (of college) a couple of years do feel the lack of spontaneous feelings and thought. You will not be angry if I say something to you? It is just this. I think women lose interest in life, at least they feel a distinct lack as though they have been cheated out of life, if they do not marry.[10]

"I know I sound brutal, as though marriage were to be entered into lightly or with such cold-bloodedness or as a panacea.... What I do mean is that if you fall in love, marry the man, provided there are no unsurpassable obstacles in the way. You will then stop being discontented or there will be at least two individualities in which you are interested."[11]

Assignments in the more stimulating operating room revived Emma's flagging interest in military nursing. Ten operations one morning were tiring but challenging work. Even at home her grandmother and namesake Emma De Long—a dominating family relic from the Victorian age—railed against her choice of careers, calling it degrading, a waste of brains and college education. The money for her four years at Wellesley, it seems, had come from grandmother's deep pockets. (Her father, James Avery Wotton, founded the family fortune as part-owner of the New York and Havre Steamship Co., forerunner of the French Line.) Emma wondered if she had a right to make her feel her money wasted. Grandmother waited to see her take an interest in clothes and dances, tea parties and bridge.

On April 25, 1919, the discontented student nurse penned:

> Here I am, the sole occupant of impossibly cold quarters. All the other girls have gone to our first dance. I'm all broken up again & hate everybody. I didn't want to go in the least & wouldn't be there now for a good deal, but Florence looked so lovely as she went out, it roused seven devils of envy, jealousy, regret, etc., in me. Why can't I be one sort of a person, or another, definitely? It always seems that when I'm frivolous, I'm inwardly disgusted; when I'm serious, I'm ravingly jealous.... Teddy suggested the other day that our troubles arose from the fact that we were both old maids, but it goes farther than that; there must be some reason for our being old maids. I think mine is chiefly that I'm always too aware of self & instead of just going ahead & doing things, always listen to my own opinions, likes & dislikes.[12]

Mayling readily diagnosed her "case" and responded with a "working hypothesis." She first told Emma that she need not worry whether she would ever amount to anything. "I grant, though, one does get horribly confused when one does not feel solid ground underneath. I think matters with you stand as follows: you do not like your life at camp, but still less do you like the one in New York, because at camp, although you feel that the work is not congenial and hence you can not put the best of yourself in it, still it is making you learn something and in a measure the work itself absorbs your time and hence you do not feel so useless as you would feel were you without it. Then, if you were in New York, there are the wishes of the family to consider, and when you are actually there you more or less rebel at their taking for granted certain things about you. As, for instance, they expect you to agree with them in their attitude towards life and their expectation that you would fulfill what is expected of you."[13]

Mayling wisely concluded that Emma was losing her self-confidence and direction as to what path to take: "I think I can understand what you are going through, for since I have been back, I have had something very like the experience you are having, only in my case I was sure what I wanted, only the gods did not see fit to give it to me."[14]

At age 24, Emma needed to get back her self-confidence—the overflowing abundance of faith in herself that "really was the most unique characteristic you had in differentiating yourself from the rest of the gee-gabbing crowd." Mayling observed that the most successful men were usually not the ones with great powers as geniuses but the ones who had such ultimate faith in their own selves that invariably they hypothesize others to that belief as well as themselves. She advised Emma to go into civic work. At the same time, added Mayling, the role of being a wife to a lawyer or other professional spouse would bring satisfaction. It would bring a lot of empathy that is "running to waste unless you find a fit channel to bestow it." Mayling asserted that the profession of marriage was the one most important for every woman, and could not be subordinated by any other calling or inspiration.

"Push the self who doted on Henry James a little more to one side," urged Mayling. "You had enough of that in college."[15]

Emma stayed on at camp, but admitted being starved for music and books, weighty discussions, and homey comforts, even good clothes. And perhaps sex, if one can gauge Mayling's feedback in several follow-up letters. There was, it seems, an unpleasant incident that awakened in Emma

> the knowledge of brutal passion as distinguished from the academic view of passion which we in our college days knew absolutely nothing about. Most of us fancied sexual desires as something apart from ourselves, a subject on which we could and did make downright statements theoretic and speculative. But except from that angle, we had not seen it nor seen it manifested in life. And I think the shock was a bit too sudden and startling for you.

I think the best way for you to become normal in your attitude towards men would be to ignore the question of sex entirely. Of course, that is difficult, for almost without exception when a man becomes interested in a girl, he becomes sentimental. And do not shirk from threshing out the question with yourself. Love is partly sexual in its composition, and there is nothing disgusting about it if you consider it in conjunction with the other elements which make up Love in the real sense. For instance, physical love is like certain parts of Bach or Beethoven works which if considered by themselves are discords but which it combined with the parts the authors meant to have considered, they become harmonious and beautiful. In all probability, the man who looked at you so disgustingly was only attracted to you by your physical attractions, and a man who is that sort is certainly a beast, a brute and an animal. ... but, Dada, not all men are like that.... The best thing for you to do would be not to view love from the sexual side; just be normal, and when you really feel in love with a man worthy of you, everything will come clearly and naturally to your mind....

Do not begin to think that you are disgusted with life, for you aren't. You are only disgusted with a certain element. ... an attitude quite natural to all pure-minded girls who are what you are. For example, I like camping out, while every time I camp, I despise the beastly mosquitoes. Yet the mosquitoes are so small and evil when compared with the pleasure I derive from camping that I do not take them at all into account when I express enthusiasm for camping. All this is inadequate, I know, but I am such a duffer at expressing my thought.[16]

The oppressive summer heat of Shanghai, more than the opposite sex, vexed Mayling. She was amused by rumors of her being engaged, with each rumor roping in different men. Her mother was not amused, and thus stopped her from seeing her gentlemen friends. "I am almost willing to be engaged out of revenge," she wrote Emma. "The truth is, I am dreadfully bored, outrageously so. I have even had teas unchaperoned a couple of times, just because ... I feel so wretchedly oppressed. And the funny part I do not care a snap about any of the men."[17]

Yet the men of Shanghai pursued Mayling continually. They called and wrote letters. They invited her to dinners and dances. At her birthday and on Chinese New Year, they sent presents. One ongoing suitor even joined the Soongs' church.

But it was virtually impossible for her to go out driving with a perfectly decent man without chaperone. Mayling begged her mother to let her leave home and do something besides volunteer work. She sought a real job, a satisfying occupation. She had a position offered on a newspaper, but anticipated the family fuss if she were to take it. They believed a young woman couldn't be decent morally if she worked with men. "Damm it all," she wrote, "I think that if I had my way, I could amount to something, but hampered with a respectable family whom everyone knows about, it is impossible.... I know you are surprised at this outburst of mine when you have been thinking for the past few months that I am calmly settling down to respectability. Instead you find me crazy to attack the Gorgon's head and not his domestic hearth."[18]

With courtship and marriage on her mind, Mayling related an incident of two Chinese students who sought the approval of parents to wed. The young man's vastly wealthy mother and father were asked permission by their son to become engaged to a girl whose family lived in Honolulu. The girl, a student overseas, had no social standing nor dowry. So the father refused. The couple came to China, where the girl had a married sister in Nanking. The man's family were non–Christians and very superstitious. They lived in a large house of over 100 rooms but in a very crowded part of Shanghai where one had to enter the dwelling through a narrow dark alley because the mother believed the location brought good luck.

> And this woman never goes out of the house without first consulting her family fortune teller to ask whether the date is propitious or not. The man's family finally asked for the date of the girl's birthday, and to what family of animals she belonged. Everyone in China is born under an animal family, something like the western idea of belonging to a certain constellation. The girl's brother-in-law found out from the prospective groom what his birth day, year, and animal kingdom were, and then consulted a professional fortune teller, asking him to work out a birthday for the girl which in every respect would be favorable when put alongside of the man's birthday. For a few dollars, the fortune teller worked out a fictitious birth date for the girl, making her some years younger than the man.[19]

Mayling explained that the brother-in-law went to the young man's family and told them the made-up birth date. The mother then consulted her own fortune teller, and discovered to her surprise that from every point of view the match could not be better. She relented. "So the couple are to be married this Sunday, and as the groom has not finished his studies they are to sail for America in October.... This wedding will be very large, over 4,000 people are invited. ... it is lucky the girl is going to sail with her husband for his family is so old-fashioned that they would make her live with them, and with all the secondary wives, sisters-in-law...."[20]

Mayling turned to her civic, educational and social activities at a dizzy pace. Once the year-long period of mourning for her father ended, her engagement book opened to page after page of dates, commitments, and milestones, including the birth of a niece, Jeannette May Kung, in August 1919—the third child of Ailing. She helped receive guests with her sister, Mrs. Sun, at a very large official gathering on October 10 to mark the founding of the Republic. The 100-member American College Women's Club of Shanghai elected her vice president, and she served as secretary of the McTyeire School sorority, the largest association in Shanghai for Chinese women, and a part of the foreign-style primary school she had attended before her year at boarding school in Summit, New Jersey. The Girls Club at the Y occupied many hours a week, and there was talk at the Y of Mayling giving a series of lectures on modern philosophy. And she returned to study of the Chinese language in its classical mode.

"The schools in Shanghai," she noted, "are in need of teachers, and really some of them made me very attractive offers, but I am so swamped with work as it is now that I am not getting enough sleep.... I have been out to dinner or had guests six nights a week ... besides innumerable teas and theatre.... My circle of friends in Shanghai is getting to be almost too huge for me to be able to keep up with them. The funny thing is that when I do have a moment to myself now, I am so awfully restless that I cannot sit still ... besides all these things, I am trying to settle a serious question in my mind. I do not know what the outcome will be, but I think I know.... I just have to weigh matters carefully from every point possible."[21]

5

New Callings

For a woman who would live well beyond the century mark, Mayling in her younger years endured numerous bouts of ill health and periods of chronic sickness. A number of the diseases of childhood caught up with her as an adult in China. Her exhausting round of activities in early 1920 included shepherding visiting Wellesley president Ellen Pendleton to receptions and dinners in Shanghai. Pendleton's itinerary included a sojourn at Wellesley's sister college, Yenching, in Peking. Mayling's extended social commitments led to a near nervous breakdown (as in her words, "found myself nervous as a cat and irritable as an uncovered electric wire"). "I began by having hysterics, and being unsociable and snappy, and contrary." The family realized that she was physically spent; it had played a part in her collapse by making outside engagements and obligations without her consent.[1]

By early February Mayling showed symptoms of an impacted wisdom tooth and tonsillitis. "The only compensation which I seem to be getting out of this," she wrote, "is plenty of leisure to myself, although I find speech a painful operation and whoever enters my room finds the lashings of my unswollen tongue still more painful." Later in the year, doctors removed the badly infected tonsils, and concluded that they had been the cause of the outbreaks on her face. "The operation went hard with me, as I was on the verge of a nervous breakdown. I am still resting," she wrote on October 11, 1920. "and not taking an active part in anything socially or in any social-service work. My mornings I spend digging in the garden. I have already planted my sweet peas. The gardener does the hard work, while I do the easy planting. By November, I ought to be setting out my rose cuttings."[2]

Books stood by as Mayling's closest companions, and Emma kept her supplied with many volumes from America. "Talking about new books reminds me of a little poem by Anne Fellows Johnston. She described her sensation in opening the covers of a new book as being similar to that she experienced in entering homes where she never had visited before. I was quite pleased with the analogy because although I have felt the truth of this in a vague and unworded haze, I never had seen it expressed."[3]

Seeing Miss Pendleton had made Wellesley and America come back with great vividness, and Mayling once again felt a zest for things intellectual. "One of the saddest things in the process of getting a more practical grasp of things in days after college is the gradual diminishing of intellectual unrest," she pointed out, "and the passive state of mind which is more or less an unresisting acknowledgment of the greater importance of material welfare as against the elusive and less tangible intellectual yearnings."[4]

Even in the midst of a full-blown social life, Mayling had hardly neglected her intellectual pursuits. Nearly every day she took reading and writing lessons in classical Chinese. Her teacher, an old-school scholar who also understood the modern forms of expression, proved strict and demanding. Her brother T.V.'s Chinese secretary, this teacher introduced Mayling to the many words and phrases that had been introduced in China with the inroads of Western civilization and new scientific discoveries. But the time-honored Chinese literature chiefly piqued this American-educated student. She memorized long passages of traditional works. By memorizing, she explained to Emma Mills, she acquired by instinct almost the "feel" of what was correct, noting that words expressed in some other way would lack the desired polish and effectiveness of writing elegantly and easily.

"Much depends upon to what degree the student has assimilated the idea and the atmosphere of good literature. Good writing in Chinese is practically unconscious writing.... At any rate, the study of Chinese is fascinating if one really means to be a Chinese scholar, and knows that the elementary period is necessary before one reaches the really artistic forms. To the average foreigner, the study of Chinese is tedious and difficult because one does not expect to go beyond the readings of easy books and newspapers."[5]

During this intense period of lessons, Mayling moved into the home of sister Ailing Kung, who had gone with her husband to Peking for a month or so. Mayling stayed at the Kungs' residence to care for their three young children, but came back to Seymour Road for her daily studies. "When Mrs. Kung returns," she noted, "I shall be free of the children and have time to 'gad' around a bit."[6]

It was time once more to advise an agitated and floundering Emma. In mid–1919 she had completed the initial segment of nurses' training at Camp Meade, and received a month's furlough.

Had she pursued a medical career this far because of her father's work as a doctor? Walter Mills had achieve prominence as professor of medicine, hospital staff consultant, health department examiner, and author of a well-recognized textbook, *The Practice of Medicine*. A World War I captain in the Army Medical Corps, he, too, served at a base hospital at Camp Meade a year before the Armistice. Emma had always been closer to Dr. Mills and his activities than to her mother, an only child and long sheltered by a well-meaning yet possessive mother. Eventually this would lead to a split between Emma's parents; about the time Emma enrolled in nursing training, Dr. Mills left his wife and mother-in-law's home to live in upper Manhattan with his unmarried sisters.

Urged to continue her career, Emma moved on to a nursing assignment at Walter Reed Hospital in Washington. But after a week there, Emma, utterly discouraged by its countless cockroaches, messy facilities, and poor food, applied for a discharge. Once granted, she began to look for work in Washington and a place to stay on her own. Through family connections, the well-read Emma met with several major newspaper editors for job interviews. They suggested the writing of freelance feature stories on a speculation basis. Emma sought out possible subjects as she settled down in the city. She, however, failed to connect with viable topics or moneymaking assignments. She turned to other employment, and investigated government work, but only typist jobs were available for most women applicants, college-educated or not. She lasted only a day or two as a department store sales clerk.

Mayling urged her not to turn down a job as cub reporter, even if it paid as little as ten dollars a week. A position as a newspaper writer on staff, she thought, would perhaps curb her restlessness. "If you have real talent, the positive work of writing and drudgery will bring it out," Mayling explained. "If you have not real talent, then you would have the satisfaction of knowing that you gave yourself a chance to try out. I believe that as long as your family looks upon you as a 'Problem' and as long as you are merely writing 'on your own,' you would not make much progress. Get out and get a $10 job, and have your articles battered up, torn to pieces and mutilated. By that time you will be too tired. ... if you really have the divine fire, the fire will roar; if not it will sputter and go out. I sound ruthless and cold-hearted, an unsympathetic brute! But Dada, I really believe that you could be a good writer if you had to work like a dog and have a regular job. More about myself next time."[7]

A long silence by Mayling was broken with the airing of surprising thoughts—the serious matter she had lightly touched upon a year earlier but not revealed. It was not "a matter of the Heart," she made clear at the outset.

"I have been thinking of returning to America," Mayling wrote in September 1920," and taking up medicine for a career." She ached for a career, and to her mind, a doctor's life had enough varied human aspects to be interesting, and certainly full. Barring teaching, there was virtually nothing on the horizon for well-schooled women in China, she claimed, "and nothing open to me without trespassing upon the traditions of the family." Business, she pointed out, would generate gossip and disagreeable annoyances. Social work struck her as too theoretical (and amateurish, with a lot of gabbing). "I want to heal peoples' physical being, and let someone else deal with their social welfare. Mother thinks I am just chasing the Blue Bird of Happiness in wanting to return to America. I wish she would come with me; but of course she would not as she dislikes leaving home."[8]

Mrs. Soong, moreover, strongly objected to a medical career. The most cogent reason centered upon an absence from her for six years of advanced schooling and training. Secondly, she voiced concern over Mayling's health, especially the effects on it from the wear and tear of a doctor's life. And she reminded Mayling that there was enough family means for her wants. What's the use of killing one's self in such a profession, Mother Soong exclaimed. Besides, she would be just as useful to China in other ways.

Mayling, who had had a comparatively brief youth in the care of her mother, realized how good she had been to her since her return from America. Mayling now experienced a real home-life—the kind she missed during her adolescent years. "I think I am beginning to be a little less individualistic, too, and understand 'family feeling' more than I ever did in my life before."[9]

Mayling now needed the advice of Emma, as Emma had sought hers.

> Dada dear, I wish you were here to talk over things with me. I have wanted to write you what I have been thinking about all these months. Yet some way, I have not been able to do so, just because I have not thought out the matter thoroughly. You wrote me that Ruth Tuthill has gone to Johns Hopkins to study. I wish I were there with her.
> Write me soon and tell me how everything is with you. For me, everything is all right, if I were only contented; but you know I am rather insatiable most of the time.[10]

Mayling came to the conclusion that she needed to be near her family and yet remain actively "involved" outside her home. Friends, she learned, were important, but when you get to a hard fix, the family was the one that would stand by you. "Coming from one who has spent a greater part of my life thousands of miles away from my family, this may sound queer. But honestly, you will find that I am right."[11]

Mayling and her family did not always agree, she acknowledged; however, they did respect each other and compromised. Her mother, for example, allowed her to go to the dances given by friends, but made Mayling promise that she would not dance! The pious Mrs. Soong believed dancing irreligious and demeaning. Mayling agreed never to dance in China. "Please note the last word; for if I ever get back to America, I am going to kick my heels off."[12]

Mother and daughter, after a decade apart, were becoming reacquainted and closer. "Really my mother is so considerate of me that every day I am ashamed of myself, and of my own behavior."[13] Yet, at the same time, Mayling had to be active and involved on her own terms. "I love to see things hum. I have no patience with a namby-pamby sort of existence."[14]

6

West to East

South of Shanghai, Dr. Sun Yat-sen in 1920 was leading his "2nd Revolution" against the warlord-backed puppets in Peking that since 1912 composed the Republic of China. These figureheads were considered the legal government of China and were recognized by the foreign powers. From Canton Sun controlled only two or three southern provinces but very tenuously. The northern provinces still eluded his dominion because of the influence of the old Peking regime, and various powerful warlords.

When the Suns lived in Shanghai before their move in 1920 to Canton, Mayling had often visited Chingling, the sister who had shared the early school years in New Jersey and Georgia. The somewhat withdrawn and studious Chingling marveled at her younger sister's energy and versatility, and friendships with foreigners. Mrs. Sun, now generally recognized as the First Lady of South China, had a growing agenda of duties and obligations in helping her husband carry out his progressive reforms and democratic consolidations. Chingling reached out to Mayling to lend a hand for a month or so at the Suns' compound in Canton. Early in 1921 she traveled south to that bustling mercantile city near the South China Sea.

The Suns resided in a roomy, well-guarded house on Kwan Yin Mountain that had belonged to the governor of the province. Just below the dwelling stood the Government House, connected to the Suns' quarters by a private covered passage resembling a long elevated bridge. Adjacent to the government offices were soldiers' barracks where some 5,000 troops lived to the sound of bugle calls and drilled daily on a marching field.

The contrast in climate from wintery Shanghai to semi-tropical Canton both amazed and physically affected Mayling. "The sun is so hot that it gives me a headache every time I go out of doors," she complained. "My face is always sunburned, too." Flowers bloomed luxuriantly, she noted, and fruit trees of every kind imaginable flourished.[1]

During Mayling's visit Dr. Sun was elected president of the Canton Provisional Government by a self-proclaimed parliament. She hoped to stay for the inauguration, but frantic telegrams from home summoned her back to Shanghai.

Nonetheless, she delayed nearly another month—until her brothers came down and insisted she arrange for passage on a boat north. The night before she sailed a friend invited her to a party, and soon she had a secret to tell Emma Mills. There she met a United States–bound Dutchman of Scottish descent whose family lived in Java and owned extensive plantations. This thirtyish, well-traveled European, identified only as Mr. Birnie, had been educated in Holland, and spoke a half-dozen languages. The next day, they rendezvoused on the same boat to Shanghai, where another ship awaited him for crossing the Pacific.

"I like him tremendously, and he does me, too," Mayling confided. "Although we were on board ship together only three days, we became very good friends. The day we arrived in Shanghai was his birthday, and so in spite of the fact that I had been away from home three months, I spent the day with him until his boat sailed that afternoon. We had a beautiful time together, and I am glad I was so rash for once in my life. Needless to say, the family was furious with me, and was scandalized. ... ever since I came home, I have been wrapped tight in cotton-wool chaperonage."[2]

The fact that Mr. Birnie was a foreigner enraged Mrs. Soong, and she accused her daughter of "picking him up" on board ship. Moreover, family pride over keeping the Soong blood "pure" aroused her mother; she said that she would rather see her daughter dead than marry a foreigner. Wireless messages from Birnie's ship saying how much he missed her passed by Mrs. Soong, who initially kept them from Mayling, causing a brief rift at 30 Seymour Road.

"I like him awfully well, in some ways better than any man I ever met, and perhaps better than the man who I may be engaged to in the near future. He has certain qualities which are exceedingly rare anywhere; but in all probability on my part the affair will not go further than friendship. In a way, I am glad he is not here, for I do not know how his presence might affect me."[3]

Mayling declined to identify the "other man," only that he was young and brilliant, from an excellent family, educated, with good morals. And undoubtedly Chinese. She did add that "one may be reasonably convinced and yet not emotionally convinced about a certain course of action as being advisable."

Aside from a shipboard romance, a worldly and ambitious Mayling felt her life had been empty and unfulfilled since graduation. What had she accomplished in the four years since leaving Wellesley? Her dreams and visions of a future had been turned into "forlorn realities." The excuses, she pointed out, were many—adjustment to family life in her homeland, her father's poor health and death, her frequent illnesses, the move to another house.

> The truth is this: if I really had something in me, I could have overcome all the obstacles, swept them aside, left the comfortable homeside, and gone into the interior and done some work "on my own," away from people who know my family, and particularly away from Shanghai where because of my family, anything I choose to do in the way of social service has the approval of the public, but where it is impossible to judge of results merely as results apart from personal achievement.[4]

Mayling's introspective moralizing did balance the downside with the positive. She had gained a fair knowledge of classical Chinese literature, raised funds for charity, promoted community good works, and revealed some executive ability. "I am also known as being 'intellectual' and 'brainy,' rather proud but pleasant. In other words," she concluded, "I feel above the average 'return student,' but not offensively snobbish—a good sport but somewhat apart from the 'common herd' because of my family's position, and because of the fact that I dress very well, and in foreign clothes, ride around in a motor, and do not have to teach to get my living."[5] Mayling wondered what could be the matter with herself.

> What could I have done, or could do not, to get that vibrant joy of life, and of living? ... I have had moments when I felt that the only way to solve my problem is by a life of self-abnegation—to become either a Catholic nun, to renounce all this "self" of my personality and to live a life of impersonal selflessness. At moments, too, I have had the temptation of getting married, and be done with the whole thing, and then just drift along, and keep myself from thinking. But here again comes this difficulty—during my four years at home, I have learned to know men thoroughly, and so when it comes to actually taking one of them, I hesitate. You know, of course, that no man really views life as we women do. If they have not already had liaisons, they will eventually have them. I have seen so many instances of this; men whom I thought more absolutely reliable. This is a terrible confession to make, I know.
>
> Oh, dada, dada, how I miss you! How I wish you were here. Three months ago, just before I left Shanghai, I had hoped that a change of climate, a change of scenery, would pull me out of myself, but, in spite of the very gay life I have had here, I cannot seem to get away from myself. And the worst is, I cannot talk to even my sister about how or what I feel, for as I told you, you are the only one I can "think aloud" to.[6]

While admitting she was envied by her friends, family and acquaintances for the comfortable and full life she led, a world-weary, rather bored Mayling believed true happiness eluded her. She wondered if solace might be found in her Methodist-based religious beliefs. She noticed the recent change in her sister, Mrs. Kung, who once had denied the existence of God, shunned the very subject of religion, and plainly said it was all old wives' nonsense. But after going through periods of agony and misery, Ailing Kung had turned to God and found peace in life and faith in living. Mayling looked upon her as the most brilliant mind in the family, and unusually keen, quick-witted, vivacious and energetic—certainly not fanatical. Yet she struck her youngest sister as deeply religious, praying to God to help for solution of her problems. Ailing urged Mayling to commune with God. Mayling took her advice—and felt a great deal happier as though she no longer was carrying a heavy burden alone.

"In having closer communion with God, the essential feature is faith that this Supreme Being is close to you, and is with you all the time," she wrote Emma Mills. "Such external forms as church worship and the Bible, etc., are good only in so far as they keep you in getting closer to God. The essential character though is this belief in the all-powerful love of God.

"I have found that the best way to get into close communion with God is to select a hymn, the meaning of which is exactly what you desire, then read or sing the words till the idea permeates through your consciousness, and you really feel that your mind is ready for communion with God: then pray, as you would talk to your father or with a very close friend. ... this is really the way how I can most strongly feel the presence of God." Mayling urged Emma to try this approach to bring solace and focus into her daily existence.[7]

Mayling also had a more down-to-earth idea for the two of them. The scholarly Wellesley duo should collaborate on turning out English versions of classic Chinese literature. Mayling would translate the essence and spirit of these masterpieces, and Emma could shape them into form. "How would the works of 'Mills & Soong' strike you!"[8]

Several weeks later, in July 1921, Mayling again proposed co-authorship of English editions of Chinese literature. She raised the question of her return to America. But she explained that her mother had recently lost $50,000 in the gold exchange market and as a result had curtailed spending within the family. Emma, however, should give serious thought to crossing the Pacific and living in China.[9]

It stood as a tempting proposal. Mills' life had been full of disappointments since leaving the army nurses' training. A writing job in Washington failed to materialize. Shortly after her return to New York, she faced an operation for appendicitis and a long recovery. Well again by the spring of 1920, she found a job at $25 a week, with the Inter-Church World Movement, writing up reports from data turned in by field investigators. That fall she began an evening lecture course taught by historian James Harvey Robinson at the New School of Social Research in downtown Manhattan. After a month or so, she dropped out for no apparent reason, and quickly filled her free evenings with theatergoing. Yet life seemed depressing, hopeless, with fits of despair and bitterness. "I never quite lose myself," she noted in her journal on July 27, 1921.

> Generally, I loathe the possibility of being swept off my feet, very rarely I long for the experience. I would probably be happier & more nearly normal if I could plunge. But always there is that on-looker, weighing values, considering consequences. I think the inmost core of my temperament is indifference. Or that familiar & oft-acted upon horror of becoming dependent upon anyone or anything, of giving anyone or anything the real power to hurt me.[10]

Work, books, and restlessness, in her own words, described her fitful life. She looked for some one, some thing, great enough, fine enough, strong enough, to lift her off her feet. Travel held the greatest allure. So she quit her job with the idea of trying the West. In September Emma began a cross-country journey, traveling to Chicago via Albany, Buffalo and Detroit by boat and train. Her efforts at finding a job there were at best peripheral. A modest bank account and a letter of credit were not exactly incentives in that direction. "Transplanting my ennui from New York to Chicago has accomplished nothing," she wrote her best friend from the wartime summer as Farmerettes, Mandy Mandeville. She soon decided to go on to San Francisco, where her brother De Long, a 1921 graduate of Annapolis just starting his naval career, and his bride lived. In California, Emma's job hunting led her to newspaper offices, where interviews produced no offers. Common sense told her that she needed a definite employable skill. So she signed up for a three-month business school course in stenography and typewriting.

Mayling's letters again urged her to come to China. "To think that only a body of water is to separate us!" she exclaimed. "I want you to come to China very much, because I want to see you! But and apart from this purely personal consideration, there is no reason why you should not catch a glimpse of the East when you are so near the Orient. I am sure you will find life here full of interest, color and movement.... Now if you can manage to get your passage out here, I can guarantee to get you back to America."[11]

Mayling pointed out that there were plenty of jobs in Shanghai, suggesting tutoring three or four hours a day for some $100 to $150 a week. Emma

The dynamic Soong sisters—Mayling (left), Chingling (right) and Ailing—had a rare and well-publicized reunion in Chungking to quell rumors of a family split. Chingling, widow of Dr. Sun, agreed to downplay her firm allegiance to Chinese communists during the Sino-Japanese conflict. (AP/Wide World Photographs.)

would live with the Soongs, then after a few months go to Canton to stay with Mrs. Sun. In the summer, Mayling and Emma might visit Shansi, where Mrs. Kung kept a house. "At any rate, you don't have to worry about anything—have a good rest, see the Orient, and perhaps do some work together in English based on Chinese fiction." Mayling wondered how each had changed in four years since college. "One cannot help changing in four years, especially as the mode of living, the standard of ideals, and external conditions here are different from those in Wellesley. I think, though, that we have kept sufficiently near to each other through constant correspondence not to be utter strangers, and shall be able to find a common meeting ground."[12]

Emma's family acquiesced on her decision to visit her college confidante an ocean away. She felt relief thus far of having gotten away from her disjointed, multi-generational and matriarch-dominated household, and invigorated by plans of an indefinite absence from America, and perhaps permanent "leave" from New York. Writing to Mandy back East, another matter crossed her mind: "If I should come back with a Chinese husband, would you receive us? I'm gathering statistics from all my friends on that point. It's a very delicate question."

Everywhere in San Francisco that Emma looked there were reminders of China and what lay ahead. "Ultimate destination?" she asked herself in a letter to Wellesley classmate Helen McKeag. "God knows! I have already been asked sarcastically if I am intending to take in Heaven & Hell on this trip, too." And as to such an adventure as a young, single woman, she replied, "Afraid to travel alone? Bah! There's even an added spice to it."[13]

Then, in early January of 1922 came thrilling news from Mayling. A job awaited Emma on the English-language *Shanghai Gazette* at $200 a month, mostly reporting women's clubs' activities. "The dream of a life coming true," she told her friends. She telegraphed home for a few hundred dollars in order to book passage—and, surprisingly, Grandmother came through with the funds. "My temperature has been 120, my pulse 400, for the past 24 hours," she jokingly related to Mandy. "I beam upon the world at large. ... meanwhile, to get a passport, my teeth fixed, typhoid inoculation, vaccination, permanent wave, buy a trunk, clothes and a Corona; make an expert typist of myself—that is the one adamant requirement."[14]

7

Among Movers and Shakers

On the morning of March 26, 1922, Mayling met Emma's passenger ship, USS the *Hoosier State*, at Shanghai, delayed several hours because of the low tides at the mouth of the Yangtze River. Looking down from the deck of the ship to the bustling, crowded docks and clusters of waterfront junks, Emma had the feeling that "these are my people." And this land would be her "home." In China, Emma believed, she'd discover her "calling."

Mayling hustled her college chum through customs and into the family automobile, and on to the Seymour Road house. Emma had originally booked passage on the SS *China*, a boat recommended by Mayling and set to sail in February, but labor troubles delayed the ship from leaving Hong Kong for the United States and returning to the Far East. A Japanese liner could have transported her to the Orient a few days later. Emma, however, felt uneasy about traveling on a Japanese boat as it might expose Mayling to criticism on her behalf. An American vessel was neutral ground, so to speak, and on March 4 she boarded the Pacific Mail Steam Ship Company's *Hoosier State*. The voyage of three weeks encompassed 12- to 24-hour stopovers in Honolulu, Yokohama and Kobe.

Mayling celebrated Emma's long anticipated arrival and her newspaper job with a full-scale luncheon of eight or nine different dishes on the table, set with both silver knives and forks and ivory chopsticks. Later that afternoon, Mayling proudly took Emma to see the family's spacious, country-styled Avenue Joffre house, still owned by Mrs. Soong but unoccupied. Mayling indicated that she was about to sell it because of hard times.

Mayling had initially invited Emma to live with the Soongs, but her American classmate quickly discovered that she would be living "on the economy" in a furnished top-floor room in a three-story gray-brick boarding house at 103 Bubbling Well Road, a main thoroughfare just beyond the city race track and opposite the Belgian consulate. Emma, thought Mayling, would more fully experience life in China and the vibrant mix of Oriental and Occidental without the isolation and comfort within the Soong household. Perhaps, too, Mayling wished to maintain her own independence and privacy.

7. Among Movers and Shakers

Shanghai's portside, the Bund on the Huangpu River, teemed with junks and other small craft when Emma Mills landed in 1922. (Mills–DeLong collection.)

In Emma's eyes, Mayling seemed nervous and jittery, in perpetual motion. She couldn't sit still, she observed, nor even stick to one topic of conversation for more than five minutes. She steadfastly tracked the presidential activities of her brother-in-law and sister in Canton, especially the political and military shifts that affected Dr. Sun's leadership. She spoke of mysterious travels; stories had circulated before Emma's arrival to the effect that Mayling might become governor of a province.

Nonetheless, she never faltered as a consummate hostess and eager guide. Invitations to luncheons, teas and dinner parties placed Emma in a swirl of sumptuous meals in exquisite settings with heady conversation by an array of urbane movers and shakers, both Chinese and foreign. Mayling insisted that her non-dancing classmate accompany her and T.V. Soong to dances, usually given by returned students, chiefly from America. "All the latest steps, including cheek to cheek dancing," the observant Emma wrote her mother. "I was much interested in this exhibition of what we have done for China. Mayling doesn't dance, so that lets me out nicely as far as that was concerned."[1]

Upon Emma Mills' arrival, Mrs. Soong—non-family addressed her as Madame Soong—had not appeared to greet her because the family matriarch bore a facial blemish and wanted it to heal before meeting her daughter's classmate. A week or so passed before she emerged. Gradually she got used to having Emma around the house, became quite friendly, and even ventured a bit in speaking English to her. Mrs. Soong then told Mayling she wished her daughter was as sweet and quiet as Emma seemed to be. To which Mayling remarked, "I don't blame her, knowing me as we do."

Mayling dutifully wrote to Dr. and Mrs. Mills of their daughter's safe arrival in Shanghai.

> I cannot tell you how glad I am to see Emma! She certainly is a nice jolly companion.... Oh, yes, I must tell you that some of my Chinese friends who have met her say she is very beautiful, and even I have to admit to her, that she is good looking, altho I hate to make the admission, because she is such a conceited little minx anyway. I can well see that before very long, I shall probably have to be Emma's bridesmaid, only as I told her, she is so conceited that she thinks nobody is good enough to be the master of her heart and hand. But probably she might take one of them to be her household coolie and door mat all rolled in one. Can you imagine it?
>
> Mother asked me to tell her that foreign bachelors are very flirtatious in Shanghai. I told Mother that Emma knows fairly well how to use her strong right hand if the occasion demands it.

Mayling's closing words reassured the Millses that "the lady of the boarding house where she is staying is very nice and so Emma will be well protected on every side."[2]

Mayling's involvement with investigative studies by a women's club committee into degrading factory conditions gave Emma a first-hand look at a Shanghai plant. The manager at the Edison light bulb factory, an American, expected labor troubles from such meddling; Mayling suggested a comprehensive roundtable conference of Chinese, as well as Japanese and other foreign mill owners. The manager, however, vowed to have nothing personally to do with attempts to ameliorate working conditions, believing whoever meddled would be blamed for the inevitable catastrophe. Mayling pointed out that 45 percent of the country's industries were controlled by the Japanese, and they stood poised to grab a larger interest at any opportunity. Chinese owners, she thought, should especially be aware of the role that better-treated labor played in the economic advancement for a stronger and unified China.[3]

On their forays into downtown Shanghai, Mayling and Emma caused a good deal of commotion. Mayling sometimes wore Chinese dress but added a foreign cape and shoes. And with her hair done in Western style, she was the object of many stares by Chinese, who discussed whether she could be Chinese or not, especially with Emma at her side. "When we were getting gasoline the other day," noted Emma, "quite a crowd stood about the car commenting upon us." And when Mayling was completely outfitted in American clothes, passing Chinese peered into her face, again wondering if this attractive young woman was foreign or Chinese.[4]

Mayling indicated that she felt freer in foreign clothes. Her family, except T.V., she revealed, considered her ugly because she was more energetic and animated than most Chinese women, whose hands, she added, usually remained limp when one takes them. "She has no interest in an attempt to write in the vernacular," Emma noted, "and no interest in the new phonetic alphabet, which do well enough for 'the common herd.' If she is so conservative here, what hopes?"[5]

Shopping with Mayling revealed her exalted local status. In an underwear shop, she bought two white-silk, embroidered petticoats for $12. She had no money with her, but simply wrote an IOU, gave her name and address, and was permitted to walk out of the shop with her purchases.

Mayling often vented anger against servants. One day she overturned a scrap basket on her number one house boy. Another time she confronted Emma's rooming house boy over his slowness in doing her laundry. She demanded his name and where he came from—with the result that he quickly became most attentive in his duties.

Mayling rarely hesitated to ask Emma to do special tasks, usually shopping and handling merchandise orders from overseas. She once arranged for a shipment of milkweed cream from the States and saw it through customs. Banking and delivering messages became routine, as did tracing sources of gossip. "They call these creatures private secretaries and pay them a salary!" Emma thought to herself.

Work at the *Shanghai Gazette*, for which she was paid $215 a month in five dollar bills, entailed writing all personal and social items, and co-editing the women's page. Her beat in the International Settlement ranged from the American consulate and British police headquarters to art exhibits and garden parties. She sought to include a book review column as there was little or nothing like it in China. But with no copyright laws there, many journals merely clipped and reprinted reviews and other articles from foreign papers without a thought. At one point, the *Gazette*, with Emma's encouragement, published Mayling's English translations of Chinese short stories. After two months on the job, Emma briefly took over running the entire shop—editing, layout, headlines, and printing supervision—when the editor and his assistant went out of town.

Emma's zeal as a journalist soon waned. She took a dislike to *Gazette* publisher and editor-in-chief Eugene Chen and his indifference to her and "lack of humanity." Educated as a lawyer in England, he had abandoned a legal practice to become a crusading journalist in support of Dr. Sun and a political climber—and a reputed suitor of Mayling. In due course Emma lost all interest in the *Gazette* following a staff change. "Li-T'sai began to assert his powers of editor. He interferes with everything—& his own work is execrable.... I take a book along with me, & spend much of the day reading."[6]

Chingling Sun suggested to Mayling and Emma that they start a weekly of their own. "Mayling doesn't take it a bit seriously," Emma wrote home. "But I think something might be done, in the course of time. If I stay out here any great length of time, and in newspaper work at all—you know my

Mayling visited Peking in 1924. Emma snapped this photograph of her wearing "fearfully dignified" Chinese clothes. At left: American journalist Dorothy Gould Bess. (Mills–DeLong collection.)

sticking proclivities—that is just what I should want to do, go in business for myself."[7]

With the arrival of spring, Mayling planned a six-day holiday in the old Ming dynasty capital, Nanking. She needed rest, and believed the change of scenery would help break up a cold Emma had had for weeks. They traveled by train to the walled city and settled into the Nanking Garden Hotel. A set of notices, in Chinese, neatly framed on the wall of their room, requested that occupants not be noisy, talk loudly nor giggle with the prostitutes after midnight. Emma asked Mayling if they were supplied by the hotel. "Oh, no," she replied, "but of course they can always be sent for."

The two college companions enjoyed their leisure, going to bed early and sleeping until noon. An excursion to the Ming Dynasty tomb, however, necessitated an early wake-up at 5:30. They set off in a pony-driven carriage along a broad rural highway toward three massive stone structures, the portals in the old wall of the Ming palace enclosure of the 15th century. They visited a museum for Ming relics, and its displays of stone tablets, fragments of columns, mirrors of bronze, pieces of pottery and porcelain, and scroll portraits, and finally, the tombs themselves with their row of centuries-old stone figures, and gateways and courtyards. The day's itinerary ended with stops at several Confucian temples. There, street vendors and beggars called out, "old lady," in Chinese to get the attention of the 27-year-old Western tourist in their midst.[8]

Emma as an extended member of Mayling's household quickly gained an insight into the struggles between the North and the South for control of China, and the cabinet crises, street protests, factory strikes, and military encounters—and face-saving tactics. In Canton, China's most southerly large city, Dr. Sun remained committed to crushing corrupt provincial warlords and unifying the disjunctive country. To the North, in Peking, military leader Wu Pei-fu and his private army controlled much territory, including the vital Peking-Hankou railway and its revenues. British officials and merchants downplayed the nationalistic push of the Canton government, preferring the status quo with its international concessions and extraterritorial conclaves in China's major cities. Dr. Sun soon joined forces with the governor of Manchuria, General Chang Tso-lin, to further a plan for unification. Chang sent 70,000 troops from Mukden southward to support contemplated pro–Sun changes in the Peking government. All parties seemed anxious to get rid of the president of the northern alliance, old Hsu Shih-chang. Meanwhile, W.W. Yen, minister of foreign affairs, fled to Tientsin, adding embarrassment to increasing disorder within the Hsu administration.[9]

Mayling spoke of her family's possible involvement with the Northern government. Her brother-in-law, H.H. "Chauncey" Kung, had been asked by Peking to take charge of the commercial aspect of the return of Shantung from Japanese control, following agreement at the multi-nation Washington Conference in early 1922. Mayling thought Kung had been approached because it was known he was thoroughly honest, and Peking decided honesty was the better policy when it came to bringing Shantung back into Chinese sway. "He is a Shansi man," Emma recorded, "his family originally from Shantung, but his sympathies are with the Southern party, and known to be. He is considering accepting, however, for the sake of China."

Dr. Sun's legal adviser and proselyte Eugene Chen, however, opposed the idea. Not seeing beyond party lines, Mayling, too, made it clear that anything that led to success for the Peking government simply hindered the Canton cause, which always came first. A Chinese aristocrat, Kung reminded one and all of "my ancestor, Confucius, whose tomb is in Shantung." For that reason alone, he'd be comfortable in the North!

The savvy Kung had been born into a family of merchants and bankers with a strong bent for education. He studied at the American Mission Board School in Shansi (where he later became principal), moved on to North China College at age 16, and then pursued degrees in the States at Oberlin and Yale. With a BA in chemistry, and an MA from the 1906–07 term in New Haven, he returned to China in time to participate in the beginning phases of the 1911 revolution. His first wife, a Shansi girl, died shortly after their marriage the year before. When the revolution encountered a setback, Dr. Sun, Kung and the Soongs fled to Japan. That influential country had often served as a refuge and gathering place for Chinese intent on upsetting the status quo in their own land. For two years they lived as political fugitives apart from China. Returned students in alliance with Dr. Sun's goals, Kung and Ailing soon met (although apparently they had first been introduced at a party in New York in 1906 when both were studying in the States). The Soongs placed no obstacles to the courtship of 33-year-old, Christian-raised Kung and their eldest daughter. They wed in a church in Yokohama. Pauline, the first of their four children, was born in 1916 soon after their return to China.[10]

The Kungs with their vast financial resources played an increasingly major part in the affairs of state, be it in the South or the North of China. By 1922, with an mercenary eye on the northern domains, warlords Wu Pei-fu and Chang mobilized and hurled invectives at each other. Both factions seemed to be trying to gain popular support by propaganda. "Rather a new departure for mandarins!" Emma noted.[11] Hostilities ended with the defeat of pro-unification Chang by the unenlightened Wu. As a result, Kung declined the job in Shantung.

Real, close-at-hand danger enveloped the Suns in June 1922. Living at their hillside residency in Canton, with minimum protection from assault or artillery barrage, Chingling and her husband were attacked in an about-face by Dr. Sun's military commander, General Chen Chiung-ming, the warlord of Kwangtung province. Sun had urged his general to lead his army north to help bring unity to China. Chen, worried over his weakening hold on South China, however, secretly believed a thrust from there to the North unwise. Purposely misinformed by their own advisors for their personal advantage, the Suns soon left Canton to prepare for a northern expedition without Chen. They camped nearby in the town of Shaokuan to organize the loyal Kuomintang (KMT) troops. In their absence, General Chen wasted no time in taking control of Canton in what was called "that mutiny at Canton." The Suns hurried back to the presidential quarters, but now realized their precarious position and fled to safety on a KMT gunboat, their floating garrison.[12]

At first word of the mutiny, the Kungs drafted a newspaper editorial backing Dr. Sun's efforts. Later that evening, Mayling, T.V. and Emma sat around the family dining room table working on this statement for immediate publication. A kimona-garbed Mayling compiled suggestions from the others. Tea was constantly brought in, and at nine, ham and eggs. Shortly before midnight, the sleepy trio had polished the paragraphs supporting the Suns in their hour of turmoil.[13]

On June 25 Chingling Sun arrived in Shanghai, incognito, in the disguise of a round-shouldered country woman without belongings. Both Suns had landed in Hong Kong a week or so earlier, where Chingling had wired Mayling for $500 to book passage on a boat to Shanghai, a safe haven. "Small, slight, very pale, and altogether the loneliest thing I have ever seen," observed Emma at their first meeting at 29 Rue Molière, the Suns' Shanghai quarters. Emma stayed for supper and later helped Mayling with a tailor who came by to put together some clothes for Chingling, who only had the outfit on her back—an amah's trouser suit of shiny black. She bemoaned the loss of various possessions left back in Canton—the diary of her eight years of marriage, a sable coat, trunkfuls of silver, a pair of elephant tusks presented by the king of Siam at Dr. Sun's inaugural. Mayling, in particular, expressed dismay at the Suns' loss of a batch of new books just sent out from New York's Brentano's and forwarded to Canton a short time before.[14]

On August 14, 1922, Dr. Sun landed in Shanghai aboard the *Empress of Russia*. Mayling, Chingling and T.V. huddled in a launch to meet him, and elude officials and crowds. Sun needed a haircut. To Chingling's remonstrances over the neglect of his appearance, he replied that the thought of anyone fussing around his head was more than he could bear in his present state of mind. Nevertheless, she had a barber sent for, and his hair was cut—at a charge of three dollars, nearly ten times the usual charge.

Mayling expressed the belief that Dr. Sun might be "re-elected" president by a broader mandate from the current Parliament. But his wife groaned that she hoped not. "I'm anxious to have him retire and enjoy life." And there was talk of the possibility of asking Emma to be Chingling's private secretary.[15]

Emma would soon be looking for another job. There were more staff changes and cutbacks at the *Gazette*. Financial support for the paper had shrunk, especially from those political backers of Sun who now believed it poorly served the "southern cause." Mayling confronted its owner and Sun ally Eugene Chen as to why her American friend had been dropped. She learned the *Gazette* was letting her go because she "hadn't the faculty for nosing out news." Chen suggested magazine writing, or teaching.[16] (The *Gazette* soon folded when Chen bought the American-published *Shanghai Star*, and combined the two papers into the *Evening News*.)

To Emma, the job loss was just another bump in the long road of careers. "The Soongs and numerous other friends," she wrote home that summer, "would help me out at a moment's notice any time should any sort of necessity ever arise." And with a jab at her New York household, she continued: "You can't imagine how seriously they take the responsibility of me, more so in some respects than my own family ever did."[17]

The summer heat curtailed many social activities. Friends were traveling to cooler climates. The Soongs held the promise of trips together—to Shansi, Peking and Hong Kong—but nothing materialized. Increasingly occupied with running the Suns' house, Mayling began to spend less time with Emma, who, nonetheless, continued to receive mail and packages at the Soong house. "Mayling has acquired a cast-iron, cut and dried classification of the world," Emma concluded in a letter to her mother. "The people who are interesting and have a good time are 'fast,' and one must have nothing whatever to do with them; the people one may associate with are mostly missionaries and YWCA workers—and boring. She really has grown fearfully narrow-minded and straight-laced. And when it is a question of Chinese people, dreadfully snobbish. All of which I tell her in no uncertain terms but without the slightest effect. She wanted me to vacation with one of her YW friends, a very nice, but fearfully colorless middle-aged English woman, but I rebelled. Would infinitely rather go off by myself."[18]

Mayling's increasing aloofness was underscored by a brief remark without elaboration made soon after Emma's arrival in China. "I'm likely to get married in the next two or three months." Heaven knows, Emma had thought, who it is this time!

8

Sisterhood

In mid–1922 Sun Yat-sen remained cloistered and well-guarded at Rue Molière. His very life continued to be a coveted target for those eager to maintain a weak, fractious China. Sun had been driven from Canton by his one-time-ally, General Chen Chiung-ming, on a dispute over Sun's tax policies and other issues. Sun was under great pressure from representatives of the Soviet Union who were seeking influence in China that would weaken the influence of the Western powers. A good man who was seen as impetuous and naive about politics in China, he was constantly writing to Western diplomats and leaders seeking their support and intervention for his government in opposition in Canton. The fact is that Sun was a rebel against the Peking government recognized by the foreign powers whose interest was the continued recognition of their treaty rights.

Ailing Kung and her husband and Mayling brought Sun news and bits of information on events that could strengthen his position and keep him in some degree of command. It seems natural that Mayling would become enamored with Dr. Sun, who had also been raised in America, chiefly Hawaii, and whose democratic and republican views she shared from her American education. More and more the three Soong sisters intensely debated the uncertainties of Dr. Sun's faltering political foothold and his course of action to remain titular leader of South China.

The three siblings would become the world's most remarkable sister combination—far better known in America than in most of China, where wives of important men were completely overshadowed. By standards of charm, intelligence, influence and even wealth the Soongs stood out in high circles of government. Before long, the tagline had it that "one [Ailing] loves money, one [Mayling] loves power, and one [Chingling] loves China."[1] The sisters and various members of their family often disagreed politically, but they had close personal relationships. This was especially true in the latter days of Sun's life.

With a hand in helping to run two households in Shanghai—her mother's and sister Chingling Sun's—Mayling curtailed her fervent involvement in social gatherings and charity proceedings. In the midst of fast-changing administrative and military polemics centering around Dr. Sun, she witnessed and, indeed, participated in discussions and decisions impacting her country's fate and future.

The slow-growing but clearly vibrant Communist Party in China was a frequent subject of argument. The party was founded a year earlier, in July 1921. Started by intellectuals and students, it took its cue from neighboring Soviet Russia. Reassuring skeptical Chinese that it had no grand designs on its government, Soviet Communists voiced sympathy for the quandary faced by China. They promised to support Dr. Sun's goals and help organize national changes. Sun now looked to them for aid to sustain his movement towards a modern China.

Although supportive of her brother-in-law's revolutionary ends, Mayling stood apart from the Suns' advisors who favored a liaison with Communists within China and in Russia, a subject that sparked fiery words inside the walls of 29 Rue Moliere. Dr. Sun needed Soviet support—politically, militarily and monetarily—and he reluctantly joined with his revolutionary neighbor. Communists soon were allowed to join the Kuomintang as individual members.

On-the-scene advice stemmed from Moscow's agent, Mikhail Borodin. This charismatic and experienced communist pushed policies to organize peasants and workers in the name of a united China, yet with aims of ultimately Sovietizing the country. "As children of a revolutionary family whose father was a close associate of Dr. Sun," wrote Mayling in her 1978 book, *Conversations with Mikhail Borodin*, "we saw much of the Borodins, be it in Peiping (then called Peking), during Dr. Sun's last illness in that Northern city or in Canton when it was the center of the Nationalist movement and government, or still later in Wuban."[2] Long and ingenuously revealing political-philosophical discussions and colloquies with Borodin only strengthened Mayling's anti-communist views then and in the years ahead.

Emma Mills referred to ideological and procedural tiffs between Chingling and Mayling—to the degree that they didn't speak to each other for days. Sun, too, had his ups and downs with the Soong family as well as with his advisors, who often quarreled among themselves. Illness again struck Mayling. Her anxiety and frustration led to a nervous and physical breakdown. At one point it necessitated a drastic step—electric shock treatments. And before her full recovery, she was bedridden from an outbreak of boils.

By then, Emma, lacking employment, had left Shanghai. In late summer of 1922 her sisterly friend and fellow Farmerette, Mandy Mandeville, had written from New York of plans to journey to the Near East. She sought adventure underscored by a modicum of work. Emma, with time on her hands and some money in her pocket (from Grandmother) suggested they meet in Japan and briefly explore the countryside, and maybe look into possible jobs.

Mayling and her family chauffeur drove Emma to her Yokohama-bound ship on August 31, a Thursday morning, but a fierce typhoon delayed her sailing. So Mayling brought Emma back to the Soong house on Seymour Road. "She reclined on the couch most of the day," Emma remembered, and "flew into a tantrum when she discovered the servants had given me some of their food for lunch, but gradually grew more cheerful thereafter. ... it was blowing furiously and raining in torrents. So they made up a bed on the couch in the corner room downstairs for me. Two women tailors were put on the floor in the parlor, also owing to the storm. Quite a houseparty.

"Their telephone was out of order, so we couldn't find out ahead about the ship. ... later we were not surprised to find she was waiting still another 24 hours." The storm persisted. "Mayling laughed, and predicted that we would not get away till Monday." Mayling was nearly right; the ship sailed on Sunday, after a three-day delay.[3]

Emma and Mandy joined up in Yokohama, and the two traveled to Tokyo, where they spent their first night at the newly opened Imperial Hotel. "It was designed by a Chicago architect [Frank Lloyd Wright] in a sort of Aztec style," Emma explained in a long letter home. "A low building of yellow brick and tile, with gilded mortar, queer carvings, courts with pools of water. The interior looks like a futurist movie. The bathtub you step down into, rugs and furniture covering are of cubist designs. I love it, myself, but opinions differ. At any rate, it is well worth going half around the world to see."[4] As tourists, the duo visited the temples at Nikko, the bronze Buddha at Kamakura, the imperial gardens at Kyoto. Anxious to show her eager companion China, Emma booked their passage on a boat to Korea, where they went by train to Seoul, and finally to the old capital of China, Peking. They were among some 9,000 foreigners living or visiting in that city; nearly half were Japanese. "Foreigners come here for gain," observed Emma, "or from a desire to inflict their standards on others, or because here they may enjoy a greater sense of importance than would be possible at home.

"Foreigners in general in China are provincial, mutually scornful of each other, & really not anxious for China to progress," she concluded. "And yet people, or rather, nations, can't let each other alone—there is a meddlesome desire to reform China. It is hard for foreigners to realize that in China they still have a living patriarchal society.... It is absurd, & may prove disastrous, to try to fit Western institutions into such a background. China has already tried out many of these ideas, at any rate, & found them wanting."[5]

In Peking, Mandy quickly found a secretarial job. Emma, with few leads to continue as a journalist, failed in her efforts to find any sort of employment.

The outgoing and gregarious Mandy attracted a host of attentive men, both Chinese and foreign. Emma went along to a constant round of soirees and afternoon teas. Legations created much of the social atmosphere for detached youths, government secretaries, interns, and bankers. Mandy's paycheck subsidized the Mills-Mandeville social life, and their room and board. Yet, having experienced life in China for six months, Mandy was ready to move on. She decided on a leisurely trip back to New York by way of India and England.

Frustrated by lack of regular work and income, Emma often voiced dismay over Mayling's inattentiveness, especially her lack of communication and chronic delay in forwarding mail and packages sent to her from America. "She is just constitutionally irresponsible about other peoples' affairs," Emma concluded.

In her desuetude, Emma raised eyebrows and questions. "It seems that everybody in town is much interested in my plans and the source of my income. They can't imagine anyone can be out here without a definite job, and imagine my indefiniteness covers some deep laid scheme. If this were Japan, I should probably have the secret service camping on my trail."[6]

Perhaps employment at that point mattered little for the phlegmatic Emma. China stood on the brink of anarchy, with Peking in a vacuum. There was no president; Li Yuan-hong was driven out of office by another warlord, Tsao Kun. The disarrayed government, moreover, lacked a premier and a finance minister, leaving only three members of a defunct cabinet as regents in charge. In outlying provinces troops engaged in civil war. China was experiencing a series of factious wars among most "warlord" groups. Peking residents wondered how soon aggressive troops would march in and take possession of the city. Chinese bandits, too, profited by the governing chasm. In early May 1923 they wrecked a train near Lincheng in Shantung province and restrained about 200 passengers, including a score of foreigners. Among them was Lucy Aldrich, sister-in-law of John D. Rockefeller, Jr. (the bandits released her and two female companions plus several others the next day). The remaining captives faced weeks of uncertainty, and negotiations among the predators, Chinese officials, and foreign legation representatives. Jacob Gould Schurman, American minister to China, resisted outcries for foreign military intervention, believing the government of China must take the initiative for freeing the captives. It agreed, then took strong action, and in early June the bandits released the remaining detainees.

Emma and most foreigners seemed unperturbed, viewing it as just another episode in the woof and warp of China. And by October, northern China at least had Tsao Kun duly elected president by the Peking Parliament—with the aid of generous bribes.

Early that year 26-year-old Mayling wrote of another pending engagement—a family-arranged marriage to a man to whom she seemed quite indifferent. "It would mean her living in Peking, perhaps, or abroad, as I believe he is in the diplomatic service."[7]

The Kungs turned up in Peking on their way north from the Kung ancestral estate in Shansi, and contacted Emma. But Ailing added virtually nothing to the vague rumor of the possible marriage of her sister. Later, in the summer, Mayling accompanied Ailing and her brother-in-law to Peking. Delighted to receive a message from Mayling, Emma met her for tea at a hotel. After nearly a year apart, Mayling, she noted, now wore Chinese clothes, except for foreign shoes, and looked "fearfully dignified." As in times past, they spent many hours in shopping excursions and gab sessions. The Kungs sometimes were there. "They tell amusing stories of some of the dinners they go to, where the Chinese officials are all afraid to talk about anything and consequently the conversation is nothing but one joke after another, till Mayling says she knows all the old chestnuts by heart."[8]

With lines of correspondence somewhat re-established, Mayling related bits and pieces of her life in Shanghai. She had had trouble with her eyes. Then, after successful treatment, she took up writing Chinese poetry in the classical style. She kept busy with a new commission on child welfare. And before the year ended, she left on a visit to the Suns, now back in Canton. But she remained closemouthed on her pending engagement and possible marriage.

Chinese friends urged the increasingly bored and restless Emma to utilize her days without a job by studying the Chinese language. It would be invaluable for a journalist, they pointed out. Grandmother agreed to pay the $75 tuition, and to remit a modest monthly allowance. Daily lessons in speaking Chinese began at North China Union Language School. As did dancing lessons! Of this breakthrough, Emma wrote: "I poured at a tea yesterday, and then they made me dance, and I danced all the rest of the afternoon, and they made me say I would take it up.... Can't say I see any fun in it, but if it makes other people so much happier and simplifies the social end of things so much, suppose I may as well submit gracefully."[9]

The most satisfying role for Emma came about as a guest at a birthday party in July 1923 for a venerable Manchu grandmother. Emma and three other women were the only foreigners in attendance. During the festivities, she learned of the dowager's teenage granddaughter's wish to learn basic English in preparation for her marriage to 16-year-old Pu Chieh, younger brother of the ex-emperor, Henry Pu Yi, who had sat on the Manchu throne from age two to six (1908–1912). Would Emma consider teaching her at the nominal sum of $10 a month? After several private meetings where she was thoroughly scrutinized, Emma got the nod and readily accepted the challenge to instruct the bright and eager young pupil. The lessons with Annabel Tong continued for the remainder of the year, until shortly before the marriage ceremonies in January 1924.[10]

Emma was privy to ten days of preparations for the wedding and shared the growing excitement, which was as great as though the bride were an American girl, marrying the man of her choice, rather than a Manchu—who was someone she had never seen.

On the wedding day family and special guests in impressively elaborate dress greeted each other in ceremonious manner, augmented by Chinese music.

Emma taught English to teenage Annabel Tong, bride-to-be of Prince Pu Chieh, brother of ex-emperor Henry Pu Yi. A traditional Manchu wedding ceremony in Peking in 1924 remained a cherished memory for Emma. (Mills–DeLong collection.)

The bridal chair, with a gold phoenix signifying the imperial household, was first set down in a court-like chamber while the bride's brother lighted incense to drive away possible lurking evil spirits. With carrying poles, the chair, with the bride hidden inside, was transported to the street where a large procession formed, led by lantern bearers, a foreign-style band, and mandarins on horseback. Meanwhile, Annabel's family skipped off in automobiles to be at the groom's house when she arrived.

Three days later the bride came back for the traditional visit to her father's house. The bridal couple sat at a dining table but didn't touch the food. "They never looked at each other, either, and gave no indication that they were aware of the other's existence. I shall not see her again now till she makes her next visit home, a month after the marriage."[11]

At times Emma despaired over not finding and holding a regular, well-paying job in Peking or Shanghai, such as a reporter. Nonetheless, she kept her hopes high, be it short or long range. A determined Emma Mills wrote home, "There is no question of my coming back to America till I have made good at something out here, if it takes me twenty years."[12]

Although Mayling had initially opened doors for employment in China, it had fallen to 29-year-old Emma to seek out and negotiate on her own a niche in the workaday world of the Near East.

9

In the Thick of Things

Mayling's circle of friends from Wellesley stayed in touch with her well into the 1920s, a half-dozen or more years after graduation. But their letters from America soon decreased as family and jobs took precedence in their lives.[1] Engagements, marriages, children and, indeed, careers inevitably loosened these old school-chum ties, particularly with those overseas. Mayling had urged them to visit her homeland. Only Emma had answered Mayling's faraway call to travel to the Far East and experience life in China.

Emma truly relished the Chinese culture and ongoing encounters with Chinese, not to exclude foreigners from all corners of the globe. Both Peking and Shanghai beckoned as a crossroads of the world for tourists and expatriates, missionaries and medical workers, artists and writers, students and diplomats, tradesmen and mercenaries. Moreover, there were many more men than women in Peking and Shanghai, a port city, with a demand for "extra" girls for the social swirl.

Of her days there, she relayed to college chums a local saying about women from abroad: the first year, she loses her hair, the second, her complexion, and the third, her morals. She was relieved to know she was preserving her youth although the dry air—and occasionally a hot, parching wind—and dust storms were a constant threat to one's complexion.

Living at the North China Language School in Peking, Emma enjoyed the acquaintance of men and women of varied backgrounds and occupations. And among them, there was often a possible suitor. A captain in the Marines became an occasional bridge partner. And following a tea dance, she dined with two recent Harvard graduates "who weren't afraid to show that they had brains and I think were as glad to find me as I was to find them." She took up mah jong and chess with fellow boarders at the school hostel. Rarely lonely and never homesick, Emma, nevertheless, continually found "perfect companionship" in reading books. For most of her long life, she read on the average two books a week; in 1923, her first year in Peking, the annual total reached 140.

Of books, she concluded: "I read books, endless books, & pour other people's thoughts endlessly into the hopper of my mind. But there they simply disappear. With all the material I make nothing myself. I don't suppose I ever thought a remotely original thought in my life. My imagination is active enough, but there are no ideas in me. I could not even put two & two together intellectually & produce such a sorry thing as an editorial."[2]

As to marriage, she once observed in her journal that "a life that achieves nothing but a solving of the mating problem may be a waste of the cosmic energy, but a morning thought prompts me to add, one that does not may be an even greater waste."[3]

Finding and keeping a job or two to pay basic living expenses—and have some extra money for clothes, travel and social activities—remained an abiding challenge. While tutoring the young Manchu bride-to-be, Emma secured part time employment as a reference librarian at the language school. And she soon broke into journalism again. Grover Clark, the American editor of the Chinese-owned, English-language *Peking Leader* (circulation 750), hired her to assist in writing headlines, doing layout, and "putting the paper to bed" three nights a week. Virtually all of the content came as pickup from news agencies, and thus involved no actual writing or reporting, yet the job paid a fair salary. Many front-page stories that year summarized the U.S. presidential contest between incumbent Calvin Coolidge and Democratic candidate, and ultimately loser, John W. Davis. With two jobs, together with periodic tutoring, there remained little time for much else besides work and sleep.

Working side by side with the middle-aged Clark, she often had to endure his double entendres. Tossing aside his puritan inhibitions, he got up courage one day to suggest to Emma that they walk together on the Great Wall after work late that night. She accepted the tryst jeeringly, causing him to call off the amorous interlude—and go home to his wife. A day or two later, he asked Emma to dinner at the Hotel du Nord. She agreed in a matter-of-fact manner. But Grover persisted in voicing an itch to do something beyond dinner, something unconventional—wild and reckless. Emma didn't respond, not being the least bit interested in an affair with her married boss.

Not long after, Emma's supervisor at the library confronted her, perhaps out of jealousy. She was overworked, he exclaimed, and getting herself into poorer physical shape with the passing of each day. She would end up in the hospital, he predicted. So unless she gave up the newspaper job, he would fire her. Emma made it clear she wouldn't quit the *Leader*. "The first time I have ever been fired for my own good," she remarked in a letter to Mandy. "Well, I lose my four months vacation pay ... and have to look for something else with summer coming up and jobs not so easy to find, or content myself with $175 Mexican a month [the prevailing currency, worth approximately 85 U.S. dollars] which is what I get from the paper."[4]

To augment her modest wages, Emma persuaded Mandy and other friends back in New York to sell Chinese goods that she purchased. Taking a commission on such items as mandarin coats, strings of beads, silk embroideries, throw rugs, pieces of brass and cloisonné, Emma, in turn, managed to pick up extra dollars, even after paying shipping charges and customs duties.

She now could add goods merchant to her long list of occupations since receiving her college sheepskin. To Grandmother, she summarized life and work in a somewhat philosophical vein: "It only goes to show again that you might as well do something while you are young for the sake of the training, even if you don't need to. It gives a great deal more point to life, anyway. I have never made very much money at any of my ventures, but I certainly am versatile. Laboratory technician, nurse, farmhand, statistician, newspaper woman, advertising, teacher, librarian and buyer."

Continuing to look back, she wrote, "The thing that makes me perfectly furious every time I think of it, though, is that way I wasted my summers while I was going to college. I never worked less in my life than I did during those winters and had no more need of a vacation than a katydid, and if it hadn't been for the family tradition of my great delicacy—which I have at last shaken myself free from—I could have turned all those lost, wasted months to some account."[5]

Expounding on wasted summers, Emma explained that she could have gone on with a study of German, or taken up Greek or Russian or Italian in earnest, or added other varieties of occupation to her considerable list and seen more of the country and of people. "Instead, I brooded up in my attic and nearly wrecked my sane outlook on life for all time. That is all past history, but I am only fully realizing now what tremendous waste there has been in even my less than thirty years."[6]

In this unusual and frank analysis to the head of the family and her long-standing chastiser, she made no mention of Mayling and her magnetic pull over her, nor the impact of China in her life. Mayling's chummy and boundless advice by 1924 had waned. Her letters now were comparatively infrequent and inconsequential. Emma apparently felt they lacked substance, and discarded them upon receipt or shortly thereafter.

Mayling made virtually no comment on the calamitous political and military situation faced by the Suns, although she was with them in Canton in early 1924. Mayling, it seems, believed that letters in English between Canton and Peking would be censored, as she did earlier with her letters from Shanghai to Emma in New York and San Francisco. There was no evidence that such correspondence was ever screened; the Chinese government post office even told Emma that no foreign letters were ever touched.

Reports of the death of the fifty-eight-year-old Dr. Sun periodically spread across China; some newspapers even ran long obituaries on his demise, which proved false. However, Chingling Sun, Mayling briefly explained, was ill, not her husband. This required Mayling's return to Canton. Once there, she discovered that her sister only wanted company and had actually suffered no sickness. Emma surmised that Mayling would stay in Canton until her mother got lonesome and telegraphed her to come back to Shanghai. "Such is life for the unmarried daughter without occupation who lives at home," Emma concluded in a letter to *her* mother. "In the meantime, Mayling is having an article in one of the Shanghai papers on the Chinese woman and industrialism."[7]

In 1924 Peking experienced one of the hottest summers on records. The thermometer on June 22 reached 108 degrees. The heat wave continued into July. Then, suddenly, the weather turned rainy, cooling down the scorching temperatures. The usual season of daily showers became one of downpours. Fifteen inches fell in eight days, and one afternoon an inch in just 20 minutes flooded many streets. The incessant rain caused the clay walls and tile roofs of some Chinese houses to collapse, downed telegraph lines, and washed out railroad tracks. Other parts of the country suffered, too. Kal-

Emma, age 30 in 1924, posed for a studio portrait while living in Peking. (Mills–DeLong collection.)

gan's business district stayed under water for days, and some 500 people drowned. Property and crop damage proved extensive in other northern areas. The Westernized Mayling, Emma remembered, often spoke of natural calamities in these and similar words: "I know, good Lord, we prayed for rain last spring, but, my God, this is simply ridiculous!"

The horrendous devastation of farmland and widespread homelessness from the worst flood in 35 years led Emma to a new supplementary job. She was hired for six months as publicity director of a drive by an overseas Chinese group to raise two million dollars for flood victims. Under the auspices of the National Flood Relief Drive, Emma began to turn out two or three articles each week for distribution to newspapers in China and other countries.

Just as soon as the rains subsided, pockets of man-made troubles broke out, from Canton in the south to Peking in the north. Battles among provincial military governors put troops on the march in cities and outlying regions. There was fighting near Shanghai between two opposing factions—skirmishes that were halted by heavy rains. To cope with the weather, one general purchased 8,000 umbrellas for his soldiers at the front.

Merchants in Canton vied against Sun Yat-sen's soldiers by organizing a general strike to protest excessive taxation. That, in turn, led to threatened bombardment by Sun's gunboats. One thousand tradesmen died by bullets and ensuing fires. At the same time, more than 1,000 U.S. Marines landed to guard foreign settlements in Shanghai as leaderless armed troops looted deserted Chinese homes and shops.

In Peking, General Wu Pei-fu, the city's military ruler, showed signs of losing control, causing his nemesis, the Manchurian warrior Chang Tso-lin, to jump in and declare war on the city. With Wu away in battle, Feng Yu-hsiang, "the Christian General," double-crossed his friend Wu by occupying Peking and trying to set up a president of his own choosing to replace Tsao Kun. The attempt seemed successful, so Feng invited his ally Dr. Sun to come north for a unification conference in Tientsin to work out a cessation of hostilities.

Newspapers in America eagerly carried accounts of the turmoil in China. Foreign correspondents had instructions to cable all the news they could gather. They often needed to guess at what had transpired on the battlefield and behind the scenes. Reporters on the road wrote of slow and erratic railroad travel as troop movements monopolized the rails. A trip between Peitaiho and Peking, normally taking seven hours, consumed 56 hours, and civilian passengers had to ride in baggage cars. Some 35 miles of railway rolling stock soon ended up jammed in at the end of the line near Shanhaikwan on the Chilian-Manchurian front. Wu Pei-fu struggled to clear up the congestion, but various generals there would not permit a single car to be moved. If a retreat became necessary, they wanted plenty of trains to fall back on.

Serious fighting continued sporadically at the northern front. Artillery fire, not only by day but through the night with the aid of gas-powered searchlights, brought heavy casualties. Adequate means of caring for the wounded remained a constant challenge on all sides.

In Peking Emma faced no food shortages; most staples came into the city by donkey carts, not railway cars. Regular mail delivery, however, worsened. And from her rooming house window, she looked upon a courtyard filled with 100 tons of coal, a precaution for a possible winter fuel shortage. Emma seemed in no physical danger, and expressed little concern over the outcome of the territorial flare-ups. On October 28 she wrote Dr. Mills: "We are all quite safe and comfortable and serene and having the time of our lives being for once in the thick of things."[8]

One immediate and direct effect of the territorial battles left Emma with one less job. The flood relief program abruptly ended; her publicity work was no longer feasible in the midst of a civil war.

If Mayling had apprised Emma of possible peril to foreigners in Peking, no record of her concern exists. Travelers from overseas continued to visit the city, including nine Wellesley graduates and two former faculty members who were welcomed at a collegial tea. With most time and energy focused on the travails of the Suns, Mayling again lived with Chingling. By late fall, as negotiations between Christian general Feng and the victorious Chang Tso-lin got underway in Tientsin, Chingling and Dr. Sun traveled there, and at year's end to Peking. Sun, in declining health for many months, now required constant medical care at their spacious suite at the Peking Hotel. Their attentive brother-in-law, "Chauncey" Kung, joined them, and Ailing soon left Shanghai to help her sister.

Early in 1925, Sun's doctors urged an immediate operation for cancer at nearby Rockefeller Hospital. Newspapers reported the procedure a success, and Sun's staff cautiously spoke of a speedy recovery.

By January Emma's spare time now focused on packing. A decision had been made. She would visit home for three or four months that spring, then return to China in early summer. Her various jobs—they again included work on an hourly basis at the language school reference library—had brought in nearly $500 a month in wages, albeit for a short period. She put aside enough to book passage on the *Empress of Russia*, sailing in February from Shanghai to Vancouver. Among her pieces of luggage stood a trunk jammed with Chinese goods that she expected to sell to friends in a number of cities as she crossed the United States. The leftover items she would thrust upon others in New York. She fully anticipated a profit of a thousand dollars, perhaps more, from this merchandising venture.

While Mayling had welcomed Emma Mills to China with open arms three years earlier, in 1922, she had no time to spare from family concerns for a bon voyage party of any sort. Without fanfare, this new "old China hand" boarded the Canadian Pacific ship bound for a reunion half way around the world—and a world apart from the life she relished, but struggled to sustain.

10

Sun's Successor

Before Emma Mills left Peking for the long voyage home, she had an impromptu get-together with Chingling Sun. It came about when Mayling in a letter to Emma enclosed a letter for her sister with instructions to deliver it in person at the Suns' hotel. There, Chingling, through an aide, declined to see Emma, then suddenly changed her mind. Chingling explained she had been teaching a nurse the particular way her husband liked his back rubbed, and that took priority. Emma ended up joining her for dinner in the Suns' suite. Chingling spoke of being in Canton when Emma returned in June.

In a letter home Emma wrote: "The doctor is getting better she [Chingling] thinks, but the general opinion around town is that he is not going to survive.... I haven't seen him, of course. They have two nurses on the job, and all the doctors.... There is hope of Mayling coming up some time, but not till after I go, I am afraid."[1]

"Fat Mr. Kung came in when we were about the nineteenth course," she noted in a journal entry, "and seemed pleased as a child over his many invitations to lunch and dine. When I said I liked living in Peking but couldn't really explain why, Chingling laughed and said it was because at heart I am an imperialist."[2]

Sun Yat-sen's condition took a definite turn for the worse by February. Daily bulletins offered very little hope for his survival as cancer spread from his liver throughout the rest of his body. Against the advice of his physicians, he was moved to the residence of Wellington Koo, erstwhile foreign minister. There, the Father of the Republic—"the George Washington of China"—died on March 12, 1925. Although Dr. Sun had sporadically controlled affairs in south China, he had failed to unify the country under his leadership, and bring together in any meaningful measure its population of some 400 million. Nonetheless, virtually all political and military factions would look upon him as the founder of modern China, a symbol of the Revolution, a catalyst for national revival. Chingling, who would survive her revered husband for 55 years, devoted her life to promulgating his "three principles of the people": nationalism, democracy, and people's livelihood. In the process this credo aligned Chingling with left-wing policies and the Chinese Communist Party. In so doing, she revealed the failure of the Western powers to support a truly democratic government in Peking and Western intransigence in reforming the "unequal treaties."

On the transpacific ship bound for North America, Emma encountered a U.S. naval officer. She was completely captivated, and he, apparently enamored with the bright and engaging fellow passenger. A shipboard romance ensued. Uncharacteristically, Emma failed to make any reference to the voyage or affair then or later in her journals. She only spoke of it years later to a small handful of friends.

Shortly before the ship reached port, her would-be suitor dealt the liaison a devastating blow: he had a wife, and divorce was out of the question. More sad news awaited Emma upon her arrival in New York. Her mother's health had deteriorated. A mastoid operation a year earlier proved only partially successful. On April 18 Sylvie Mills, age 53, died. Her health had not been a reason for her daughter's decision to travel home that winter. But her unexpected passing quickly changed Emma's intention to return to China. Her aging grandmother needed her at home. Emma faced reality. If she opted for life in China, her future inheritance clearly would be in jeopardy. By staying at West 89th Street, her ongoing need for full-time employment could subside; a small monthly allowance from grandmother would give her leisure and wherewithal to attend concerts and theatre, dine out and visit with friends, and, above all, buy and read books. And later that year to enroll in a Columbia University Chinese studies program.

Keeping track of events in China drew her to scan New York daily newspapers, and various periodicals, and cut out articles for classroom writing assignments and future reference.

Throughout 1925 a kaleidoscope of unrest in China swirled around disunity and personal politics, coalescing and opposing each other with speed and often purposelessness. Military intervention, mob violence, communist agitation, and anti-foreign hostility and resentment of imperialist exploitation accelerated in the wake of the continuing wars. Yet political discord and frequent civil strife failed to affect the lives of most people forced to live under the conditions which such disorders created. It was generally business as usual. In the *New York Times* feature "China: An Odd Paradox of War and Business," Margaret De Forest Hicks wrote that "the vast majority of the Chinese," are so used to a world where civil conflicts have long existed and so totally unconscious of a government and untaught in the fact that it might be blamed for them, that they pursue their duties day in and day out without giving the problems an anxious moment's thought."[3]

Mayling and Chingling, the two youngest Soong sisters, stayed close in the months after Sun's death—perhaps as close as in their early school days in Georgia. Mayling was often by the side of her widowed sister, traveling back and forth from Shanghai to Canton. Mayling also turned to writing, preparing articles for the Shanghai newspaper controlled by the assiduous Eugene Chen. But as she neared a publication date, the paper folded. Besides, Chen, suddenly kidnapped by Manchuria's "Old Marshall" Chang Tso-lin, remained captive in Tientsin. Chen, it seems, had been creating a hero legend around rival "Christian General" Feng. "It is understood that Chen is being treated like an honored guest," journalist Dorothy Gould Bess wrote Emma, "but he is being kept out of mischief at the same time."[4]

Correspondence by Mayling to overseas friends now played little or no part in her life. It wasn't until January 1926 when one of Mayling's long handwritten letters reached Emma from Canton. "Dear Dada," she began on stationary of the Central Bank of China. "I came here some two weeks ago with Mrs. Sun as she had to attend the Second Congress of the Kuomintang. We are visiting my brother T.V. who is Minister of Finance. Since he came into office four months ago, he has increased the government revenues from $1,700,00 to $4,200,00 per month ... without increasing taxation on necessities. Even all the Hongkong papers which jeered at him four months ago when he announced his intention to stabilize finances now say that he had accomplished the seemingly impossible," she proudly added.[5]

With Mayling, it was business as usual vis-à-vis Emma. A refund check from Macy's was enclosed. Would Emma use it to buy more milkweed cream and send the jars to Shanghai?

Mayling described Canton as clean and peaceful, and very different from what Emma had been reading in newspapers. "I wish you were here," Mayling concluded, adding those familiar words that first brought her to China. "If ever you want a job, there are plenty in Canton—*if you are not afraid.*"[6] Which belied the calm and peacefulness she depicted in that city!

Military troubles and complications clearly accelerated and spread from Canton to other cities. Peking, the internationally recognized central government of China, was no exception. Increasingly, all factions rallied under the banner of China for the Chinese, a slogan clearly expressing China's vibrant new nationalism. While Kung was in the States receiving an honorary degree from his alma mater, Oberlin College, his wife and children felt it unsafe to stay in Peking in 1926.

That year Mayling made several long visits to Canton before returning to Shanghai in July. By September, "restless," she wondered where her next trip would take her: back to Canton with Mrs. Sun or possibly north to Peking, where conditions had stabilized to the degree that sister Ailing now considered enrolling her children in the Peking American school.[7]

That fall Mayling's youngest brother, T.A. (Joe) Soong, returned to Harvard for his senior year. She sent with him fabric for a dress with instructions to deliver it personally to Emma.

The number of Georgia-educated Wesleyan College alumnae in China, chiefly in missionary work and teaching, had grown to the extent that a Wesleyan Club evolved in Shanghai. Members elected Mayling its first president.

Chinese university students and recent graduates were viewed as the best gauge of emerging power bases. In 1926 they generally moved in two directions: one, toward the vigorous and colorful "Christian General" Feng in the North and his call for nationalism, augmented by an army he regularly led in hymn singing and baptized en masse with a water hose; and the other, toward Canton where the Kuomintang had been building its strength with the backing of the Communists, and promoting a united national government for all of China.

A new military leader came forth in the South that year—a general who would lead well-trained, disciplined troops in a quest to bring together the disparate provinces of a country in turmoil. General Chiang Kai-shek, an aide of Dr. Sun since the beginning of the downfall of the Manchu empire, had been appointed by Sun to head the new Whampoa Military Academy. Chiang's training and experience contrasted with those regional warlords who, for the most part, lacked regimental training in molding a combat-ready army.

Chiang, born October 31, 1887, at Chikow in the province of Chekiang, south of Shanghai, attended local schools at Fenghu before entering the Paoting Military Academy. A soldier of promise, he was selected to study military science in Japan in 1907. There he first met the exiled Sun Yat-sen, learned the tenets of the revolutionary movement, and joined the forerunner of the Kuomintang (KMT). Sun quickly recognized the military skills—and political aptitude—of Chiang, not to mention his keen commitment to the advancement of China. Small in stature with a close-cropped head, he struck many as the scholar type. Chiang's career progressed with the command of a brigade of Shanghai troops, but for a time he drifted into the mode of a typical old-style Chinese officer, drinking, gambling, and womanizing. For some ten years he paid more attention to speculative investments than military affairs. In due course Dr. Sun brought him back into the revolutionary fold, and at one point sent Chiang to Moscow to facilitate Soviet aid to the Nationalist movement. Russian support ranged from guns and ammunition to military and propaganda advisers, among them the political exhorter Mikhail Borodin. After the death of Sun, Chiang reached for his mentor's mantle, emphasizing Sun's and the Republic's broad goals: nationalism, democracy and economic strength. The aggressive warrior became Sun's principal interpreter to the Chinese people. Tied to these ends were the unification of a vast population, and a campaign to arouse China to abrogate the long-standing, troublesome extraterritorial treaties which gave foreigners their dominant hold of the country.

T.V. Soong, well versed in economics and finance from studies at Harvard and Columbia, and with hands-on experience working for commercial enterprises in China, joined the Nationalist movement as its banker and monetary guru. The revenues he brought in as general manager of the Central Bank and backing from Shanghai's formidable segment of racketeers put Chiang's army on the march; its objective, to crush the warlords to the north and unite China.

"Unity is our first job," Chiang stated in a *New York Times Magazine* profile of November 14, 1926. "Ours is part of a world revolution, and we can use people from any nation if they sympathize with and are ready to serve our nation." And Chiang concluded: "We will cancel the unequal treaties and set China free. It will not be difficult. In one, two, at most three, years it will be done. And, to be sure, Canton has already begun to revise the customs duties without consulting foreign powers." To the American journalist-interviewer Lewis Gannett, Chiang added, "Your statesmen talk in a more friendly way, but in the end they sign the same treaties as the British and the Japanese, and we like an attitude of straightforward opposition better."[8]

In 1926 Chiang Kai-shek, now commander of the entire southern army, led an expedition northward to unify the country once and for all. The troops, totaling nearly 100,000, were divided into three parts, branching out to Hunan, Kiangsi and Chekiang below the Yangtze River. The Nationalists went on to many victories. A number of hostile warlords, thugs and renegades joined the politicized Nationalists. Chiang's well-trained men were paid on a regular basis, in contrast to the soldiers of intrepid warlords who requisitioned local dwellings, conscripted villagers, and demanded merchants pay for their keep. An unconscionable despot, and often at odds with his party's central leadership, he repulsed the strong Communist influence that more and more surfaced in anti–Chiang measures.

General Chiang Kai-shek at the same time had been carrying out a campaign of another kind, highly personal and very secretive. It commenced about five years earlier when as an aide of Sun Yat-sen, the general's path had crossed that of the younger sister of Chingling Soong Sun. The general and Mayling, it is thought, first met at the Suns' quarters in Canton in late 1921 or early 1922. He was smitten by the attractive, unmarried daughter of the Soongs. She represented an affluent and influential, well-educated and cosmopolitan segment of an emerging China. A devout Buddhist, at age 15 Chiang had entered an arranged marriage. His plain country wife, Mao Fu-mei, and the mother of his son Ching-kuo, seemed happiest to remain at home apart from the travels and demands required by the advancing military career of her husband. Politics, too, left Fu-mei bewildered. Chiang divorced her in 1922.

The cultured Mayling paid little attention to the soldierly Chiang. A steady stream of suitors knocked on her door. None had ever been an army officer. Rumors of an engagement, as Emma realized, constantly swirled about her Chinese friend. Mayling felt she would marry but on her terms and in her own good time. The only man who is known to have emerged beyond the marital gossip stage, Liu Chi-wen, later became mayor of Nanking.

Occasions arose for Chiang to be in the presence of Mayling, and the aggressive general moved quickly. He asked Dr. Sun if he might propose marriage to his sister-in-law. Sun advised him to wait. Moreover, she expressed no interest in Chiang. Sun pointed out that Mayling had refused proposals from several young men more suitable and acceptable than Chiang. But Chiang persisted. Finally, Mayling agreed to receive his letters if he wished to write. More and more, as she responded, he felt a kinship in ambition and point of view with the strong-willed and savvy Soong daughter. For some five years, Chiang pressed on in his campaign to win her over. Then in the wake of his great military successes, Chiang formally proposed to Mayling, just weeks after her 30th birthday in the spring of 1927. He had just set up governmental offices in Nanking, and had broken away from the Left wing of the KMT, which set up a headquarters in the industrial city of Wuhan, the commercial hub of central China. The Communists, who had engineered worker uprisings and anti–Chiang confrontations, now faced a purge by the strong-armed general. Nanking would not permit the development of a communist state within China. The Russian-backed opposition forces gradually lost their grip and backed down from the increasingly dictatorial Chiang who, starting in Shanghai, crushed the Communists and workers' revolution. The Reds were driven into the countryside. The Nationalist Party now shouted, "On to Peking!" and "Out with the foreigners!" The successful military campaign of 1926–28—the Northern Expedition—ended in Peking with a degree of reunification.

For Chiang the road to matrimony with Soong family obstacles probably paled in contrast with his military and political twists and turns. In China, he knew, arranged marriages remained the norm, really a family duty. With luck, couples, however, could come to like each other, even fall in love, after getting wed. Mayling's more Westernized family permitted offspring to choose a spouse. Nonetheless, permission of one's parents for granting this freedom had not changed. And in Mayling's household, it loomed as a formidable hurdle.

Mrs. Soong opposed the match. Soldiers were looked down upon as very low on the social ladder. For the most part, they lacked education, and many subsisted as spoils-seeking mercenaries and renegades. A Chinese proverb placed them as undesirable mates: "You cannot make a good nail out of bad iron or a honest man out of a soldier." A high-ranking commander-in-chief or not, Chiang remained an inadequate future son-in-law. Above all, he was not a Christian. That disturbed the pious matriarch the most. She avoided all discussion of the matter, and declined to see him privately in his quest for Mayling's hand. This was the Chinese way of saying "no." But Chiang was no quitter. He already had won over Mayling; the family, he believed, would accept him. He decided to change his tactics.

Madame Soong virtually fled to Japan to seal the matter, as well as escape Shanghai's summertime heat. But Chiang with his military and political career on hold followed. He finally persuaded her to at least grant an interview. At the meeting, she asked him if he would become a Christian. No, he would not convert as part of any matrimonial agreement. However, he would study Christianity and read the Bible, and then perhaps be led into the faith. Mayling's mother, impressed by his honesty and forthrightness, dropped her antipathy to the marriage. Surprisingly, she seemingly overlooked his status as a divorced man, and the rumors of a second wife and assorted relationships. She could take comfort that at least he was not a foreigner.

By the time Chiang convinced Madame Soong of his highly possible conversion to Christianity, he had resigned from all his posts in the Kuomintang—theoretically for the good of the Party and its cause. Publicly, he spoke of study abroad, honing his interest in politics and economics, perhaps learning to speak and read English. Meanwhile, he retreated to a Buddhist monastery in Chekiang, near his birthplace. Putting aside his military uniform, he donned a long, scholarly-looking Chinese robe.

Although Chiang had divorced Mao Fu-mei, there was a second spouse by the name of Ch'en Chieh-ju (Jennie). Doubts about the validity of this second marriage arose—spread by Chiang and his aides. Would it prevent him entering still a third?

Opposition to the alliance surfaced from other members of the Soong family. Brother T.V., who had worked closely with Chiang factions as financial adviser and banker, spoke of him as a loathsome warlord and scheming opportunist. T.V. leaned toward the leftist branch of the government, making his views unpopular in the general's camp in spite of its admiration for his fiscal skills. Chingling Sun reflected her brother's stance. She voiced dislike for Chiang and his anti–Red tactics. She felt he had parted from Dr. Sun's belief that the people were the true strength in the struggle to overthrow imperialism, cancel unequal treaties, and unify the country. Chingling would call the Chiang-Soong link-up "a marriage of opportunism on both sides." For Mayling, it had the lure of power, of becoming First Lady one day. For Chiang, it would forge a link with wealth and Western knowhow and connections.

Chingling left the country for Moscow with Eugene Chen, giving rise to rumors of a pending marriage of her own with the peripatetic journalist and Party gadabout. Ailing and H.H. Kung offset family disfavor with outright support of Chiang. They declared Chiang the emerging leader of China, but that he needed some western influence. Mayling, in a spirit of patriotism, must marry him. Mayling relied on the Kungs to persuade Mrs. Soong to agree to the marriage.

In late August of 1927, American newspapers noted that Madame Chiang Kai-shek, second wife of the recently "retired" commander-in-chief of the Nationalist troops, had sailed for the United States aboard the S.S. *President Jackson*. Three weeks later, this woman, "fashionably gowned in Occidental attire," arrived as a "tourist" in San Francisco. Replying in English to questions concerning her visit, she explained that three young Chinese girls accompanied her, to be placed in schools in the States and in Paris.[9]

Who was this attractive, well-groomed woman? The wife of the General? Or an imposter? On September 20 Chiang in an interview at Fenghwa stated that she was not his wife. He branded the madame's name and travels as the "work of political enemies" seeking to embarrass him in any way possible and did not know the woman. He asserted he had no wife, having divorced Fu-mai five years earlier. He made no mention of an engagement to Mayling.

That very week, rumors of a Soong-Chiang marriage reached the press. A special cable to the *New York Times* explained that Chiang had divorced his first wife only *several months ago* by the old Chinese custom of merely proclaiming that she was no longer his wife. The report continued: "It seems that he has sent away two other 'wives,' as well as his original wife, and is now ready to marry Miss Soong." Days later Chiang followed up his denial of a second marriage by saying that since breaking away from Fu-mei he had "set free" two concubines. "I was surprised to learn that one of them went to America as my wife."[10] Be that as it may, the traveling concubine-wife signed her passport applications as Chiang Chieh-ju, not stating whether she was Miss or Mrs. She gave her occupation as student, her age as 20, and said that the purpose of her visit was to travel.

Even before Chiang won consent from Mrs. Soong in Japan, Mayling, at a dinner with close Chinese and foreign friends, spoke of her intentions to wed. "I sincerely love the great General," she stated, then explained that Chiang was off to get her family's permission.[11]

In October an official engagement portrait of the couple began to appear in newspapers throughout the United States. Mayling's American friends wondered how different her life would be as the wife of an army general and political heir to Sun Yat-sen. Yet they believed her background and experience would make her an apt, eager and self-reliant partner in shaping the destiny of China.

Mayling (and the Kungs) believed Chiang was destined for a greater role in uniting the country. He represented "power." Chiang, long smitten by the beauty and intelligence of the American-educated Mayling Soong, knew acceptance into that family could ease his way strategically into the highest level of government. With the English- and French-speaking Mayling to compensate for his lack of knowledge of those languages, the two of them could reach out and gain the support of foreign interests and governments, and put to rest the prevailing notion that the general and his backers were committed to drive out all foreign enterprises and settlements. Mayling would soften his image as a heartless warrior, and show by example the importance of membership in the world community as well as Christian good works. She took very seriously her role of interpreter of the West, and its dogmas and "isms," to her stern, Chinese-bred partner.[12]

On December 1, 1927, Chiang and Mayling were married in a double ceremony in Shanghai. The first ceremony, that of the Methodist church, took

In 1927 Mayling married Generalissimo Chiang Kai-shek, a trusted aide of Sun Yat-sen. The nuptials in Shanghai linked Chiang's military and political agenda with the affluent and influential Soong family. (Mills–DeLong collection.)

place before a small group in the library of the Soong home; the second, a Chinese civil ceremony with a sprinkling of traditional rites, followed at the city's Majestic Hotel before more than a thousand friends, military officers, and Chinese and foreign dignitaries—and under a huge photograph of Sun Yat-sen and between a display of Nationalist Party flags. Escorted by T.V.

Soong, the bride wore traditional Western wedding dress and veil; the groom, a cutaway coat. His wedding gift was a string of costly pearls that had belonged to the Dowager Empress.

Some two months later Mayling wrote a lengthy account of the nuptials, and touched upon her view of the marriage to an unenlightened husband. "I have been married almost two months, and just as I started this letter to you [Emma], again the question flashed across my mind whether marriage has made any difference to me. I really do not know, because I wonder whether the difference is due to marriage, or just due to natural development." But first she related the proceedings of the wedding day, noting it was the biggest wedding Shanghai had ever witnessed. "Everybody was admitted by card only, and anybody who was anybody was present. All the consular bodies attended en masse, etc. But I was so dazed and frightened that I did not see anything or anyone.

"About a month after we were married, the General re-assumed the Generalissimoship. Most people think we had a honeymoon. We didn't! The day after we were married, he began attending political meetings, and seeing guests — and it has been that way ever since."[13]

The marriage, to be sure, helped to swell immediate and popular clamor for Chiang's return to power.

Mayling confided to Emma that her marriage would be far from the traditional Chinese cohabitation and would not impede her own constructive outreach and community work. "I do not think that marriage should erase or absorb one's individuality," she made clear. "For this reason, I want to be myself, and not as the General's wife. I have been Mayling Soong all these years, and I believe I stand for something, and I intend to continue to develop my individuality, and to keep my identity. Naturally my husband does not agree with me. He wants me to be identified as his wife; but I say nothing, and I am going to stand for something myself. I am not a believer of the Lucy Stone League [viz., publicly using a wife's maiden name] — but I do want to be recognized as a factor because I am I and not because I happen to be his wife."[14]

Mayling even went as far as to point out that she had declined special traveling privileges as the general's spouse. She did not want such perks until such time "as I have proven myself worthy of special privileges extended to me."[15]

At Nanking, the new Nationalist capital, she was now Madame Chiang Kai-shek. But Mayling Soong of Shanghai remained just below the surface in her life as the general's wife.

11

First Lady

Chiang's plans at the time of his engagement concentrated on a proposed lengthy stay in America just as soon as he had married. The out-of-uniform general told Mayling of his hope to study politics and economics in Washington for at least a year. "I want to study American government and military science and tactics," he added, "and learn something by inspecting the naval and military academies. My primary interests are related to the future of a united China."[1]

An overjoyed Mayling, away from her adopted homeland for a decade, envisioned reunions with her college friends back on the Wellesley campus, as well as in and near New York. Perhaps a visit to Macon with her earliest school companions and faculty mentors. Living in Washington would reconnect her with her idyllic youth, and along with Chiang make friends for the new China they wanted to bring into being.

By the time of the wedding, the American homecoming slipped into a distant hoped-for dream. Chiang's party insisted upon his immediate return to an active and full role in government and military affairs. And Nanking, not Shanghai or Canton, became the capital city of the Nationalists. The first major city upstream from Shanghai, Nanking retained historic ties with Sun Yat-sen and his rise to leadership of the Republic's provisional government. There, the impressive mausoleum for Sun would soon rise to dominate the outlying landscape. Yet the city was best described in 1928 as rundown and decrepit. Government officials and their families tended to avoid Nanking; many wives refused to live there. But for the new bride of the head of state, the city provided a diverting challenge.

Mayling now had a mission, a crusade, a destiny. Biographer Elmer T. Clark in his *Chiangs of China*, published in 1943, describes her initiation into life in the real China, apart from the comparatively modernized coastal cities. "Nanking, still early in the process of being made into a modern capital, was a mixture of ancient ruins and new ugliness, with all the dirt, crowding, and squalor which Madame Chiang has since done so much to reduce throughout the country."[2] Mayling threw herself into the work of changing a village of narrow streets and primitive houses into a permanent and attractive metropolis. In a post-wedding letter to Emma Mills, Mayling reminded her of their visit together to Nanking and the Ming tombs soon after she landed in China.

"It is an awfully dirty place, absolutely terrible," Mayling wrote. "And so I am going to work for a Municipal Public Health Department. I think I have a good man to head it. And then also I am planning for a public garden, and a home for disabled soldiers where they may recuperate and learn a trade.

"There is no decent hotel here," she complained, "and so I am establishing a Government hostel where foreign guests of the Government may be entertained. I have been here only ten days, but I see where a lot of work needs be done, and I am going to see what I can do."[3]

Fed by Chiang's undeniable power and financial resources, his wife's early hopes and plans became solid reality. To Mayling's credit, transformation of Nanking and areas beyond the capital continued apace for some ten years until the start of the Sino-Japanese war.

Marriage to Chiang had changed Mayling, in the eyes of Far East journalist Dorothy Gould Bess. On a visit to New York Bess brought news of her which, in turn, Emma duly recorded in her journal on January 31, 1929. "She seems to have succumbed to the general Chinese point of view, each man for himself." Dorothy told Emma there had been some talk of an orphanage for children of soldiers killed in the Nationalist campaigns. It all seemed very vague, and finally sifted down to the fact that Mayling had bought land in Peking which she later hoped to sell to the government for this purpose.

"Chiang is devoted to Mayling, and manages her in the following manner. When there is a meeting or conference he wants her to attend with him, she pleads indigestion as an excuse for not going, to which he immediately replies that if she is ill he couldn't think of leaving her and won't go himself. She knows that won't do, so submits and goes along. Dorothy doesn't think there is anything to be said for the Nationalists—they are all in it for what they can get out of it."[4]

Any news—even trivia—of Mayling's life gleaned from American and British friends overseas fascinated Emma. Mayling's secretary, Florence Pomeroy Brown, an American, revealed a bit of her experience as an insider in the presidential household. One of her responsibilities—to see that the lawn was watered—led to the discovery of a lack of water hose. She finally unearthed a Chinese official who said he'd provide a hose, and when Brown returned, she found the city fire department watering the lawn.[5]

Chiang often revealed a jealous streak. He was especially piqued over Mayling's conversations in English, which he could not understand. Moreover, the General demanded constant companionship, to the degree that Mayling had to cancel a lecture tour to the States in the fall of 1929. Her bookings included her alma mater. Unrest in China became the official reason for scrapping the visit.

Apparently there would be no children born of the Chiang-Soong alliance. Soon after his marriage to 15-year-old Jennie Chen, he had infected her with gonorrhea, which left them both sterile.[6] And during Mayling and Kai-shek's brief honeymoon, he told her that he did not believe in sexual relations except for the purpose of producing a child. He seemed uninterested in having more children, apart from his first marriage.[7] Six months or so later, Mayling looked very ill and feared she was pregnant. Doctors assured her she wasn't. But she appeared obsessed by the thought of it.

Apart from the physical reconstruction of Nanking, Mayling turned to the education of China's youth, an area she had hankered to improve and expand since her return to Shanghai in 1917. Now she had the backing and resources to impact teaching, and started a program called Schools for the Children of the Revolution. Many of those who had fought for a new China had died in battle or suffered severe wounds. Their children must be taken care of, she thought. These schools would combine book learning with practical preparation for living. They emphasized the necessity of developing job initiative in cooperation with observance of textbook knowledge and self-discipline. It proved a learning process for Mayling, who professed not to be a born teacher or even a good one. She experimented with educational ideas and training classes, and the results benefited a number of deprived communities.

In Nanking she also observed that young officers lacked recreation facilities and social outlets while they waited for orders for the front lines. These soldiers often complained that there was nothing to do in the city. The Chiangs listened, then formed the Officers' Moral Endeavor Association. Partly inspired by the YWCA that her family in Shanghai had nurtured, the new organization gradually brought in skeptical officers through its club-like atmosphere and cultural activities.

The Chiangs' most ambitious undertaking touched the basic roots of Chinese life—its customs, appearance, outlook and morals. Called the New Life Movement, it laid down principles of conduct and attitude in everyday life, both personal and official. The movement called for an awakening of the people to a full sense of their individual and collective rights, duties and responsibilities—and for China, a regeneration, a reformation, a renaissance. For Chiang, it would be an ideology to set against communism. For Mayling, it embodied social consciousness. Her Methodist upbringing stressed good works in a community and society at large. Be doers of the Word, and not merely hearers, her Bible studies emphasized. Some 400,000 volunteer workers would join the New Life Service Corps by 1940. The New Life Movement, she explained, could be traced back to contact with hill-country classmates in Georgia, and then evolved to fruition by frequent observation of the needs of her people while accompanying the general on his military campaigns. The more she saw of the country, the more determined she became to stimulate a spiritual reform—a broadly encompassing process not without keen attention to such details as modesty in dress, improvement in table manners, moderation in smoking, and suppression of opium. Above all, in Mayling's eyes, cleanliness demanded utmost attention.

Author and Mayling partisan Emily Hahn explained it in 1940, a half-dozen years after the New Life Movement began: "For Madame Chiang that cleanliness where age-old dirt reigned before her coming is a symbol of all that must be done for China." Mayling's desire to "clean up" represented an old weakness.

> The energy with which she insists today upon scrubbing the floors and tables, washing the linen, cleaning the windows of any place where she is in charge represents more than a personal foible.... Her spirit, inherited from the redoubtable Charles Soong and encouraged by her American training, was never cast down by the magnitude of the task she set herself. It is no delicate and feminine gesture when she takes curtains and flower bowls with her to the front and decorates the house in which she is to live with the Generalissimo, no matter how poor a hut it may be. It is an outward sign of her defiance, the war she is continually fighting against sloth and *laissez-faire*.[8]

The New Life rules faced much skepticism and ridicule, especially by the foreign press. The vast majority understood little of its precepts; many never tried. Chiang, nonetheless, wholeheartedly supported the movement, which took on the character of a Christian missionary program. Indeed, he had dutifully studied the Bible as a bridegroom. He prayed together with Mayling, and she tried to answer his questions regarding Christianity. Once he asked her, "What exactly is a Christian?" And she replied, "My mother is the finished product. I am a Christian in the making."

The Soong family pastor, too, provided spiritual guidance and explained the gospel teachings. Slowly but with sincerity, Chiang embraced his new religion. Three years after his promise to Mrs. Soong, he announced his readiness to convert from Buddhism. In October 1930, the Rev. Z. Kuang, pastor of the Young Allen Memorial Church, baptized the general, who in the ceremony joined the Methodist congregation of the Soongs. When the time came for the vows of membership, Mayling rose quietly and walked to the side of her husband. As he spoke in answer to the pastor's questions, she said the words in English in unison with him, rededicating herself. Among the small group gathered at the Soong home, Chiang's mother-in-law had been the strongest influence. His journey to Christianity now bound together all members of her family in one faith.

Mrs. Soong would not live to witness the New Life Movement. Ill with cancer, she removed herself from the summer heat of Shanghai to Tsingtao. On July 23, 1931, she received news of an assassination attempt on the life of her son T.V., as he was returning by train from Nanking to his office in Shanghai as finance minister. The shooting there at the railroad station fatally wounded his young Yale-educated secretary; T.V. escaped injury. Apparently, word of the incident so shocked his mother that she died later that day. Described as the "Mother-in-Law of the Chinese Revolution," Mrs. Soong had lived to see her six children educated in America and each in positions of influence in government and industry.[9]

This plot by dissident Cantonese extremists followed an earlier attempted assassination within the family. In 1929 a bold would-be killer sneaked into the Shanghai bedroom of the Chiangs. Both were asleep. The intruder raised his gun and was about to fire when Chiang turned, groaning restlessly. The assailant, thinking the general had wakened, fled in a panic. He was quickly apprehended, and revealed to be a bodyguard for Chiang, and part of a 24-man plot to kill the presidential couple.[10]

With beefed-up security, Chiang ordered a specially built limousine with a body of half-inch thick navy steel plate designed to shed bullets or bombs of would-be terrorists. Described as the most expensive and luxurious automobile ever brought into China, at a cost of $47,000, the vehicle added two extra seats projecting from the rear of the car, high enough to permit special armed guards to see forward over the hood. Not long after its import, the auto faced its baptism by fire. Chiang in a drive through a wooded park at Nanchang near Shanghai encountered several gunmen. They fired at him as he passed by in his open car. The bullets went wild, and no one was injured. His bodyguards arrested the assailants—again Cantonese rebels who had been sent to kill Chiang during his customary daily outing.[11]

When Chiang Kai-shek was named president of the Nationalist Government in October 1928, Mayling assumed the role of China's First Lady. The general's periodic resignations and "sabbaticals" from this office never seemed to have relinquished her hold on that position. Nor did they dilute her influence, an authority rare for a woman in the Far East. She joined the Legislative Yuan, a governmental body "somewhat on the order of your Senate for the passing of laws," wrote Mayling to classmate Marian Jones McCandless. "We have three woman representatives of which I am one."[12]

Her partnership with her husband took her on many risky trips to battlefields, and involved her in key interviews and meetings. If English or French was spoken, she reviewed the interpreter's notes to make certain the exact meaning was given to what had been said. "She may at first [have] shocked the older generation of Chinese women," Wellesley instructor Helen Hull wrote in a 1943 biographical sketch, "because she moved about with the freedom she had learned in America."[13]

Forceful, energetic and fearless, Mayling was called "Madame Dictator," and the strongest influence on the generalissimo. Behind the scenes, he often was viewed as the dupe of a clever and designing woman. It became commonplace when grievances were discussed *sub rosa* to interject the tag line: "If Mayling were at the bottom of the Yangtze, then China would suffer less."[14]

Cynics referred to her as the royal consort, living a lavish life on a parallel with the pre–Revolution emperor and his family. On the day when the former Manchu ruler Henry Pu Yi moved to a smaller house in Tientsin because he could not pay a high rent of $650 a month, the Chiangs paid a bill of $17,000 for their two weeks at the Grand Hotel de Peking. Their entourage occupied more than 30 rooms. The First Family's public image soon became more controlled. A major public relations coup focused on Charles Lindbergh and his wife Anne and their goodwill visit to Nanking in 1931. The trans–Atlantic pioneer on an extensive air trip around the world stopped in China, had tea with the Chiangs, and in a private ceremony received the first Chinese medal awarded for distinguished service in aviation.[15]

The Lindberghs offered their services to aid victims of the devastating Yangtze floods to the north—the worst in decades left millions homeless. Lindbergh volunteered to deliver by air vital medical supplies. His seaplane landed in flooded rice fields. This attempt to bring medical packets to the desperate Chinese attracted hundreds of sampans that quickly jammed around the plane and put it in harm's way. The crowds doomed further landings along the river. His caring gesture, nevertheless, made him a hero among the Chinese and garnered worldwide headlines for both the Lindberghs and the Chiangs on measures to relieve the suffering of the Chinese people. Several days later the Lindberghs' air expedition met serious trouble. A mooring mishap in the Yangtze flipped their craft onto its back, nearly drowning the couple. Wing damage ended the goodwill journey and its land survey flights, and both the plane and its celebrated pilot and navigator-wife headed back to America aboard ship.

Mayling took a special interest in Wellesley's sister college, Yenching College for Women, in Peking. The school, accepting its first class of three students in 1905, provided Chinese women their initial opportunity for higher education. By the mid–1930s, some 250 women had enrolled in what had become a coed institution, having merged with Peking University. Wellesley alumnae provided funds for Yenching, taught there, and served on its board. In turn, a number of Yenching students studied at Wellesley. Mayling spoke of her pride in this bond, an association that had begun soon after her graduation, and one, no doubt, strengthened by her own enrollment at Wellesley— let alone her outstanding academic performance there.

The adopted Chinese sister school made her alma mater conscious of political events in Asia earlier than otherwise. Mayling's visits to Yenching inevitably brought together Wellesley graduates residing there or nearby with those traveling in and about Peking.

Her once prolific personal correspondence slackened in the early years of Mayling's marriage. As China's First Lady, she turned to official activities and special projects. Even with a secretary or two to handle her mail and facilitate her appointments and duties, the writing of letters to classmates had fallen to one or two a year, if that. Emma Mills did not hear from her for a half-dozen years—and that contact was a presidential Christmas card sent in 1935 in care of the Wellesley alumnae office.

Emma indirectly sought her out when the Chiangs "came" to New York via a Fox Movietone newsreel segment—one of the first "sound" film clips of the couple. Emma and her father went to the Roxy Theatre on June 27, 1929 to see and hear them. First the general made a brief speech in Chinese.

> He spoke very distinctly and the tones came out beautifully—translated for him into English with an accent by [Minister of Foreign Affairs] C.T. Wang.
> Then Mayling and he were shown sitting together, and she spoke in English. She looked very natural, and her voice sounded almost natural, too, though she was speaking with unnatural slowness and distinctness. Something bothered her— perhaps what sounded like a bird really was one—and she forgot her next word. She hesitated, laughed easily and said something to him in Chinese, then repeated her last sentence and went on.

Emma failed to record the content of their talks.[16]

Publications soon started to ask Emma to write "a bit of personal reminiscence" on the wife of the president of China. Emma refused, even when requested by the Wellesley alumnae magazine. She explained, "I do not wish even to appear to exploit my intimacy with her or the kindness to me of the members of her family while I was in China."

Despite the inroads of a deepening Depression, with few jobs to be had, Emma Mills lived a comfortable and cosmopolitan life, enjoying a vacation in England a year before the stock market crash (at Canterbury the old city walls made her think of Peking's Great Wall). New York's cultural treasure-trove continually beckoned. Grandmother's monthly check of 25 dollars provided just enough for lesser-priced seats at concerts, plays, movies and lectures. If she budgeted carefully, there were a few dollars left to augment a modest wardrobe and buy cut-rate books and other reading matter. Graying school acquaintances and out-of-town friends passing through the city usually stopped by Grandmother's West Side townhouse to visit Emma. There were shared meals both at home or at nearby restaurants and tea rooms. In turn, Emma visited these chums, often at their homes outside the city, in New Jersey and New England. The Westchester household of best friend Mandy Mandeville and lawyer-husband Gil Ferris and their two young daughters, Mary and Rita, exposed Emma to moments of genuine domesticity. Yet on many days, she bore the weight of time alone.

Something was missing in this sphere of sociality and solitude. One winter afternoon, she walked along Riverside Drive, as the Hudson River was lost in a milky twilight. "I walked hard and enjoyed it—physically, mentally," she noted. But after an evening of reading, she felt somewhat depressed by a sense of the passing of time. It sometimes afflicted her to a morbid degree. It must, she thought, have some physical basis, some physical maladjustment at the bottom of it. Emotional frustration is the easy answer, she concluded. Perhaps an operation for the removal of an ovarian cyst—her second such procedure by age 35—gave rise to discontentment and mood changes.

Nearing age 40 and unmarried, she looked back over the past decades, extracting incidents of living within a fractured, multigenerational household and all-girl sequestered schools. She read from her journal the whole account of her army nursing experience, and was a bit amused, sometimes pleased, but mostly shocked and indignant. "My extreme sensitiveness to peoples' reactions to me and my apparently somewhat formidable bearing towards most of them were a direct result, of course, of the morbidly anti-social household in which I was brought up—& the lack of anyone among the elders around me who could see into me deeply enough to help me," Emma concluded. "It was no atmosphere for young people. And that, at twenty-four, I was reduced to falling more or less in love with other girls indicates that some one failed very badly at their job, for the trouble was not at all with me, as subsequent events showed. Four years inured in college had something to do with it. But upbringing more.... I gather that Mother rather consciously tried to train me away from any thought of marrying. She had been unhappy in her marriage, & thought I would be happier single."[17]

Emma continued in her introspective soliloquy: "I was brought up to regard any normal association with boys of my own age as silly, & of course never had any idea what to do about the few I accidentally met. I remember more than once being delegated to gather girls for De Long [her brother] & his friends to take out when he came from Annapolis, but if I went at all, it was among the chaperones. Once, at least, I suggested I might do myself as a partner for somebody, & I wept & Mother was indignant at the very idea, for the other girls were mostly my contemporaries & no older than De Long & his friends.

"I might, if given half a chance to associate with young people of anywhere near my own interests & taught how to get on with all sorts of other people as naturally as breathing," she concluded, "I would probably have been spared the tragedy love was to be to me, for I would, almost surely, have married fairly early."[18]

Her parents had separated shortly before Emma's journey to China. Dr. Mills moved in with his two unmarried sisters. His medical practice shrunk, as did his income, which never had reflected his professional standing in the city. Emma relished her time with him, particularly as he aged and fell ill. Walter Mills died from congestive heart failure in early 1934. Thereafter, Emma re-read the letters she had written to him and to her mother. As a child, she seemed so eager for a more stimulating life. "I still think I was rather a promising young girl, & somebody should have seen it & attempted to give me a chance. Father was proud of me, of course, but unable to do much about it. I needed a decent home, to begin with, which would have provided me with nourishment intellectual & emotional."[19]

Going through the letters from China stirred up a desire to take steps to return. "It seemed easy to make money there once, perhaps it would still be possible," she thought. "Perhaps I should try to develop the old idea for the Language School library. One could devote a lifetime to becoming an expert on the bibliography of China. A fairly interesting lifetime." Six months later, by June of 1935, Emma had changed her mind about a return to Peking. The very quiet surrender of Tientsin and other areas to the Japanese had left her disillusioned. "It puts it so beyond a doubt that Mayling's husband, & Mayling, have sold out to the Japanese."[20]

Virtually since the beginning of their marriage, the Chiangs had faced a three-way struggle in China among the communist party, the Koumintang and the Japanese. In all, a period of rebellions, ruses and reversals. And more were yet to come.

12

Trouble Spots

In a brief statement at the close of 1935, Scripps-Howard newspaper publisher Roy Howard warned Western nations to be realistic about Japan's imperialistic strategy. During a tour of the Far East, he observed the growing threat of that country as a major, indeed, menacing, military power. "It is becoming increasingly evident that the plans of Japanese militarists in the Far East are more or less limitless. Unless a common basis of understanding is reached by the major powers with interests in the Far East, the United States," he predicted, "will do a permanent fadeout from the Far East picture."[1]

China had faced the expanding influence of her neighbor for decades. But often it had reacted rather casually to Tokyo's inroads. China's stand against Japan had consistently lacked teeth, and thus the United States placed greater importance on border transgressions in Europe. Moreover, Chiang's primary focus remained on internal dissension, strife and unrest. During his early years as China's chief leader he continued his drive to bring Peking fully into the Nationalist fold, curb labor uprisings in Shanghai, and stem the Communist-encouraged peasant movement to rebel against those with command of money or land. Both Mayling and the Generalissimo sought firmer support from the country's merchant class and more recognition by foreign powers, and downplayed the anti-foreign feelings in many quarters. Above all, the Nationalists permitted no opposition party. Although strife among regional warlords continued, Chiang had emerged as the recognized master among China's militant commanders.

Chiang once had predicted that the elimination of the Northern militarists would chiefly come in time by their dying a natural death. But their ongoing survival proved otherwise. His nemesis, Marshal Chang Tso-lin, who exercised control over Peking, and much of northern China, left the old capital to build up leverage in his stronghold, Manchuria. En route to its capital, Mukden, in June 1928, he, for one, died from injuries suffered by a bombing of his train. Japanese troops, it seemed, planned the incident to gain more control over Manchuria. However, the Old Marshal's demise actually strengthened the Nationalist movement there. But three years later, in 1931, the Japanese in full force came in to occupy the area and declare it an independent state called Manchuko with ex–Manchu emperor Pu Yi as token ruler. Briefly before the take-over, Marshal Chang's son, Chang Hsueh-liang, and a supporter of the KMT, had led the Mukden government. Known as the "Young Marshal," he was driven from Manchuria by Japan's forceful creation of this puppet state on the Chinese mainland.

To the southeast, within Shansi province, Feng Yu-hsiang, the so-called Christian General, and once a strong rival of Chiang, became a Nationalist ally. The Generalissimo had crushed his military strength on the battlefield, and Feng realized his days as a powerful warlord had waned.

Wu Pei-fu, another important militarist, had seen his potency diminish. He lost ground on the battlefield, ending his years in a Sichuan exile.

Chiang outwitted his foes by warfare as well as through political intrigue. Yet the Communist faction remained potent in spite of its ouster from the KMT. The Soviet-guided Chinese Communist Party nurtured its vision of land reform in rural areas and blocked Chiang's struggle towards a more united country. The Communists formed a fringe government in Kiangsi in 1931, and soon took a decidedly anti–Japan position. Chiang failed to resist Japan, they clamored. Bringing in German military advisors, he concentrated on wiping out opposition led by Marxist Mao Tse-tung, who had formed a revolutionary army of his own. By 1934 Chiang's periodic "bandit suppression" campaigns to eliminate Mao and his comrades in south China led to a momentous step by Mao. He took to the road north with some 100,000 followers in what became known as the Long March—a vigorous trek over 6,000 miles of mountainous interior terrain. The Nationalists gave up the chase, and Mao and the survivors of this monumental trek set up a soviet base in remote Yenan.

The League of Nations had earlier attempted to curb Japan's occupation of Manchuria and penetration into parts of northeastern and coastal China, albeit unsuccessfully. The league, which the United States had not joined, condemned Japan, which immediately resigned from the international body. Chiang, along with the United States and other major powers, failed to stand up to his fascist neighbor. Secretary of State Henry Stimson in a letter to the Senate Foreign Relations Committee in February 1932 declared that the United States would stand by its treaty rights in the Far East, and urged other nations to follow the Stimson Doctrine of nonrecognition. Several weeks later the League of Nations adopted a resolution incorporating this doctrine. Boycotts of Japanese goods sprung up in and outside China. In March 1932 Emma Mills jotted down her thoughts on the Japanese-Chinese confrontation. "Japan," she wrote, "is in the pathetic and ludicrous predicament of not knowing what to do with her military victory now that she has it. She has driven the Chinese army from Shanghai, but complains that any suggestion she makes for liquidating the situation, China will never consent to." Then Emma did an odd thing for an old China hand. She went into a Japanese knick-knack shop in midtown Manhattan and bought an imported cotton kimono from the Japanese saleswoman. Her explanation: so that Japanese lives would not have been sacrificed in vain! And, she added, "in spite of my theoretical approval of an anti–Japanese boycott."[2]

For the first time in her life, Mayling now saw parts of China she had only read about. As Chiang's partner, she traveled thousands of miles within her native land. Together, they made their temporary homes in far-flung, and sometimes dangerous, interior locales. On the trail of Communists and bandits, they journeyed with troops to trouble spots by auto and airplane. In December 1934 they carried out a long and weary trip through the craggy mountains of Fukien where the Nationalists crushed a threatening rebellion led by disgruntled leaders of the Nationalist's 19th Route Army. At Chiang's field headquarters in adjacent Kiangsi Province, Mayling and her husband encountered enemy fire. In the dead of night, they heard the crack crack, crack of several hundred gun shots. Chiang was up instantly and called to her to dress quickly and prepare to move out from their encampment. With zeal, Mayling later related moments of danger: "Shivering with cold, in the feeble candlelight, I threw on my clothes and sorted out certain papers which must not fall into enemy hands. I kept them within reach to be burned if we had to leave the house. Then I took my revolver and sat down to wait for what might come. I heard my husband giving orders for all available guards to form a cordon, so that we could shoot our way out if we were actually surrounded by communists.... While we were in apparent danger I was not frightened," she wrote in an account published in *The Forum* of February 1935. "I had only two things on my mind: the papers giving information of our troop movements and positions, and the determination, should I be taken captive, to shoot myself. I would prefer death to the fate of women who fall into the hands of bandits. But, fortunately, the attack was repelled, and we went back to sleep." At the end of the journey, Chiang reproached himself for submitting his wife to such hazards.[3]

A month later the Chiangs encamped in the isolated southeastern city of Puchen in a bandit-infested region accessible by harsh footpaths through almost impassable mountains. Chiang's troops advanced daily, and at the end of a week he boarded a military plane for Kien-Ur, a point farther south and a mere hour by air. On his arrival he wired Mayling to follow by sampan. Her party— an American nurse, a secretary, an amah, men servants, and guards—numbering in all about 60 or 70—required five 20-foot-long and six-foot-wide sampans, plus five bamboo rafts. Their prodigious trip, through rapids and over water so shallow that the boatmen poled the sampans from rock to rock, took four days and nights. The party passed scores of abandoned farms and ravaged villages. Cramped in the narrow sampan for hours at a time, Mayling frequently insisted on going on foot, rejoining the little fleet several miles downstream. And when the swaying sampan made her seasick, she again walked, passing field after field of blackened stubble and numerous deserted villages. "Everywhere we were reminded of death. And this is a province rich in fertile soil and blessed beyond many with hills and valleys and rivers and trees. All had been devastated by the hand of man grown cruel and merciless beyond belief."[4]

Mayling envisioned a long, slow process of rural rehabilitation. Lost land and property and farm animals and household goods called for a gallant spirit to carry on and wrest a livelihood from mother earth. A co-operative reconstruction program "will not make front-page news but it will mean a contented peasantry," she predicted.

Chiang's increased field movements away from Nanking came about after heeding strongly worded advice from a longtime Australian newspaperman and astute observer of China named William H. Donald. He came to work for the Chiangs in 1934. This courageously outspoken counselor—who spoke no Chinese—pointed to graft everywhere and inefficiency in abundance, and minced no words on facing this situation. "Personnel of every government department had to be talked to, sat on, kicked in the pants when necessary, and backed up," Donald declared. "A rigid system of control and auditing would have to be instituted. Finally, supporting the entire program, the Generalissimo himself would have to get out into the country, travel about, make himself known to officials and to the public."[5] Although Chiang continued to overlook a number of his government's deficiencies and abuses, he did take to heart the need to move about, be visible as a leader in the field, and gain firsthand knowledge of activities of his army on the move.

A visitor to New York, just back from China in late 1935, told Emma of the Chiangs' recent unreported absences from Nanking and journeys into the interior. "No one knew quite where or why.... But everyone took a try at guessing—that he was running away from the Japanese, that he was running away because he had been negotiating with the Japanese, that he was secretly amassing a huge army to use against the Japanese." This acquaintance of Mills explained that "Peking was quiet, but the Japanese had increased their legation guard to 15,000, & had them quartered in Chinese government buildings, which they had simply appropriated, & drilled them in the city streets, notifying the mayor beforehand that such sections were to be closed to traffic."[6]

A month later Emma heard a bit more of the encroachments of the Japanese into China. A Chinese general on leave in New York felt that the rank and file of the Japanese army did not really want to fight. With two thousand men this commander had held a town against 20,000 Japanese until ordered to retreat by Chiang Kai-shek. He spoke of individual Japanese soldiers running from unarmed Chinese civilians. "We felt the oldest men in the command, too, were not much interested in fighting, either, because they are near retirement, and their careers made. It was the younger officers, anxious for promotion and fame who were the main instigators," Emma recorded. "His feeling was, apparently, if Chiang would only make a stand."[7]

Chiang's fighting spirit received a major boost with the injection into his military arsenal of 50 new airplanes, a 50th birthday gift paid for by public subscription. A gesture spearheaded by Mayling, this outpouring of generosity in the form of air power had all the earmarks of an American public relations–styled occasion. Some 100,000 people gathered in Nanking on October 31, 1936 (celebrated in Chinese tradition a year ahead of his 50th birthday), in a highly visible outpouring of popular support and acclaim for the general, and viewed a sky-full of some 50 US–made fighter planes. And several thousand delegates from all parts of the republic attended the ceremonies and bowed before a huge picture of the Generalissimo. Chiang accepted the gift on behalf of the nation, responding with words that evidenced a firm, defiant stand against Japan, and appealed to the officers and men of China's air force to "take cognizance of the hopes their countrymen reposes in them to carry out the task of national salvation."[8]

Mayling looked upon modern-day aviation as an essential means to help bring China together in peace and war. She pointed out that by air one could travel from Shanghai to central China in three hours instead of three days. Letters posted in Shanghai for Chungking, located up the gorges of the Yangtze River, would arrive in two days instead of two weeks. Air travel made Chinese Turkestan accessible in three days instead of four months. By 1935 passengers and mail were carried over more than six thousand miles of air routes in China. And it meant victory over remote pockets of bandits and Communists. "No other country on the face of the earth," she wrote in the article "Fighting Communists in China," "has stepped so quickly out of the medieval story book into the twentieth-century airplane."[9]

China's First Lady, indeed, embraced the airplane—and personally felt more disturbed traversing the crowded, dirty streets of an interior city than by the hazards of flying with poor visibility. The general was less enthusiastic about flying, preferring travel by land. The most important "unifying force" in China seemingly was not Chiang himself, but the airplane and its utilization. "Rebellions always take time to hatch," noted the well-traveled scholarly observer Lin Yutang in 1936, "and a swift airplane journey to a distant province is often enough to force the rebellious war lord to reconsider."[10]

Mayling's commitment to, and promotion of, air travel led to her appointment as secretary-general of the Commission of Aeronautical Affairs. She took this job seriously, as did her husband. It seems Chiang trusted only his wife to purchase war planes; other officials attached personal graft to every transaction. Mayling poured over aircraft catalogs, dickered with hard-bargaining salesmen, and was reputed to have had several Chinese officials of her air ministry shot to reduce thievery.

Above all, Mayling realized China's aircraft would not be effective war machines without well-trained and experienced pilots. Filling that void was crucial in the months ahead.

Back in New York, Emma's Chinese friends continued to discuss the impasse between China and Japan, and the latter's encroachment that had given it dominion over Manchuria, Inner Mongolia and a large part of north China. Chiang and his government were now "heart and soul in preparations to fight Japan," one central government insider revealed. "For two years they had been accumulating vast war supplies. Airplane and ammunition factories in the United States were working entirely on Chinese orders. Originally it had been planned to start hostilities this month [June 1936], then it had been postponed six months, but recently it was felt China could not wait so long. So it may be quite soon," Emma recorded. "All agreed Japan would immediately blockade the coast & China would lose her coastal cities & the coastal population in general would have to be sacrificed. China was concentrating on defense of the Yangtze valley & the northwestern provinces."[11]

Apart from the veiled arms buildup, Chiang pursued negotiations toward a treaty of friendship with Japan, on a basis of full equality. Tokyo came close to an agreement, but would accept it only if the Chinese would exclude Western powers and rely on Japan as its advisor and protector—and master strategist of the Far East. But Japan turned away from peaceful solutions. It would not withdraw its soldiers from Manchuria and other Chinese regions. Japan believed China lacked the willpower to reclaim and govern its northernmost territory.

Chiang's suppression of the Chinese Communist Party began to run out of steam. His own generals now balked at the killing of their own countrymen in what had become a civil war. Both sides—the Nationalists and the Red army—suffered heavy losses long enough, they protested. The greater threat, Japan, needed to be faced. The Communists sent word that they wished to end the internal strife and unite against Japan. The Young Marshal, Chang Hsueh-liang—virtually Chiang's vice–Generalissimo—played a deciding role in this turnabout.

In 1936 the Chinese Communists secretly contacted Chang, not Chiang Kai-shek, and Chang invited them to meet at his headquarters in Sian. Among the Red leaders at these clandestine meetings was Chou En-lai. Soon a plot came into place that would shake China to its very core.

In early December Chiang Kai-shek traveled north to Lintang, a hot springs mountain resort 12 miles from Sian. There, he strategized with area commanders in an effort to inject new vigor into the military campaign against the Reds. In the pre-dawn hours of December 12 disloyal KMT soldiers broke into his quarters and prepared to placed him under house arrest. With the help of his guards Chiang escaped. In fleeing he fell 20 feet into a shallow moat, injuring his back. He retreated to a cave but within hours Chang's men discovered and captured him.

Taken prisoner by the Young Marshal and Shensi province commander Yang Hu-cheng, Chiang was confronted with the demands of his rebellious troops. It was time, they proclaimed, to negotiate an agreement with the Red leaders to bring about a united front against an invader who already occupied a sixth of China.

Once Chang's denunciation of the Nationalist administration and his demands were made public, the kidnapping aroused both political and military circles throughout China. Telegrams urged the Generalissimo's release; others, his rescue. His loyal troops rushed to a staging area outside Sian to await word to move forward into combat and free their leader. Chang backed down a bit, becoming subservient and respectful in the presence of Chiang. The two warriors talked politely over tea.

"If you recognize me as your superior officer," Chiang made clear, "you must immediately escort me back to Loyang. Otherwise you are a rebel. If I am in rebel hands, then you can kill me immediately. Apart from that, there is nothing more to be said."

Chiang then remained silent. Others would have to "speak" for him. His position was clear: no signed or formal agreement to any demands. The impasse soon took on aspects of a theatre buffo. In most circumstances, Mayling would have been at her husband's side, or close by. But his visit was to have been short and chiefly one of rest. And Mayling had gone to Shanghai to recuperate from the flu. As soon as she heard of the kidnapping, Mayling rushed to Nanking to confer with her brothers and the Kungs; brother-in-law H.H. took charge of the situation—and the central government. She felt that had she been with her husband the incident would not have occurred. Had she been at Lintang, Chiang, she believed, might not have been so abrupt and censorious with his commanders. "There has been a mutiny," Kung explained, "and there is no news of the Generalissimo."

William H. Donald was given authority to go to Sian as chief go-between, and he flew there immediately. Before his advisorship to Chiang he had served a stint as a sounding board to the Young Marshal. Mayling urged calmness of judgment and an avoidance of precipitous action. Most of Nanking, however, opted for revengeful action. She explained that without Chiang the country surely would fall into a disastrous civil war—a conflict inviting further inroads by the Japanese. Her courage, self-control and advice prevailed.

Donald relayed the news to Nanking that Chiang was alive and well treated. Chiang, he added, did not want his wife to go to Sian. Nonetheless, T.V. Soong flew there to arrange for Madame Chiang to follow. The dashing young Chang was no stranger to Mayling; he had courted her some ten years earlier, just before she accepted the Generalissimo's offer of marriage.

At Nanking on December 22 Mayling prepared the Chiangs' private plane for takeoff on the 700-mile flight to Sian. T.V. and Donald, who had returned together to Nanking for a council of aggression, if not war, boarded the plane with her. Once airborne, she mulled over the many different undercurrents with which she had to battle: the extremists, the plotters, the standpatters.

There were the old-style Chinese whose minds could not see beyond a tangle of petty intrigues, whatever their intentions may have been, and cluttered up the time to an extent that had been annoying for her quick, Western-honed mind. "Many of them could not conceive of any woman's taking action for other than personal, sentimental reasons, and this idea colored their opinion of Madame Chiang's attitude and went far to nullify her speeches. It was small wonder that those very natural feelings that they felt they must guard against were stifled in Mayling's heart until she herself could not guard against them."[12]

As the aircraft started its descent over Sian, she handed a small revolver to Donald. "Shoot me if hostile troops seize me when we land," she instructed. Donald took the gun, but later declared he had no intention of actually pulling the trigger. Chang met the plane at the airport and Mayling accepted his invitation to have tea with him and co-conspirator Yang. Eager to see her husband, she hurried through the welcoming formalities. She surprised Chiang by her appearance in the midst of his captors. "You have walked into a tiger's lair," he exclaimed. In response, she opened her purse, handing him a new set of false teeth to replace the ones lost in his attempt to escape some ten days earlier.

Mayling's bold move was not her first encounter with a camp of enemies. Some three years before, she had played a daring role in negotiation with rebels in northern Fukien. There, she flew unaccompanied, except for her pilot, from Chiang's headquarters in Chuchow, apparently without his approval. Mayling returned to Chiang with word that she had met with emissaries of rebel commanders—and they now sought to surrender.

At Sian she, in essence, prevented a possible civil war by reassuring the military that Chiang would be freed with "face-saving" by all parties. Her friendly but firm diplomatic skills came into full play. Chiang never formally agreed to the Communists' demands to convene all parties for "national salvation," and he signed nothing in his 12 days of captivity. He had spent much of his imprisonment reading the Bible that his mother-in-law had given him and praying often for guidance. When Mayling came to his rescue, they first asked for seclusion to join together in prayer for divine help.

Mayling broke through the barriers to a resolution of the impasse. The Generalissimo agreed to stop the suppression, the extermination, of bandit-communists, and to take steps toward a unified front against Japan. The Communists were invited to send a delegation to the National People's Congress in 1937 (and as such gain wide respectability and solid opportunities for future strength).[13]

On Christmas Day, 1936, Chiang Kai-shek, with Mayling at his side, left Sian a free man. Two hours later his kidnapper, Chang, also flew to Nanking where he continued on as a house guest of T.V. Soong in Shanghai. The Young Marshal admitted his guilt as "an impudent lawbreaker who committed a great crime.... I shall never decline what is beneficial to our country even if it means

The Chiangs struggled to unite China, engaging in conflict with warlords and communists. The kidnapping of the Generalissimo, and his release with Mayling's help, brought a measure of consolidation as the country faced an enemy invasion by the Japanese. (Mills–DeLong collection.)

my death."[14] The repentant Chang's ultimate punishment fell far short of execution. Chiang had him court-martialed and sentenced to ten years in prison. Later granted amnesty, he remained under house arrest for the next 55 years. (Mayling regularly corresponded with Chang, inquiring as to his needs, be it clothing, medical supplies, even money. When her dog had puppies, she offered him one.) Co-conspirator Yang Hu-cheng spent years under KMT "protection" and suffered the loss of civil rights. W.H. Donald as intermediary had completed his greatest mission for the Chiangs and persuaded the Generalissimo to satisfy Chang by uniting China in opposition to Japan.[15]

The Generalissimo, too, admitted to "carelessness" in the pursuit of Chinese unity. He accepted some blame for the situation and action of subordinates. There is little doubt that Chiang's diary, perused by Chang and his coterie, contained writings that revealed Chiang's true thoughts on the strategy and plans he had already developed to stand up against Japan. It was chiefly a question of when and where. The kidnapping accelerated the timetable, and reinforced the necessity of merging the two opposing armies—the KMT and the Communists—within China.

The thought lingered that the entire Sian incident—as it became known then and in history—had been a mapped-out melodramatic plot, an arranged put-up job, to build popular support and expose Chiang's enemies.[16] If true, then the general was never really in danger.

The Sian incident brought the Chiangs national and international attention, and greater backing from virtually every quarter of their vast country. The deep gloom over his capture turned to jubilation upon his release, and enhanced stronger-than-ever loyalty to his, and Mayling's, leadership. And the incident sent a pointed message to Japan—one that would be answered in full force within the year.

13

Pen and Sword

In early January of 1937 Emma Mills received a Christmas card from the Chiangs—a formal "head of state" greeting with a photograph of a large country house overlooking a placid lake. The caption read: "Residence at Chikow, Chekiang Province." No handwritten message from Mayling was added. It was the first direct communication, more or less, Emma had gotten from her in nearly ten years. (A year earlier, however, Emma had received a package with a Christmas card, sent to the Wellesley College alumnae office, and forwarded to her. It contained a small brocade panel, but no note. Nonetheless, it seemed to signal plans to come to America.)

The holiday greeting for 1936-1937 marked the tepid rekindling of a bond and correspondence that had flourished in the immediate post-college years. Yet it would be months before Mayling reached out to her American friends from across the sea and back over time.

In the mid–1930s Mayling embarked on a prolific outpouring of writing and speechmaking. Her magazine and newspaper articles, and talks before special gatherings of educators and missionaries, often heard over the radio, reached receptive readers and listeners, chiefly overseas. Her American education had honed her well in formal English as well as its vernacular. She was an editor's delight, requiring few if any changes to her typed material.

But Mayling, it seems, had been slow to pick up the pen. Certainly her mother's ill health and death led to dark despair. She wrote of this period of depression in a *Forum* article, "What Religion Means to Me." "A terrible depression settled on me—spiritual despair, bleakness, desolation. At the time of my mother's death, the blackness was greatest. A foreign foe was on our soil in the North. A discontented political faction in the South. Famine in the Northwest. Floods threatening the millions who dwell in the Yangtze Valley. And my beloved mother taken from us. What was left?"[1]

A devout Christian, Mrs. Soong had spent hours a day praying. Whenever her family had problems, they would go to her and ask her to pray for them. She repeatedly told them that they should pray also. Yet she often emphasized that one should not ask God's help if the request would hurt someone else. "Vengeance is mine, saith the Lord," she'd say. "It certainly isn't yours."[2]

In helping her husband and his cause, particularly in his quest for a Christian life, Mayling in her own way grew spiritually. "Life," she revealed, "was all confusion.... Out of the feeling of human inadequacy, I was driven back to my mother's God." Mayling observed that she had entered into a new state where God's will prevailed.

"My firm conviction is that one's greatest weapon is not more deceptive falsity, more subtle diplomacy, greater expediency, but the simple, unassailable weapons of sincerity and truth.... I wait to feel His leading, and His guidance means certainty."[3] Turning to writing provided a comforting balm, a release for her anxieties and frustrations in a country that was far from unity and peace.

Mayling eagerly told of life in China, its progress, along with personal descriptions of her own travels. She wrote byline pieces for the *North-China Daily News* and *Asia*, as well as the *Forum*. She spoke to the National Christian Council of China and to students at the School for Children of the Chinese Revolution, and via specific short-wave broadcasts from Nanking. As war entered the daily lives of China's people, her words regularly appeared in American and British dailies.

Mayling made tentative plans to visit the United States in spring 1937. When word of this proposed trip leaked out, she became "terrified" at the pile of invitations for her to speak and be honored. She had hoped to come to America for a quiet rest and to see her Wellesley classmates.

Chiang's back injuries from his fall while escaping from his Sian abductors necessitated a leave of absence from government. Mayling canceled her trip because of his recovery needs.

The turbulent drama of the Chiangs in China even played out in the pages of *The New York Times* when Mayling in collaboration with her husband agreed to write their account of the Sian kidnapping and release. The extraordinary tale began on page one on April 16, 1937, and continued for eight more installments. The *Times* described the story as a "saga of a veritable battle and a striking victory ... a great historical document."[4]

The couple had sold the articles to the *Times* for $5,000, a sum they donated to the widows and children of 21 members of Chiang's bodyguard who were killed at Sian. Later that year the series appeared in a biography of the Generalissimo when Mayling and Doubleday Doran published the absorbing narrative, based in part on his own diary of the puzzling abduction. (Because his outspoken recollections of the coup were offensive to high-ranking friends, Chiang agreed to a Chinese-language edition only when told a Japanese publisher planned a pirated version; he quickly sold the rights to a Shanghai book publisher for a reputed $30,000.)

A basic theme of Mayling's writings—a concern for the standard of

Prolific writer, and later artist, Mayling knew her words could rally overseas support from friends. After Japan's attack in 1937 she corresponded frequently with Emma Mills who, in turn, wrote back the feelings of isolationist America. (Mills–DeLong collection.)

living and the quality of life in China, along with an abiding interest in education—reflected the social betterment activities of another contemporary First Lady. Eleanor Roosevelt assumed a partnership role with her husband Franklin, who had never recovered from polio. His disability curtailed his travels as president. Mrs. Roosevelt acted as FDR's "second self" with a stand on certain public issues. She, too, engaged in an enormous output of the spoken and written word. With a deep interest in youth programs, educational reforms, vocational guidance, and humanitarian matters, Eleanor assumed a reportorial role that expanded into speeches, articles, books, press conferences, and newspaper columns.

Both Mrs. Roosevelt and Mayling subscribed to the belief that education stood as the primary route through which progress is made towards the goal of useful citizenship for all people. Each helped to establish a school. Mayling started the Nanking school for children of fallen KMT soldiers, securing funding, selecting teachers and developing its year-round curriculum with its emphasis on practical aspects of Chinese farming and learning a trade.

Eleanor joined several friends to found the all-girl Todhunter School in New York, becoming assistant principal, and teaching literature, history and current events. Each loved reading, keeping a steady stream of books close at hand. They championed air travel; Eleanor flew wherever and whenever she could. As did Mayling, who often faced hazaardous flying conditions.

Nevertheless, they met criticism for interference in their country's domestic affairs, and broke the unwritten law that a First Lady avoids public statements. They were emancipated, ambituous women of a new century in new roles—Mayling more so, when viewed in a context where young ladies and wives in the Far East were seen but not heard. And with these unprecedented steps came threats and physical danger. Both at one time or another carried a revolver hidden in a purse.

Mayling's first direct contact with Eleanor Roosevelt came about via telephone. To inaugurate radio-phone service between America and China in May 1937, the Bell System invited the two women to talk to each other over some 10,000 miles of wire and radio circuits. Speaking from the State Department office of Secretary Cordell Hull, Mrs. Roosevelt greeted Mayling, standing by at the Palace Hotel in Shanghai.

America's First Lady expressed the hope that this new method of communication would draw the two countries closer together in understanding and sympathy, and mobilize the women of the world for peace.

"I have often wondered," Mayling responded, "what we women of the world could do to encourage science to keep people alive, instead of mowing them down in masses. The world should maintain the machinery of peace. The munitions makers do not want peace. Can't we women step into the breach?"[5]

Mrs. Kung participated in the ceremony, speaking hopefully of the things which her sister expressed, and inviting the Roosevelts to China, with promise of a warm welcome.

The two famous First Ladies would later meet in a historical setting at the peak of world war.

A decade removed from her journalistic work in China, Emma Mills again re-focused on her writing, hoping to sell stories, perhaps to build a self-sufficient career with the skill she felt most comfortable with. She had enrolled in a creative writing class at New York University in early 1935. The teacher, Sylvia Chatfield Bates, presided over what was perhaps the city's leading advanced writing course. Emma entered wholeheartedly into the assignments, producing four full-length stories each term. Bates had close ties with *Story* magazine, and tried to groom students as contributors, realizing it was one of the few fiction outlets for the efforts of beginners. She spotted a certain "authenticity and naturalism" in her middle-aged pupil's initial work. But the undeniable head-of-the-class proved to be a very young Southern girl who in record time polished off and sold a handful of short stories. This creative wunderkind—Carson Smith—was on the path to literary greatness. As Carson McCullers, she wrote such best-selling novels as *The Heart Is a Lonely Hunter* and *Reflections in a Golden Eye*, and became one of Emma's closest new friends—assuredly the most refreshing and spontaneous spirit in her life at that time.

Emma's published output paled by comparison with Carson's. Emma sold three or four China-related articles in all, to *Asia* magazine, the *New York Herald Tribune* (a book review) and the *Christian Science Monitor*. Although often encouraged to utilize her personal recollections of China, she felt uncomfortable about borrowing or extracting material from her journals and tapping reminscences when so much of it focused on her friends and acquaintances, both Chinese and non — especially Mayling and her family. Yet, for *Asia* magazine she recounted a brief, conjectural dialogue between Mayling and a young household servant who had run away from a missionary school supported by Mrs. Soong, then gravitated to her doorstep for work. Above all, Emma's journals and letters remained a powerful and productive outlet for expression.

"Sometimes I have such a hunger to put words down on paper—it comes in that form & not as an urge to say this or that specific thing," Emma explained in a journal entry. "Might lead somewhere if it were the latter. It seems absurd all these Chinese studies, for instance, lead nowhere.... I doubt if I could lecture on it [China] any better than I seem able to write. And yet I do so want to put words on paper, if only here."[6]

Physically, she swung from energetic vivacity to weary enervation. "Only today [January 25, 1937] I begin to feel somewhat normal again. The line is so sharply drawn, for me, between sickness & health. During even a slight illness, I feel as though an alien inhabited my body. The change is sharp & definite."[7]

With China more and more on the front pages of most daily newspapers and the subject of discussion among many Occidentals and Chinese, Emma's views were sought out, as, indeed, were her experiences of living in China. She attended talks and forums on her adopted land. Such topics as the threat of war there and the need for overseas aid engaged most speakers. Emma soon re-enrolled in courses on China at Columbia.

By the spring of 1937, Chiang faced the almost complete collapse and demoralization of his air force. The Chinese Air Force was controlled and run by foreigners, primarily a group of Italians who failed to measure up. The Chinese had few planes in fighting condition, only minimal flying skills and no background in mechanics — and total inexperience with bomb sights, radios and aerial gunnery. The Chiangs discussed the need for an aviation leader, one who could give China a semblance of air defense against the Japanese. In essence, the small, ill-equipped Chinese Air Force lacked trained pilots and an adequate number of planes.

Chiang placed his wife in nominal command of the unsettled air resources, while he searched the world for a leader. The Chiangs looked in Europe but found to their satisfaction a retired American Army Air Corps pilot willing to fill the post and recruit American pilots. Claire Chennault, who had significantly contributed to the U.S. Army Air Force publication *The Role of Pursuit Aviation*, emphasized employment of swift fighting planes against bombardment from the air. He met China's vital needs. Thus began the nucleus of the first U.S. experiment with a clandestine air force, an outfit financed, equipped and staffed by the neutral United States yet under the Chinese flag. It soon would protect from Japanese bombs the supply lifeline of China—the treacherous Burma Road, stretching 700 miles through jungle and over mountains from Lashio, Burma, to the southwest Chinese city of Kunming.

The volunteer group would soon number about 300 adventurous, high-spirited men with U.S. Army and Navy air squadron and maintainance backgrounds. Mayling had long observed that Americans relished the naming of their automobiles and boats. Why not airplanes, she thought. She suggested the tiger as the unit's emblem. This formidable jungle animal—with the face of a shark on its nose—posed a surreal, menacing threat. The Flying Tigers motif captured wide attention, and its pilots gave China its first great aerial victories. To Mayling, the men were "my angels—with or without wings."

Chennault, an unpolished, outspoken Cajun, became a kindred soul with Mayling. Both stood as fighters in a common moral cause. He admired her dedication to building air strength. She, in turn, did not treat him as a mere employee nor intimidate him. Indeed, Mayling, with a concern about rank and prestige among Chinese officers, dubbed Chennault a "Colonel," although he had retired as a captain due to partial deafness. "I reckon you and I will get along all right in building up your air force," Chennault drawled at their first meeting. "I reckon so, Colonel," she replied with Southern affirmation.

With her backing, Chennault worked to have makeshift turf airfields hard surfaced, a laborious task performed by thousands of coolies. He learned quickly to deal only with General and Madame Chiang. Chennault realized that underneath her femininity she was as hard as steel, and as politically ambituous and power-hungry as her husband. The newly recruited Americans also were inspired by Mayling's hard work on behalf of the air force. She endeared herself to them by her spunk and ability to put them at ease in her presence. They observed, too, that she sometimes wept as the Chiangs watched China's cities being blown to bits.

In July 1937 the somewhat hopeful negotiations with Japan sputtered to a halt. Lengthy conversations between Chinese commanders and the Japanese military extremists had merely added confusion to tension and fear over the country's unreadiness to engage its neighbor on the battlefield. Soon Japan commenced a big push into north China, utilizing airplanes to bomb targets and provoke heavy casualties. Bombs fell on Chinese barracks at Langfang, midway point on the rail line between Tientsin and Peking. War seemed unavoidable. Chinese Ambassador to the United States C.T. Wang informed Secretary of State Cordell Hull of the seriousness which the Chiangs viewed this clash. The situation, Dr. Wang noted, might disturb the peace of the world, going far beyond a war in Asia.

A battle for Peking broke out—a city tyrannized by Japanese planes,

Mayling recruited Claire Chennault (right), a retired U.S. Army pilot, to organize and lead her husband's air force. Called the Flying Tigers, the fighter group played an important part in defending Nationalist China, beginning in 1937. (Courtesy of Anna C. Chennault.)

bombs, artillery and machine guns. An entire Chinese regiment of some 500 men was quickly annihilated. Although China claimed to have mustered more than a million and a half men under arms, they were pitted against a smaller but well-trained and well-armed military force. Moreover, it had the backing of an aggressive standing army with money and material and morale. Apart from the battlefield, China's chief weakness lay on the sea. "Japan can muster the world's third largest navy," wrote *New York Times* correspondent Hanson Baldwin, "easily strong enough to keep her lifeline open across the Strait of Tsushima, to contain the pitiful Chinese fleet, to blockade Chinese ports."[8]

Come what may, Chiang Kai-shek vowed "to lead the nation in a struggle to the bitter end." He explained that the latest devastation by Japan was only the beginning of its long-planned, large-scale invasion. There would be no compromise and no surrender in what was still an undeclared war. Chiang's statement served to bolster public confidence in his government, although there was already much evidence of grassroots resistance against the Japanese.

Madame Chiang, as secretary-general of the air force, took to the public forum, making certain her words were heard by the Associated Press and other international news agencies. In an address before delegates of numerous women's organizations which had undertaken war relief work, she spoke of the gravest crisis in China's history. "This means we must sacrifice many of our soldiers, masses of our innocent people, much of the nation's wealth and see ruthlessly destroyed the results of our reconstruction."[9] Mayling spoke to the women of China—and women overseas—to show the world they counted in the fight against aggression and invasion. Recalling World War I, when the women of many countries gave their best, she emphasized that women of her country were no less patriotic or capable of physical endurance than those of other lands.

Mayling took the lead in organizing civilian support for the army and assisting the Chinese Red Cross in their humanitarian work. The "Give one day to your country" campaign, which had been launched a year earlier when Japan moved against Suiyuan province, was revived with her backing. Chinese again were urged to contribute one day's pay each month to the nation. Collection boxes appeared in most public places to generate funds to wage war. Soon Mayling would reach beyond China's borders for aid to her beleaguered homeland.

In New York, speakers and forums on Chinese subjects had attracted larger and larger audiences in the wake of Chiang's kidnapping and his country's growing animosity towards Japan. The Foreign Policy Association discussed the question "How Can China Achieve Unity?" A participant, author Lin Yutang, pointed out that Japanese terrorism had actually been an important factor in uniting China. The Japanese, he noted, had themselves succeeded in making it nearly impossible for any Chinese to advocate cooperation with them. "They, and Chiang Kai-shek had united the country in an external sense,"

Emma Mills recorded after attending this forum. "Education and a gradual infiltration of modern ideas [has] in an internal sense. The people," in her summary of Dr. Lin's views that spring, " had been swung solidly to the support of the government, as represented by Chiang Kai-shek, when, in the summer of 1935, the military attache at the Japanese Embassy in Nanking said, 'Chiang Kai-shek must go.' Lin considers Chiang sincere, but says he is an autocrat by temperment. He has all the qualities that, in the old days, would have led him to found a new dynasty, but instead, unlike Mussolini and Hitler, he talks of democracy."[10]

The New School in Manhattan offered a lecture series on the political and economic situation in the Far East, while not ignoring the education movement in China. Uptown, the China Society showed four reels of a film called *China in Progress*, recently photographed by an English traveler. It was comforting to Emma to see how much of old China was left—the boat life, the shops and street trades—amid scenes of widened streets, increased motor transportation, school boys in Western clothes, new steel bridges. With China on her mind more than ever, she sought out a Chinese tutor to once again try to speak the language she had attempted to learn a dozen or so years before. Emma wished that she could afford more frequent lessons. "As it is, twice a week at $2 a throw is way beyond my means."

Through her American background, Mayling knew education remained a priority, even in the midst of battlefield upheavals. China's masses, largely ignorant of certain basic measures to help win the undeclared war, had to be taught rudimentary hygiene and health care, and the steps to insure proper farming techniques to boost food supplies. Mayling viewed these fundamentals as part of the New Life Movement, which now had been partly turned into a program for defense and survival.

Mayling, and sister Ailing Kung, set up two schools in Shanghai and many more in the interior. Through her husband's great wealth, she established social centers for workers, and helped refugees find work. Chingling remained less active, although pleased that the Communists and the Kuomintang now joined together in unity against the invaders. The widow of Dr. Sun exiled herself from mainstream China, preferring to stay in British-controlled Hong Kong, where she was head of the China Defense League. Otherwise, she avoided personal appearances and hands-on involvement with the new united front.

That summer the hawkish Japanese militarists sought an "incident" to propel their forces further into China. They provoked one in early July. Their troops knocked at the gates of Wanping, a walled village a dozen miles from Peking and close by the old Marco Polo Bridge. One of their soldiers was missing, they exclaimed. "We want him back." "I know nothing about a missing Japanese," replied the Chinese commander. Which side opened fire first has never been clearly established. Each claimed the other did so. Nevertheless, the Japanese had their "incident" to exploit, forever linked to the nearby Marco Polo Bridge and the start of the Sino-Japanese War.

A month or so later, in August 1937, the Japanese defeated the Nationalists' 37th Division and occupied Peking. Next, they attacked Shanghai by air and positioned warships on the Yangtze. Japanese aircraft boldly attacked British ships, and moreover sank the U.S. Navy vessel *Panay*, causing casualties; deliberate acts that might have led to declaration of war by Britain and America.

Week after week, Emma met new Chinese friends at talks and meetings. The majority were successful educators, writers and doctors. Dr. Farn B. Chu, a Columbia and Yale graduate, practiced medicine in Chinatown, and with his Shanghai-born wife, Mary, gave serious thought to China's plight and what New York's Chinese might do to help. This cooperative venture by overseas Chinese and their American medical colleagues became the American Bureau for Medical Aid to China—a medical committee for raising funds for victims of the Japanese invasion.

"It promises to be a Chinese winter," Emma wrote in September. She signed up for three courses at Columbia—one in language, one in research into the modernization of China, and one on international relations in the Far East. Soon the local Chinese vice consul Cheng Pao-nan sought her out. "He seemed sad, as well he might," she noted. "Said the Chinese women were organizing here, and asked me if I would help them, when they got a little further along."

Cheng also prodded Emma: "You know Mme. Chiang well. Write to her of the sentiment in this country." At a China Colleges banquet, she met Rebecca Geist, a worker with various mission boards. Geist wanted Emma to get a list of Mayling's classmates who might be interested in attending a luncheon to hear a Chinese government official from overseas. Emma's efforts brought together a dozen or so Wellesley '17ers. At the luncheon, they composed a letter to Mayling (who thereafter claimed that message had not reached her in a timely fashion).

A likely explanation for the failure of mail delivery stemmed from the ongoing military move of the Japanese inland toward the capital city, Nanking. The drive on that city commenced in October 1937 with a policy of "loot all, kill all, burn all." The city suffered a brutal occupation—a vicious and inhuman massacre of a hundred thousand or more men, women and children. In China, Japanese troops took no prisoners. All faced firing squads. As the war took its toll, Mayling, nonetheless, kept to an agenda of frequent travels by auto to Shanghai. The morale of the troops remained foremost in her mind. On one such trip, to inspect quarters of wounded soldiers, Chiang's adviser W.H. Donald accompanied her through a dangerous sector near Shanghai. Their fast-moving car sped along a steeply banked portion of the road. Suddenly, Japanese bombers flew overhead. The driver panicked and pressed his foot down on the accelerator. In seconds, the front wheel hit a bump that sent the auto off the road and into a trench. (Some reports tell of a rear tire blowout as the cause.)

The jolt threw the passengers out of the vehicle. Mayling landed in a muddy ditch, seemingly unconscious. Donald, too, was hurled through the air but landed unharmed. He rushed to Mayling's aid, dragged her out of the mire and bent to listen to her breathing. She was alive but limp. In Emily Hahn's account, he shook her, saying "Come on, Madame, wake up! I wish you could see yourself now; you're sure a beauty! You're covered with mud. Your face and your pants and ... Oh, Lord, she's a goner," he said to himself.[11]

At that moment, Mayling stirred. Donald pulled her to her feet. She took a few shaky steps, then pointed to a nearby farmhouse. They slowly walked to the dwelling where Mayling changed into extra clothing retrieved from the car. Returning to the vehicle, Mayling insisted on completing the inspection tour. Her military aides managed to pull the overturned auto from the ditch. By ten that evening Mayling, bruised and aching, visited the wards of wounded soldiers. There, hospital doctors examined her and found a fractured rib. Weary and exhausted, she arrived at her Shanghai home to recover from the shock of the accident and the broken bone.

At year-end, Emma received a cablegram from Mayling, filed at the relocated capital, Wuchang, saying she'd received only one of the five letters initially suggested by vice consul Cheng, and written and sent during November and December 1937. Mayling replied in three juxtaposed words: "Upkeep good work." That fall Emma had dutifully perused newspapers to summarize bits of information on the latest developments vis-à-vis the Far East and the United States.

"My last letter from Mayling had been nearly ten years ago," Emma was quick to note, "and several of mine since had gone unanswered." In mid–December Emma finally had an extended reply to the joint message from the dozen or so Wellesley friends, signed at the October luncheon and lecture. A two-page, oddly impersonal letter, it pleaded for an anti–Japanese boycott.

"The movement is spreading in all parts of the world," she explained, "and the more people adhere to it and refuse to buy, sell, and transport Japanese goods, the more chance there will be for this bloody war to terminate at an early date." Mayling indicated in this message, from Nanking, that she would not tell about the horrible atrocities her country had been witnessing for the past three months. "You will have read about them in the papers. I have seen them with my own eyes, those terribly mangled bodies. I have heard the children call their dead parents, after the bombing of hundreds of refugees at the South Station at Shanghai. My shoes were blood-smeared when I walked through there. That is why I am asking you today—you and all your friends and countrymen: Help us stop this war."[12]

Two months later, Mayling again wrote from Wuchang, where 37 Japanese planes prepared to attack that city. She reminded Emma that foreign governments stood by doing nothing to help the Chinese people. "We are fighting not only for the salvation of our own land and people, but also the battle of the democracies which seem to be afraid to move against the dictatorships which base their being upon the employment of armed forces."[13]

She concluded with the belief that Japan could not fully conquer China. "Though we are at a terrible disadvantage, though we are apparently deserted in material help by America and Great Britain, I still think if we can hold out long enough Japan will be unable to reap the fruits of her efforts and our losses. Japan can easily overrun China with superior armament and airplanes, but that does not mean she can occupy and control this country."

A number of old China hands believed that Japan could conquer China with American war materials, then would turn on the United States. American ambassador Nelson Johnson at the time remarked, "By that time they will be too exhausted!" His words seemed an indication that the major world powers might just as well sit it out and continue an ongoing imperialist policy.[14]

Emma described American feelings toward the boycott. Sympathy rested entirely with China. On the campuses of Vassar, Smith and other women's colleges, undergraduates participated in the boycott by refusing to buy and wear silk stockings. Vassar students went so far as to give up all silk apparel by tossing such Japanese imports into a campus bonfire.

Women at nearby New Rochelle College in Westchester joined in, parading by an ashcan into which they dropped silk hosiery. "The arms of Japan are to be defeated by the legs of America," they proclaimed. The movement expanded to toys and other Japanese exports, with department stores and five and dime chains pulling these goods off shelves.

Mayling regularly appeared before newsreel cameras and penned a series of front-line articles for the *New York Herald Tribune*. The recently launched *Life* magazine featured photo spreads of the war in China, and her role in providing succor to its beleaguered citizens. And *Time* on its cover named Kai-shek and Mayling Man & Wife of the Year 1937. "If Chiang and Meiling [sic] can maintain their will as China's will—the same will which said that 'any sacrifice should not be regarded as too costly,'" the magazine concluded, "Chinese prospects are good."[15]

Time-Life publisher Henry Luce, born in China of missionary parents, venerated the Christian Chiang. Luce viewed the general as the savior of China, and built the Chiangs into one of the most famous and heroic couples in modern history. From time to time, Chiang appeared on the cover of the weekly; Mayling, twice with her husband, and once alone. With the journalistic push of the Luce press, Mayling augmented her role of propagandist—the *ne plus ultra* of the word. And began to coax millions of dollars out of the United States for aid to China. Chiang once said to Luce that Madame Chiang through her fundraising was worth ten army divisions. Indeed, her lofty position, communicative skills and glamorous allure brought China to the forefront of attention by the Western world—as did a decade later Eva Peron, First Lady of Argentina.

Luce saw the anti–Communist Generalissimo as on the side of God and democracy. The New York–based media baron eagerly stepped in to boost aid to the country of his birth. He helped to organize the United China Relief, mustering his printed word resources, high-level contacts, and personal capital for the cause. He insisted that the eight or more different agencies in New York appealing for support to China be joined into a united effort.

Among these groups was the American Bureau for Medical Aid to China (ABMAC), founded by Dr. Frank Co Tui, a professor of experimental surgery at New York University Medical College; Joseph Wei, an engineer and U.S. representative of a Chinese textile trading company, and Dr. Farn B. Chu, of Chinatown. They resolved to focus their energy on giving medical aid to noncombative victims of the Japanese invasion, and enlisting American interest in and support for China. A cooperative venture by overseas Chinese and their American medical colleagues, ABMAC embarked on grassroots fundraising, primarily in New York. During its initial year, Chinese-American high school and college students collected $8,000 to buy and ship emergency drugs and bandages. In due course, donations were greatly increased by Bowl-of-Rice dinners, bridge and mah jong parties, and the design and sale of Christmas and New Year's cards supervised by Emma Mills. Mayling encouraged ABMAC's expanding endeavors by serving as honorary chairman.

Her close-knit Wellesley classmates, too, moved ahead. The original eleven grew to include more '17ers, members of other classes, faculty and staff, and *their* families and friends.*

By the beginning of 1938, the special Wellesley class fund for China had brought in $155.29 from 37 members—a modest sum by any measure. But small, localized benefits organized by alumnae soon augmented the appeal. Emma wrote that the prevailing feeling seemed to be one of worry—even terror—lest something start the ball rolling that would lead America into war again. "Some of the sincerest friends of China mistrust altruism in general to such an extent that they feel China would be made to pay for Western intervention in some, perhaps indirect, way, and end by being no better off than she will be now." Isolationism remained strong, she pointed out. This feeling made some people leery of offending the Japanese who had established viable business ties with the United States. "Several classmates have written me that we must be sure to emphasize our fund is for *civilian* relief."[16]

The Chinese armies received no medical supplies from America. As a

---

**The eleven so-called Wellesley charter members were Emma Mills, Eunice Higgins Calpin, Ruth Peel Van Nest, Mildred Smith Green, Rosella Peck Pretzfelder, Sophie Meyer, Reno Reynolds Byrnes, Carrie Bowbeer Hoskins, Sophie C. Hart, Caroline J. Porter and Augusta Wagner.*

neutral party in the conflict, the United States could only provide help to noncombatants.

Emma also briefed Mayling on the country's feelings since their graduation in 1917 when the United States was as its most idealistic. Disillusionment soon followed, she noted, and cynicism, along with an economic depression that shook self-confidence. Then, in 1931 the country was snubbed by England when it sought cooperation to halt Japan. "The administration is convinced Japan is deliberately adopting terrorist tactics to frighten us all out of Asia." Emma concluded: "We have no illusions as to the program should Japan conquer China, but we do not believe it possible."

Emma raised the question of Mayling coming to the States to further the interest in China relief among government leaders and the general public. With fast transpacific air service, she would not need to be out of China but a month. (By 1937, Pan Am clipper travel between China and California took three days.) "Mme. Sun would be welcomed by the radical groups, but no other Chinese would have the wide appeal to America at large that you would have. Only have no illusions. You have to be very tactful in dealing with the isolationist sensibilities, and you would get nowhere if you came with the idea of getting us into war, or even to get government sanctions against Japan. Japan *may* force us into it, though that is nowhere within sight now, but many of the staunchest and best informed friends of China among us question whether or not that would not in the long run be an even deeper tragedy for China than what is happening now."[17]

Mayling's letters of on-the-spot descriptions of the turmoil and suffering in China struck a sympathetic nerve. Emma suggested sharing these writings with personal friends and classmates. And she asked, might excerpts be published?

Certainly much of the country had become China-conscious. And Mayling's middle-aged friends going back some 20 years spoke of their pride "to think how worthwhile a woman she had grown" to be. Money raised by Emma from the college group increased each month. In April 1938 she sent more than $300 for civilian relief from some 90 classmates. The class's 20th reunion in June—Wellesley at that point programmed the class of 1917's gathering in 1938, not 1937—would forego the usual costumes for the alumnae parade and allocate the money spent on them to an additional fund for Mayling's work.

Nonetheless, overall response to appeals fell. Emma expressed disappointment, and placed the blame on the lack of newsworthy material received from overseas. "We need badly the concrete, human interest story," she told Mayling. "Not atrocity material, which Americans don't like because they still resent the misuse of it in the [First] World War, not bare statistics, though a few would be useful, but definite accounts of what is being done to meet the huge refugee problem, particularly by the Chinese themselves, how the dislocated population is meeting its own problems, eye-witness accounts.... For instance, the American Bureau for Medical Aid to China recently had a request for four tons of quinine [to treat malaria, one of the gravest problems in the country]. That gives better talking points than a vague general appeal for medical supplies. It catches people's imagination, and they respond more readily.

"People are generally entirely sympathetic to China, but we think we are having hard times here, particularly in New York and vicinity. There never were more appeals before us. Spanish, German and Austrian refugees, etc., and we must have the thing put in a form to appeal directly to our imaginations, we must be made to *see* what the misery means."[18]

That spring Mayling voiced gratitude over the indefatigable efforts of her loyal friend in gathering insightful information and soliciting donations. From Emma's letters, Madame Chiang learned of the attitude of the country toward global outreach. "I do not have any illusions about the attitude of mind there," she explained on April 23, "because I know that a country where big minorities exist cannot, in international matters, carry on a definite and determined policy when that policy may affect other nations. I am a little bit surprised, however, that the humanitarian aspect of the situation in China leaves philanthropic America pretty cold. ... it is difficult to abandon one's old belief that Americans are inspired by ideals connected with the well-being of the distressed and the underdog.... I only regret that the cause of millions of refugees, who have been driven out of their homes because of the failure of treaties and international law to hold a nation like Japan to the straight and narrow way, is insufficient to touch the hearts of the hitherto generous people who feared not to express themselves when it came to a question of their feelings. I have received many letters from people saying that if I could go over there no doubt I could stir up quite a lot of support. I want to go to America, but I do not want to have any visit of mine marked by a belief that I am coming on a begging expedition. The very thought of that causes me to postpone even an attempt to try to visit your country."[19]

Mayling, however, took to heart Emma's urging of a specific endeavor to convey the desperate need for overseas support. She started a program to take care of the thousands upon thousands of war orphans made homeless by bombing raids. Madame Chiang led an appeal to raise money to house, feed, clothe and educate these ragged, half-starved children. She began to place them in mission orphanages and to open new institutions. Twenty U.S. dollars would provide care of one child for one year, she explained. Personalized letters calling for $20 for the care of an orphan got results—as did publicized extracts from Mayling's correspondence to Emma.

The childless Mayling's direct involvement in caring for youngsters gave rise to the thought by Emma that this outreach evidenced "vicarious motherhood." "Perhaps," she responded. China's First Lady, indeed, participated in a hands-on way in the well-being of the increasing number of orphans, from babies to toddlers to young teenagers. After a visit to the front with the general in April, she visited military hospitals and Catholic missions. At the latter she arranged the placing of 2,000 orphans with four missions. "Of course I saw to it that the Catholics agree to our condition that we send teachers to instruct the children in nationalism as embodied in the San Min Chu I [the tenets of Sun Yat-sen] and the principles of New Life Movement.... The money that you promised to send me shall be used for the children's work. You would like that, won't you? Later I shall send you pictures of all of your orphans and they will know that you and your friends are taking care of them."[20]

In her reply that spring, Emma remarked that she sometimes knew Mayling Soong well, but didn't know Mme Chiang at all. But after reading her recent letters, she guessed they were the same person, after all. Mayling as the general's wife had seemed aloof and sometimes steely, at least from press coverage and hearsay of her activities following the widely heralded marriage. Emma had wondered if the endearing schoolmate and spirited family intimate from the past no longer existed. Now Mayling's chatty and heartfelt letters settled the matter.

Emma referred to her mesmerizing talks on radio hookups—messages from far-off China that struck Americans sympathetically in spite of generally poor short-wave transmission. "It was only by your phrasing and tricks of emphasis that I would have recognized you; your voice didn't sound natural. Incidentally, the most natural movie I've seen of you lately was the one taken as you boarded a plane to leave Hong Kong."

In January 1938, it seems, Mayling flew from Hankow to the British colony of Hong Kong. No announcement of her purpose was made. But news agencies several weeks later cabled the reasons for the flight to the neutral port city, still free of air raids and full of financial nabobs and rumormongers. Apparently, China asked Britain to mediate for peace in the undeclared war with Japan, whose troop advances neared Hankow to the west and Suchow to the north. Mme Chiang, T.V. Soong and H.H. Kung—even Mme Sun Yat-sen—gathered in Hong Kong. Peace talks fell apart; the state of Chinese finances occupied most of their waking hours. Mayling and her brother and brother-in-law attempted to arrange for a British loan of three million pounds. Negotiations dragged on for weeks, and Kung, premier and finance minister of Chiang's government, remained at the task with the Bank of China at his side.

For all intents and purposes, the Bank and the Ministry of Finance were one and the same—so London bankers kept a close watch. The possibility of China's defeat caused deep concern by the Soongs and the Kungs, and they looked beyond their homeland to a safe haven in the United States. Deposits in American banks seemed a prudent step, as were property investments in New York and on the West Coast.

Mayling, courageous and determined, full of energy and decisiveness, with an American-acquired inclination for direct and quick action, still found it hard to come to grips with the Western democracies' lack of support. Biographer Emily Hahn observed that until the moment of crisis arrived she had been pushing too hard for democratic and Judiac-Christian ideals, and hoping too ardently for the reform of China to give much thought to the shortcomings of other places beyond China. "For years she had remembered America as the yardstick by which she measured her own country."[21]

She constantly reminded the world of what Japan was doing in China. This Far Eastern enemy was sinister, ruthless, well armed and well organized and acting on a preconceived plan to conquer China even if she had to annihilate the Chinese to do so. "Curiously no other nation seems to care to stop it," Mayling concluded.[22]

"Look at the fleeing thousands of Chinese and foreigners, screaming, panic-stricken, running for their lives—indeed hundreds of thousands of Chinese mothers and children, homeless, foodless, bereft of everything, leaving their homes shattered and burning behind them when they tried to flee from the horrors of Shanghai," she vividly recounted. "Tell me, is the silence of Western nations in the face of such massacres, such demolition of homes and dislocation of businesses, a sign of the triumph of civilization with its humanitarianism, its codes of conduct, its chivalry, and its claims of Christian influence? Or is the spectacle of the first-class Powers, all standing silently in a row as if so stupefied by Japan that they do not utter a reproach, the forerunner of the collapse of international ethics, of Christian guidance and conduct, and the death knell of the supposed moral superiority of the Occidental?"[23]

Her strong feelings over China's life-and-death struggle while America and Britain aided and abetted Japan, most certainly with war supplies, brought forth a stinging indictment of the democracies in her 1940 text *China Shall Rise Again*. Aimed at overseas friends of the Chiang government, the book, with a 200-page section of official, and generally upbeat, "state of affairs" statements by its ministers of education, finance, war, foreign affairs, communications, economic affairs, health and medicine, emphasized that the calamity in China was due mostly to the breakdown of good faith in international dealings. If her country met defeat, Mayling concluded, it would not be for lack of courage, but because, by the concerted action of the democracies, China was strangled by an economic noose fashioned by Japan out of British appeasement, American profiteering and French fear.

When Nanking fell to the Japanese in the first year of the war, the general and First Lady had fled further inland to Wuchang-Hankow on the Yangtze with growing bitterness at America's continued stance of neutrality and pacifist isolation.

Mayling increasingly turned to the needs and well-being of her heavily burdened husband. She resigned from her position as secretary-general of the air force, after two years of intense work to reorganize and enlarge this fighting unit. Progress had been made in building it up into a more efficient aerial combat force. Mayling had faced incompetence in training, favoritism, loose discipline, graft and corruption. In her anger and determination, she tightened things up—to the degree that she supposedly shocked even the Generalissimo by demanding "heads" of wrongdoers—in effect, the firing squad.

> I believe I have served my purpose, so I decided to retire.... I believe my greatest contribution to the nation right now is to devote myself to the Generalissimo. Any slight burden I can remove from his shoulders will be benefiting China just that much more. Overnight, China was faced with the monumental task of creating a war machine to combat the one on which Japan has spent thirty years and billions of dollars. The strain on the Generalissimo now is gigantic, almost superhuman. I feel that I must do everything in my power to help him hold up under the strain, because I believe his leadership is vital right now to China.[24]

The strongly worded commitment to the home front virtually ruled out an overseas trip—the visit to America Mayling had long hoped for, and in turn, her American classmates and friends eagerly anticipated. Wellesley in particular was anxious to welcome her back. Seniors there in March voted her an honorary member of the graduating class of 1938. A delighted Mayling cabled her acceptance, whereupon she dreamed up unique and vicarious way to be with both her "new" and old classmates gathered on the campus that June. In a letter to Emma Mills from Wuchang, dated April 26, Mayling explained: "You are doing so many things for me that you might as well do some more. Kill the willing horse, you say. But listen or rather, read on before you make any comments."[25]

Mayling noted her inability to be at reunion, but added that '17 had occupied her waking moments for weeks. "How I should like to come back and revisit Wellesley, and have the opportunity to bridge the intervening years since we were graduated. Don't tell anybody, probably my most vivid feeling would be a supreme relief at not having to attend eight o'clock class. Heavens, how I loathed getting up on a cold winter morning to bang the window down! Ugh! You remember, what a sleepy head I always was. I still am. The other day I told my husband that most people dread dying, whereas, I do not since, then, I could sleep and sleep without disturbance for a long long time."[26]

At that point her wandering mind turned to the present. She would send a bit of China to the gathering at Wellesley. Each and every member of the class of 1917, and of 1938, that June would receive a Chinese handpainted cup, saucer and cover. The cup carried the inscription: "In the summer of the 27th year of the Chung Hua Republic, presented to Wellesley classmates as a souvenir from Mayling Soong Chiang." A package of green tea was included, along with a small Chinese silk flag—in total, some 650 cups, packages of tea and flags. In addition, for all 270 members of '17, there was a Chinese silver spoon of conventional round shape bearing three characters meaning happiness, prosperity and long life. On the back of the spoon, Mayling engraved her name and "1917 classmates souvenir."

Mme Chiang shipped the articles from Hankow to the Chinese Embassy in Washington to forward to Massachusetts. Mayling "assigned" Emma to unpack all the items from 11 shipping cases and distribute them individually at the reunion dinner—and mail the gifts to those hundred or more classmates not back on campus. "Why am I sending each '17 a spoon?" Mayling asked. "Certainly not for strawberry jam or mayonnaise, but just to show you all that a spoon may be licked, but not CHINA."

Mme Chiang's generous gift, in turn, boosted contributions for civilian relief. Money usually spent on reunion frills augmented the orphans fund. Publicity in the Boston area spurred a growing wave of interest and support. And Mayling's byline articles for the North American Newspaper Alliance (NANA) ran in many big city dailies, and met a sympathetic reception. Donations totaling a few hundred dollars earlier that year rose to the thousands. A dinner of Boston's Chinese students alone netted more than $5,000 in May.

The full story of the devastation in Nanking and banner headlines on the bombing of Canton, along with fuller newsreel coverage of China's struggle to save herself from the brutal Japanese invasion, woke up more Americans and opened their pocketbooks.

Emma assisted public relations specialists eager to convey China's plight. They latched onto the idea of exhibiting China's famed pandas for the publicity value. Would Emma pass along that suggestion to Mayling?

A week or so before the Wellesley reunion, Emma traveled to the college to work with a publicity man from Carl Byoir Associates. Pictures of the Class Baby, now a freshman [Harriet Sheldon] occupied them a good part of a day, particularly the search for a Chinese outfit that would fit the stocky undergrad. "She's her mother's build (Polly Sheldon) only prettier," remarked Emma. "She's to lead our procession."

Returning to the campus after 21 years, Emma noted the new gothic-style buildings, and trees and shrubs that had grown out of recognition. "The girls all dress alike, pullover sweaters, wool skirts of contrasting color, dirty white shoes, low-heeled and with brown trim, socks and bare legs. Kerchiefs over the head peasant fashion in the rain." For the visit Emma bought a new dress and told the sales clerk, "I don't want anything silk." The clerk replied: "None of us who know anything buy silk these days." Emma dutifully reported to Mayling that the boycott against Japanese silk "was taken for granted, pretty much now." She added: "It's been suggested that I go over and write an authorized biography of you—I'm assured you've had such a buildup here it would make my fortune—'most American women regard Mme Chiang as a sort of a saint!'—I hope it hasn't quite come to that. My publicity man going up on the train [out of] a blue sky remarked, 'You ought to get yourself sent over there by NANA. They'd jump at the chance. Anybody with your connections.' ... I'm thinking."[27]

14

A Tightening Grip

Mayling's gift of teacups caught the attention of news agencies and piqued the interest of numerous reporters. Designated to distribute the class mementos, and recognized as a close friend of Mayling, Emma found it virtually impossible to avoid interviewers as long as the American-educated First Lady of China and that country's besieged leader remained on the front page of many daily newspapers. The year 1938, too, brought much attention to Emma's own family. After more than a half century, her grandfather, Commander George Washington De Long, and his long-forgotten Jeannette Expedition was being revisited. An Annapolis-trained engineer, Edward Ellsberg, published an account of the tragic Arctic voyage. Called *Hell on Ice*, the book quickly became a bestseller. In turn, it encouraged Emma's widowed grandmother, Emma Wotton De Long, to complete her memoir, which Dodd, Mead and Company released as *Explorer's Wife* that fall. And during the very week Emma toiled over the dispersion of some 600 teacups at Wellesley, wire services telegraphed the bizarre news that a copper cylinder containing De Long's ship log, and a weather-beaten flagstaff, had been found by a biologist of the Soviet Arctic Institute on a polar island off Siberia—a bit of land Captain De Long had discovered in 1881. Emma seemed in the middle of two oddly diverse stories—one, on the 19th century Arctic wilderness and the other, the current Far Eastern battleground.

To mark the first anniversary of the undeclared war and in an effort to humanize the all-wise image of all-powerful Mayling, the *New York Times* sought copies of her correspondence with Mills. Mayling agreed that excerpts of several letters could form the basis of a lengthy feature. The material for the July 10 story revealed her in an appealing and very human light. Emma's name and address appeared in the article—the first public description of the close ties between the two college chums.[1]

The piece, with its vivid and colloquial recollections of days on campus, served to divulge a down-to-earth side of the Madame—and stirred up a flurry of donations to her favored charity: relief to Chinese orphans who were "flocking in tremendous numbers from all the fronts, dirty, ragged, pinched, emaciated little morsels of humanity."[2]

By the close of the reunion program, the graduates of '17 had agreed to care for some 35 orphans on an individual basis at $20 a year. The overall fund grew considerably. One thousand dollars in hand from classmates, their friends, and profits from the sale of Chinese costume jewelry, augmented the orphan adoption pledge. The *Times* story furthered Mayling's cause in unconventional circles. A German maid working in the summer home of a friend where Emma visited handed her $40 to pass on to Madame Chiang. The woman, who had lived in China before World War I, sold silver buckles and buttons that friends and employers had given her to raise money for China relief.

There arose rumors that summer of bombing raids over Japan by China. Travel agencies discouraged visitors to Japan. "Such reprisals would, no doubt, be natural," Emma noted, "but I for one am glad China's skirts are clean in that respect and hope they continue so."[3]

And Wellesley president Mildred McAfee, when mildly criticized for favoring China, and Mayling, in the Sino-Japanese conflict, was reported to have exclaimed, "After all, we can't help it if we have no Japanese alumna of similar prominence!"[4]

An assortment of mail reached Emma because of the July 10 article: a man who wanted to be "an ordnance expeditor" in the Chinese army; a prayer in very bad verse; a four-leafed clover; requests to talk with her about this or that phase of the war; a Christian Scientist who hoped his church would do more for Mayling. He read the article with deep interest. "I feel it will do a great deal of good in assisting to awaken the dormant thought in this country to a better realization of their duty in helping this great nation of China, and in so doing, to help themselves.... Many brutal things have happened since the human race started. I doubt very much if anything has been so cruel as this malicious attack by Japan on a peaceful, quiet nation."[5]

Readers of the *New York Times* persisted in contacting Emma. Several urged her to share with the American people additional communications from Mme Chiang. Human interest stories, they pointed out, greatly appealed to readers. Others told her that most material from Mayling's reportorial pen tended to scold the American people. But the letters to Emma gave a very different picture of war.

Moreover, *Life* magazine (August 29, 1938) upon borrowing a number of Mayling-to-Emma letters, and photographs taken by Mayling, allocated a page of "Pictures to the Editors" on orphan relief in Hankow and Mayling's accelerated work for these young refugees. In doing so, the editors praised her "latent talent for photography."

By midsummer Emma returned from a month or so of visits to friends in New England. She had the empty family townhouse all to herself. Grandmother, now age 87, and her niece and closest companion, Marguerite Wotton, were sequestered out of the hot city in rural New Jersey. Emma joined them one afternoon for lunch. "Ma [Grandmother] looks very white, walks worse than ever," she observed, "and not only her hands, but her arms are cold to the touch. We were all very polite to one another."[6]

The Wellesley reunion and teacup allocation, together with bucolic sojourns in the mountains and at the seashore, energized Emma. Without any disruptions or interference by family members, she jumped into a succession of housecleaning tasks. She started one such day by melting a couple of squares of chocolate found in a closet, sweetened it, then threw in what was left of a box of shredded coconut. To this mixture she lay her great outburst of zeal and vigor.

She cleaned out various kitchen cupboards and drawers, little touched in some 40 years. Out went empty bags and old glass jars. Putting aside one jar, she poured in the remnants of several packets of cereals. Then came a similar attack upstairs, aimed at family odds and ends destined for the ashcan—newspaper clippings, picture postcards, screws, nails, broken tools, sewing things, pen knives, faded negatives and snapshots. And from her own storeroom area, she threw out empty boxes and worthless yellowed books with loose bindings inherited from various relatives. "People should discard their own trash as they go along," she concluded. She remembered clearing out her father's files and the complaint of his sister. "Florence complained I failed to treat Father's papers 'with respect.' I feel always something of that myself—yet one has to be ruthless & throw out what the living should never let accumulate in the first place. Yes, m'am, I do try to take the lesson to myself."

Areas of the brownstone had never been subjected to such dispatch. By the end of the day Emma relaxed by turning on the radio to listen to Benny Goodman and his band, her first tune-in to "the maestro of swing—whatever swing music really is. A relentless thumping of the underlying rhythm on the basses," she thought. "He's good, & drives the audience to hysteria—as was plainly audible."[7]

The possibility of Emma's return to China to take on a writing project—chiefly an authorized biography of the First Lady—petered out rather quickly. In so many words, Mayling quashed the idea. She quoted the *New York Times* managing editor when he said that she was "writing too much." Mayling agreed. Yet she pointed to letters constantly received from publishers in America asking her to do an autobiography. A London publisher offered ten thousand pounds in advance of royalties. But she hesitated. The time had not yet arrived for that book. "Sometime ago I had concluded that I would write no more for the newspapers, and also would refrain from writing to individuals, since so many rush the letters into print. No one realizes better than I do how tired people can become of repetition of arguments."[8]

One year after the singular shot fired near the Marco Polo Bridge, the struggle for domination of China intensified. A third of Chinese territory had turned into a battlefield, with a million Japanese soldiers on the mainland. Ancient towns within the Great Wall bore the scars of war. The long, drawn-out

Letters and photographs from war-weary China boosted contributions to Madame Chiang's fund for war orphans. Here, in Szechwan, she distributes Christmas gifts to youngsters clad in sandals of straw. (Mills–DeLong collection.)

struggle impacted 12 provinces, and stretches of vital railroad links. Moreover, the invaders occupied several northern ports and a handful of inland cities. Chiang vowed, nonetheless, to fight to the finish, "even if there is only one inch of territory left and only one Chinese living." Chinese troops continued resistance to the combined Japanese naval and army advance along the Yangtze. Nevertheless, the Chiangs had fled inland to Hankow, their new temporary capital, in Hupeh province.

With the rescue and housing of thousands of war orphans under control, albeit temporarily, Mayling turned to another segment of her country's vast population. A resolute and conscientious leader, she sought to stimulate the interest of Chinese women in volunteer war work. In Hankow she gathered together scores of wives, many of whom had been active in the New Life Movement. She organized them into sewing groups to make clothes for soldiers and refugees. Her hands-on approach placed her shoulder to shoulder with them at sewing machines, a number donated by the Singer Company, those president Milton Lightner had married her Wellesley "big sister" Dickey Griffin.

A month or so later Mayling organized still another women's support aggregation: a youth corps of girls. Their training focused on the management of household tasks, especially on Mayling's forte: cleanliness and sanitation.

"We Chinese are weak on management," she explained. "We are great on making elaborate plans and poor on carrying them out. I am teaching these girls small details so that they can tackle management from the inside outward."[9]

Dressed in the blue work shirt and overalls of the New Life Corps, she joined and directed these young women in sweeping floors, washing windows, and sewing, and then supervised an afternoon's study of public health, rural administration, and the ABCs of first aid. Mayling herself conducted a class in character building.

Mayling elaborated on plans for the mobilization of women. Teams of girls in their teens and early twenties, she explained to Emma, were selected by competitive examination, and trained in first aid and other duties to help the war effort. Following this indoctrination, they were sent into villages behind the lines, where, with the help of the local administration, they disseminated the knowledge and information necessary to realize the goals of the New Life Movement in wartime. "These mettlesome, wide-awake girls are indeed representatives of the New China which is now emerging from the age-old lethargy of a bygone era."[10] Ever hopeful of a new dawn, Mayling looked beyond the war to a modern-age China—a China that would emerge as a first-class world power.

Accompanied often by her social programs adviser, the Rev. George W. Shepherd, of the American Board of Commissioners for Foreign Missions, Mayling traveled to farming districts to inspect the young women's work, and to "scold, criticize, or encourage, as the case may demand."

"What a life! ... When this war is over I think my hair will turn white, but there is one comfort: I am working so hard I am not in danger of ever becoming a nice, fat, soft sofa cushion, or having a derriere."[11]

Mayling's hospital visits, too, never wavered. Like a Florence Nightingale, she cheered up the wounded, distributed medical supplies, and often changed the dressings of battlefield casualties.

To celebrate China's National Holiday—the so-called Double Ten on October 10 in observance of the founding of the Republic in 1911—Madame Chiang set out on a tour of base hospitals and defense headquarters in the Wuchang area. Army transport wagons accompanied her, carrying 23,000 moon cakes (to mark the Mid-Autumn Moon Festival), 17,000 oranges, 1,150 catties of beef, 22,000 packs of cigarettes, and other gifts. At the hospital wards, she tucked into the pocket of every wounded and crippled soldier a new dollar bill.

By fall the Japanese pressed on toward Hankow. Nevertheless, the Chiangs maintained a vestige of normal living and mutual dependence. The general rose usually at six and, following morning exercises and bath, joined Mayling at seven for their quiet time. Nothing was allowed to interfere with this devotional half hour of Bible reading, meditation, and prayer together. Later in the day, Mayling helped her husband to keep in touch with foreign opinion by reading to him from overseas papers and magazines, or giving him the gist of their articles.

That fall Mayling wrote her classmates of a new book just off the press in Hankow—a collection of her past articles and talks gathered by the government's publicity department. Titled *Madame Chiang's Messages in War and Peace*, the volume disappointed Mayling. She apologized for poor translations into English and some duplication of material. One particular piece on the upbringing of children of revolutionary martyrs, initially written in Chinese by Mayling, led one close friend to remark that "it smacks of chop-suey, flavored with Maggi sauce, and cooked by a Main Street bride from a random recipe given her by a tourist cousin." She felt the comment justified. "Please laugh with me."[12] Mayling decided to revise the book for the general public in America and Europe. (The new edition, retitled *China in Peace and War*, was published in Shanghai in 1940.)

It again fell to Emma to distribute copies of the 1938 compilation; 293 books arrived on her doorstep for Wellesley '17 classmates and other graduates. Before year-end, another request came in the overseas mail: four bottles of Lilly's Respiratory Undenatured Bacterial Antigen, plus address changes for Mayling's nine U.S. magazine subscriptions.

Emma again hinted that a visit to the States by China's First Lady would enhance fundraising activities, and perhaps add strength to the lobbying in Congress by such groups as the American Committee for Non-participation in Japanese Aggression—a group set up to end America's supplying war materials to Japan. But isolationist and pacifist feelings counterbalanced the push for an embargo on armaments to Tokyo. This movement sought to have neutrality legislation changed to remove President Roosevelt's discretion in applying it.

The Neutrality Act of 1935, indeed, authorized the president, after proclaiming the existence of a state of war between belligerents, to prohibit all arms shipments. The embargo, however, did not include primary or raw materials such as steel and oil, easily converted to military use. Extensions of the act curtailed loans or credits to belligerents, and authorized Roosevelt to list commodities other than munitions to be paid for on delivery. In 1937 he had forbidden transport of munitions to China and Japan on U.S. government ships. Japan, with its own large merchant fleet, gained by this ruling. No declared war existed between the two "non-belligerent" Asian nations, thus ruling out quarantine measures.

Consul General Kiem Wen Yu on several occasions nabbed Emma, petitioning her to get Mayling to visit America. Her presence would deliver a jolt to the Japanese militarists. Why not have Wellesley confer an honorary degree on her? It gave a dignified excuse for her coming. The Federation of Women's Clubs already voted unanimously to bestow its annual gold medal on Mme Chiang. Mayling heard rumors of such honors for months.

By the end of 1938 Mayling dampened all hopes for a visit. She dreaded the mental and physical strain, and visualized what would happen. "All the friends I have, all the thousands of people who have written letters and contributed money, and the hundreds of thousands of curious people, to say nothing of the thousands of newspaper men and people of importance who would want either to speak to me or me to speak to them, would overwhelm me within the first few hours of my arrival. I would be a nervous wreck after the first day. This is not pessimism. It is just simple fact, for here I can stand so much and no more. I have to do my work as best I can, in stops and starts, because of the strain that has been on me for so long."[13]

The loss of both Hankow and Canton failed to discourage Mayling's travels within China. For nearly two months, she toured various fronts from Shensi down to Kwangtung—journeys marked by terrible sights and physical hazards. Planes remained a constant menace, and the results of their raids, heartbreaking. At the same time, she persevered in her efforts to mobilize women, save children, help the maimed (both soldiers and civilians) and boost the morale of the troops.

Mayling quickly corrected anyone who said the Japanese occupied the provinces of China. The enemy merely "penetrated" most areas, she protested. She put in perspective what the Sino-Japanese War was all about, at least to her.

> The Japanese jumped upon us because they realized that the unity that we were effecting and the progress that we were making would have increased the purchasing power of our people and would have developed tremendous commerce between America and our country.... The longer Japan is assisted to wreak havoc in China, the more effective will be her destruction of Occidental trade and prestige. Japan has stated definitely ... that she intends to make a realm of Asia ... with declarations that she intends to set up a league of Asiatic countries and establish a Monroe Doctrine of her own in Asia. When Japan expressed her intention of establishing a 'new order in East Asia' she was bold enough to tell the world that she would not permit anyone to do business in [East] Asia unless they subscribed to the conditions laid down by Japan.... We are hoping that now [that] Japan has shown her hand America will not permit profits to be made from the destruction of China nor consent to a condition which calls for a continuous drain on the generosity of the American people in aid of those who suffer from the effects of the bombs and equipment made or supplied by American firms.

"China will never be subjugated," Mayling emphasized, "and Japan will never be able to exploit profitably any part of China that she may be able, for sometime, to 'occupy.'"[14]

Mayling's letter was the first written from Chungking, in the remote province of Szechuan and at the end of the Yangtze gorges. This inland city, some 1,400 miles upstream on the Yangtze from Shanghai, had become the latest capital of the Nationalist government. For nearly a year the Chiangs had lived in a small house in Wuchang across the river from the center of Hankow and the government in transition. From the China coast the Japanese had pushed towards Nanking, which fell in early 1938. Hankow and Wuchang, too, came into enemy hands. But the veracious Chinese forecasted the tightening grip by the Japanese armies. Ahead of the invaders, Chinese workers carried dismantled factory machinery and equipment to Chungking and inland to safer areas. Virtually all aspects of government pulled up stakes and dug in on the steep hillsides of this sleepy but densely populated outpost, a world away both politically and economically from the mainstream coastal ports and traditional ruling centers. It would remain Chiang's seat of government until the end of the war—a city frequently bombed by the Japanese yet never conquered during six years of battle.

Mayling and the Generalissimo moved into quarters on a high peninsula at the juncture of the Yangtze and Chialing Rivers. It had housed a hotel on 100 acres, and well-fortified stone buildings were added. (In 1947 the Chiangs donated the complex to the Methodist Church as a school and home for war orphans.) A heavy fog enveloped their newest dwelling—gloomy conditions that permeated all of Chungking for the winter months and well into April. The sun appeared only at intervals as a yellowish globe through the fog. Thick clouds, and often polluted air, at least provided a protective covering against Japanese bombers for much of the year. A city built on rock offered a natural material suitable for blasting out artificial tunnels beneath narrow, precipitous streets. These underground passageways served as air raid shelters for a burgeoning population, although many people living on the city's outskirts had little chance to reach them during an attack.

That winter the Chiangs hoped that President Roosevelt and his administration would finally open their eyes, and not only move to save their interests in China, but help save Free China. "That help is due to us under treaties and agreements," Mayling dogmatically reminded Emma.[15] A month later she again voiced determination to hold to the course of resistance. "The Japanese are finding it increasingly difficult to progress though they are really doubling their efforts in every way in the hope of breaking down our spirit to defend ourselves."[16]

Then it happened. In early spring, the fog over Chungking melted into a bright, sunny and nearly cloudless sky. At noon on May 3, 1939, some 40 Japanese planes, adhering to the indiscriminate terrorizing pattern thrust upon other cities, flew over the new Chinese capital, dropping tons of bombs over a mile-long section of the riverfront district. In minutes, hundreds of jerry-built structures collapsed, burying alive hundreds of residents. Fires sprang up in every direction. Waterbucket brigades hurriedly carried Yangtze river water to fight the blazing houses. To curb the spread of fire, the city resorted to wholesale dynamiting of surrounding buildings. Not since the San Francisco earthquake some 30 years earlier had a major urban area been so ravaged by fire.

A second formation of bombers the following day inflicted more ruin. Vast sections of Chungking were laid waste, and thousands killed or injured. The devastation brought panic; nearly a quarter-million civilians fled to the safety of the countryside, many migrating by wagon or foot as far as 75 miles from the center of the city.

Mme Chiang witnessed the raids, then visited bombed areas, and personally directed rescue efforts. To facilitate this work, she and her husband ordered the commandeering of all motor vehicles to assist the evacuation. Teams of uniformed girls and women, fresh from Mayling's training programs, relieved regular policemen and enforced a semblance of order. In all, 600 women energetically and efficiently went about their prescribed duties.

Just days after the Japanese had reduced large sections of Chungking to debris and embers, and killed more than 3,000 people, Mayling wrote an emotion-filled description of one of the most disastrous raids of the still-undeclared war. "The bombs have reduced rich and poor, wise and stupid, to one common level—pieces of burnt flesh which are extracted from the smoldering piles with tongs." She called the devastation "the worst exhibition of cold-blooded mass murder that the Japanese have so far been able to perpetrate." Mme Chiang spoke of raging infernos amid houses packed tightly together on a long, high tongue of land, girt with cliffs. "Houses climb the slopes to the cliffs. They are reached by narrow stone passages, and each house has but one door. There is no escape through the back when incendiary bombs set the front ablaze."[17]

On the second day of bombing, nearly a square mile of houses caught fire, and wall after wall tumbled down. Every few seconds a roof crashed in emitting showers of sparks, and quantities of black smoke. Where two blazing streets converged, the roaring flames met with renewed vigor. And gusts of wind carried the leaping sparks into neighboring streets.

Fathers and mothers watched their children burnt alive. Other children saw their parents struggling to fight through the flames only to disappear in the ruins of falling beams and pillars. "The cries and shrieks of the dying and the wounded resounded in the night, muffled only by the incessant roar of the ever-hungry fires.... Everyone was helpless, even the fire fighters.... A bomb broke a main and the reservoirs could not be refilled. Numerous foreigners connected with missions worked all night helping to save the people. It was a terrible holocaust, and perhaps quite satisfactory to the Japanese, whose lust to kill is not yet satiated."

Mayling thought that her office and staff would be victims of the raids, as fires from three directions raged toward them, fed by a strong wind. "I had great difficulty in getting through the cordon. The police had surrounded that district and would not let anyone go through because it was considered dangerous. I managed, however ... by reassuring the police that they would not be held responsible if anything happened to me. I found the staff calm and collected." Mayling moved them outside the city. But by dawn the next morning the whole staff reassembled to serve in the various refugee stations and to collect children orphaned by the raids. Mayling predicted more attacks. As a precaution the city tore down many closely clustered houses.

She closed her lengthy account of the destruction with a plea to Emma: "Do what you can to make Americans realize that this death and havoc came to China with the help of American gasoline and oil, and materials for bombs. It should be realized that isolationism is not going to keep the Americans from meeting a similar fate, in another generation, perhaps. America's only safeguard lies in taking a courageous, resolute and active stand against all aggressor nations."[18]

Mayling agreed to Emma's wish to utilize the vivid and very moving account of the tragic Japanese bombings in U.S. newspapers and magazines, and to make widescale distribution of reprints to well-placed Washington individuals. Among the latter, Mrs. Roosevelt wrote from the White House: "Thank you for sending me the copy of Mme. Chiang Kai-shek's letter. I read it with great interest and appreciate your giving me the opportunity to see it." ABMAC sent out some 13,000 copies with an appeal note. It netted thousands of dollars from the eyewitness description.[19]

As the war neared the beginning of its third year, China had suffered approximately two million uniformed casualties—killed, wounded, crippled or unfit for further service. Japanese losses reached between 500,000 and 700,000 soldiers. China prepared for a long war. The country already faced the loss of seaports to import armaments and other war-required supplies, and turned to vital imports via the mountainous Burma Road from Rangoon and by overland caravan routes from Russia. "China, badly beaten in all frontal clashes and with all her attempts to counterattack apparently frustrated with heavy losses," wrote *New York Times* Shanghai correspondent Hallett Abend, "nevertheless refuses suggestions to discuss terms of compromise."[20] A former high-placed ally of Chiang, Wang Ching-wei, took matters into his own hands in an attempt for peace with Japan. Tokyo merely saw an opportunity to strengthen its hold over China. Wang, a former Nationalist premier and foreign minister, took the bait, and headed a new Japanese-sponsored and -controlled "national" government at Nanking. The puppet regime failed to crack the apparent unity of China's remaining pro–Chiang leaders.

American public sympathy for China increased sharply; an overwhelming majority of Americans favored a boycott of Japanese goods and an embargo on the shipment of American war materials to Japan. A Gallup Poll in June 1939 recorded a marked decline in sticking to neutrality. More than six in every ten individuals said they would join a movement to stop buying goods made in Japan.[21]

Mayling took to the short-wave radio to urge economic sanctions without delay. "The domination of East Asia," she exclaimed, "meant the closing of the Open Door to the West. They, if only because of their own right, should take a more positive action," she pointed out during the NBC hookup from Chungking. To augment this plea, Emma Mills, through the American Committee for Non-participation in Japanese Aggression, personally solicited funds to carry out the committee's work: publish facts, mail action letters, provide speakers, prepare newspaper stories and radio programs. Mills also made public Mayling's latest letter with the belief that U.S. isolationism wouldn't keep America out of war in the near future.[22]

Emma's fundraising for Mayling's orphans—now called "warphans"—also occupied a dozen or so hours each week. Emma's role in the sale of 1938 Christmas cards by the American Bureau for Medical Aid to China had brought in more than $2,500. As a result, the organization persuaded her to serve as executive vice-president of its women's auxiliary. She expressed dismay over being immersed in detail instead of breaking out of it. "I don't like office holding, am not good at it," she voiced to Mayling. "[Frank] Co Tui, the director, and his wife—both Filipino Chinese—are both trying to play silly little politics in it. I shall probably end up by losing my temper in a big way."

At the conclusion of a letter relaying a summary of year-end contributions and comments from college connections, who more and more expressed amazement and admiration over Mayling's heroic role as First Lady, Emma added a personal note.

"A Shanghai refugee, Joseph Tuck—yes, Chinese—when he was cleaned out there borrowed money, bought an amazingly miscellaneous assortment of Chinese goods and came over here to try to establish himself.... We have been able to buy some things from him to resell for the fund. He has told another Chinese friend of mine that I have 'Chinese virtue' in my face!"[23]

Emma long ago had lost her heart to China. Soon her very soul would belong to the land that now occupied most of her waking hours, and even her dreams.

15

Agitation and Angst

The collective face of the British hierarchy evidenced little probity for the Chinese nation, when compared to the helping hand of Americans. The British expressed only a token of sympathy for China; some were outspoken with criticism of the Chinese government for precipitating a stalemate which interfered with business and trade. The English still were strongly imperialistic, and thus sympathized with the Japanese empire builders. Thus, a pro–Japanese sentiment prevailed. Even those British in beleaguered Shanghai seemed oddly incapable of recognizing the long-range motives behind Japan's aggression.

Moreover, the British press gave such devastation as the rape of Nanking less attention than most newspapers because it was fearful of offending Japanese trading partners. Some editors expressed doubt of the authenticity of the reports of Japanese atrocities. Overall, there remained a genuine need for the presentation of China's point of view.

A small yet growing number of British, however, did voice mystification over their country's attitude toward the Sino-Japanese war. Why were their nation and her commonwealth allies, they asked, so solicitous of trade with Japan that they did very little to assist China, and supply her arms? One pocket of encouragement and support on behalf of China's well-being was the China Campaign Committee in England. Organized by individuals of all shades of opinion, it had three main aims: collect funds for sending medical aid, press for political measures to assist China, and supply Chinese speakers to groups all over Britain and arrange public meetings in London.

American grass-roots support of China had grown sporadically, yet aversion to war remained strong. And Japanese propaganda cleverly exploited the country's desire to "keep America out of war." Japan tirelessly distorted the situation in China. Part of the job of Japanese propagandists was to try to discredit the China relief campaigns.

Concurrently, the Japanese government urged an end of hostilities and a single, united Chinese government under former Chinese premier—and pro–Japan—Wang Ching-wei, longtime rival and now arch enemy of Chiang. Wang considered himself the rightful heir of Sun Yat-sen, not Chiang.

In the United States, Secretary of State Cordell Hull made it clear that Japan had no right to dominate China as part of a new order in East Asia. Transpacific trade relations turned in a new direction when Hull abrogated the commercial treaty which America had signed with Japan in 1911; trade between the two nations would now rest on a day-to-day basis. In effect, the move condemned Japanese policy in China and gave notice that Washington did not intend to assent to it. And by mid-summer of 1939 when the Japanese realized that England now seemed drawn to the side of the Chinese, they quickly moved to stir up anti–British agitation. Hong Kong was becoming less and less of a safe and neutral haven.

In hot and enervating Chungking, Mayling expressed dismay over the lack of cheer, encouragement and sympathy from overseas. The democracies, she felt, were sitting on the sidelines. She pressed on to finish training 450 women for junior staff work and to send them off to the front. "They are undergoing a three months' practice period and if they are able to stand the baptism of blood and fire, as well as the ravages of cooties, flies, mosquitoes, cholera, malaria, and any other diseases rampant in the summer, we shall give them their diplomas this autumn."[1]

In the United States, support of German refugees, and a boycott of Nazi goods, became extensive—by far exceeding the impact of anti–Japanese boycotts and the dollars raised by Chinese relief campaigns the prior year. And there were occasional negative outbursts at pro–China fundraising events. Emma remembered a friend's outrage against the amount of printed material from Chinese sources asking for money. "They say $1 will save a baby's life, and then they spend a $1 a week on propaganda mailed to me," he shouted. His complaint continued: "I am tired to death of reports of speeches by the Chiangs. They haven't any right to ask for money when they are throwing so much of it away on useless propaganda."[2]

Appeals for cash donations for medicines, orthopedic devices and woolen blankets brought the best results from the general public, as well from pharmaceutical houses and physicians. Malaria outbreaks became the basis for a need for quinine, spearheaded by ABMAC. It brought extraordinary returns. "The circular was written by an expert," Emma reported, "and we had the privilege of using the subscription list of *Asia*, which has never given its list for any such purpose before."[3]

"No matter how much the people in Europe suffer, I do not believe there could be such suffering anywhere on earth as there is in China," Mayling wrote from Chungking in an appeal to the Golden Rule Foundation in New York.[4]

She certainly had cause to worry about funds for the 20,000 or more children under her care. She expressed this concern to Emma:

> I certainly do appreciate the check [$1,000]. ... with Europe in conflagration, naturally our contributions from there in the future will be entirely nil. It is possible, too, that some of the funds which were coming from America will now be

diverted toward refugee work in the European countries. As we have been carrying on this war for over two years and the cost of living is mounting increasingly, and as many of the big businesses within the country have been displaced by our having to move into the interior, I am quite worried as to how these 20,000 children are to be cared for. All I hope for is that this work so enthusiastically begun will continue to function properly.[5]

Charitable groups asked Madame Chiang to broadcast via short wave, and to make some recordings for overseas appeals. She felt some distaste for such solicitations. "I hate this begging business," she explained to Emma. "Telling listeners of actual conditions should leave them to act according to the dictates of their conscience. I resent people asking me for contributions. If I see a need, I feel that I should give to the very utmost without being approached. That anyone should ask me affronts my self-respect and sense of what is fitting." Turning to her basic Christian tenets, Mayling added: "I feel that every decent person recognizes the fact that what she has does not belong solely to her but to all who are in need and that she is merely a caretaker of what she possesses and that some day she will be made to account for all omissions and commissions. But, perhaps, I am a bit peculiar."[6]

The contents of Mills' mailbox expanded as she increasingly became a conduit for messages to Mayling, as well as money. When Chungking was pounded by bombs, accounts of devastation made many of the old campus crowd heartsick. Dickey Lightner, for one, phoned Emma to find out if Mayling was still in the Chinese capital as she had the impression the city was "leveled."

Greater and greater attention focused on Europe that summer. A Russian-German pact linked the two governments in a non-aggression treaty. Roosevelt appealed to both Germany and its neighbor, Poland, to arbitrate their differences; the Poles accepted conciliation, yet soon decreed partial mobilization in the face of German threats. On September 1, Germany invaded Poland, having annexed Austria a year earlier and taken over most of Czechoslovakia in March. Britain and France quickly honored their pact with Poland, and declared war on Germany. The United States remained neutral, but before the close of 1939 Congress repealed the arms embargo, and authorized a cash and carry basis for exports of arms and munitions to belligerent powers.

When war broke out, Emma was visiting friends in Ontario, Canada. She marveled that the Canadians evidenced so little bitterness. "They are grim, very sure, very determined," she observed, "but if there is no flag waving and band playing this time, there is also no depression or hysteria." She found New Yorkers more gloomy when she returned to the city. Yet business people, she noted in the latest letter to Mayling, "tell me that everyone is so busy rejoicing at making a little money again at last, or taking profits, that they are not thinking much beyond that at present. Some of this upswing dates from before the opening of hostilities; it is not all cynical."[7]

In the days before Hitler's invasion of Poland, Chiang Kai-shek had reiterated his resistance against Japan. International developments in Europe would not deter him; he added that he hoped peace in Europe would be maintained. Japan viewed the war there as closing sources for their supplies of raw materials and machinery. Tokyo believed that events would draw Japan closer to the United States as the only great power whose hands were free for trade with the Far East.

To reinforce his determination to continue the struggle, the Chiangs made an inspection tour to the Hunan front, a 2,000-mile trip by plane, auto, sedan chair, sampan, and shanks' pony, all of which were threatened by Japanese aircraft. Several times Mayling dodged into ditches and hid in dugouts to avoid being seen by enemy machine gunners, who, she pointed out, "consider it sport to mow down people on the highways."[8]

The early November travel itinerary encompassed visits to field and base hospitals for the wounded. "Some of them have been wounded two or three times. I addressed one group of four or five thousand just ready to leave for the front lines. They were full of high enthusiasm, and so were the people. There is a remarkable change in the attitude of the peasants. Now they are co-operating with the Army. There is no robbery or violence. The soldiers regard themselves as the protector of the people, and the people regard the soldiers as an army of their own—as it really is.... We may have to fight a long time, but there is no doubt that in time we shall win unless we are overwhelmed by some further violation of treaties by some other Power who might come to the assistance of the Japanese."

The Japanese, Mayling inferred, were pushing cooperation with Russia in an endeavor to counteract the consequences of any American move to deprive Japan of munitions and gasoline and oil. Japanese military leaders also hoped that an agreement with the Soviets would enable her to withdraw her troops from Manchuria to be used to the south in China. "There will be no peace until Japanese troops and Japanese puppets such as Wang Ching-wei are off China's soil."[9]

Mayling's letter to Emma added a handwritten postscript, urging Emma to send by air mail a refill of six bottles of respiratory medicine. Overwork, frequent speechmaking, sleeplessness, and rigorous travel had taxed her strength, and made her extremely susceptible to colds, especially in the foggy Chungking climate, "where the sun so rarely shines that when it does, the dogs bark at it."

Her health took a downturn by December. A case of painful, inflamed sinus led her English doctor in Hong Kong to journey to Chungking to perform an operation. The procedure was successful but left her weak and shaky. Emma offered a bit of cheer tied to relief activities. Imports of Chinese jewelry continued to sell very well, with an average profit of 100 percent. And ABMAC Christmas card sales—a projected 12,000 boxes in contrast to 5,000 in 1938—competed strongly with organizations raising funds for Europe. Later in the month Emma, following a conversation with an informed China friend, noted that China's cause was well understood in America, and no amount of increased publicity, propaganda, or pressure would increase American good will or help. "It comes down to the fact that Europe is after all much nearer to us all; most of us are second or third generation overseas Europeans. (My own Mills grandfather was born in Ireland.) ... I don't think publicity can accomplish miracles, but some *is* necessary in connection with any attempt to raise funds, and it seems to me that China's case need no longer be argued— but information on her development and specific needs is useful."[10]

Nearly three months passed without a reply from Mayling. Then, in March 1940 she answered, this time from Hong Kong, pointing out that people had failed to see the connection between the war in Europe and the Sino-Japanese conflict of 32 months' unrelenting ferocity. "The 'right of way' given to the Japanese by the democracies inspired others to act and overwhelm weaker countries. Now the democracies are paying the price for allowing Japan to have a free hand.... She has not been able to exploit China. ... the Chinese people are adopting methods of passive resistance which are robbing the invader of the fruits which they expected to harvest in the so-called 'occupied' regions. The Japanese," she concluded, "can kill and burn, but that they cannot with equal facility, produce the necessities of life. Nor can they compel the Chinese people to do so. And in that failure lies their defeat."[11]

In a personal vein, Mayling added that she required additional treatment following her sinus operation in Chungking. A cauterization could not be performed there, apparently because no medical instruments were readily available. She also needed a complete rest, and thus came to Hong Kong. Mayling stayed with sister Ailing Kung at her house on Sassoon Road. Soon the third sister, Chingling Sun, joined them for a reunion apart from their public roles. They pushed aside political differences; gossip, anecdotes and jokes filled hours of each day. Mayling regained her health, and one evening the sisters appeared together in public. China's dynastic women dined at the Hong Kong Hotel—they had not been seen together in a decade.

The Soong sisters were seated in the main dining room where the British establishment, and a few wealthy Chinese and their wives, ate and danced. Couples glided past their table, and turned their heads to witness the rare public reunion of the three. "Madame Kung quietly splendid, Madame Chiang glowing with new-found health, Madame Sun in black, her hair glossy, her eyes amused. Three Chinese ladies who sat quietly eating their dinners just as if they were no Symbols."[12]

Mayling insisted that her sisters come back with her to Chungking. "We need to be seen together in the capital. It would squelch those nasty rumors as to a split in the family, and strengthen the Government in the wake of the Nanking inauguration of that traitor Wang Ching-wei." Both sisters consented.

On April 1 the three Soongs boarded a DC3 of the China National Aviation Company at Hong Kong's Kai Tak airport. They left amid much secrecy, yet their arrival in Chungking led Kuomintang publicity aides to pull out all the stops. Ailing and Chingling had never been to that city, and for Madame Sun, it was the first time in many years that she had set foot in the headquarters of the Nationalists. She settled into Foreign Minister H.H. Kung's large house, occupying the top floor of what had been a warlord's concubines' quarters. And with two Soong brothers, T.V. and T.L., in Chungking, the gathering had all the trappings of a family reunion.

Madame Chiang eagerly introduced her guests at meetings of various associations and committees, and at receptions for official groups. Chingling, as the widow of the Father of the Chinese Republic, and an ally of the Communists, carried particular significance. Her presence ended rumors that relations with her brother-in-law and his government were at or near the breaking point. Madame Sun added to the importance of a session of the People's Political Council and dampened pending recognition of the newly installed Wang regime in Nanking where stood the shrine-like tomb of Dr. Sun.

The American-educated sisters traveled about the city visiting hospitals and schools, orphanages and bomb shelters. The newsreel cameras photographed them at every move, most dramatically amid the ruins of Japanese-destroyed buildings. Mayling had persuaded her older, more traditionally dressed sisters to wear black slacks on their scouting treks about the city and nearby Chengtu.

Their appearances magnified the unity of the Soongs in the war effort, and the enhanced toughness of the sisters in adversity. On April 18 they each spoke over the NBC network in an overseas broadcast—the first time the sisters had gathered together before a microphone. Madame Sun opened the hookup with a brief comment. Speaking in English, as did her sisters, she said "the future history of the peoples of the Pacific and of the whole world will be different and brighter because our 450,000,000 people, instead of becoming the helots of an all-conquering slave empire, have taken up arms for their own freedom as well as yours."[13]

Chingling then turned the microphone over to Mrs. Kung, who acknowledged the help of friends of China, especially those people in the remote areas of her vast country. She pointed to Japan's ill-starred aggression and failure to conquer, and the futile, turncoat government at Nanking. "An array of facts stands out as clear as crystal. The chief one is that Japan has already shot her bolt in China. China, without any assistance at all, and with comparatively feeble armament, has fought Japan to a standstill."[14] Ailing spoke proudly of the hundreds of factories dismantled and carried or shipped to the interior from the eastern provinces. The country had also created some 1,400 industrial cooperatives in places that could not be bombed. They, she noted, represented about 30,000 worker-members, and were part of a region successfully transformed by engineers, technical experts, educators, mill managers, and artisans. Madame Kung next echoed her youngest sister's frequent description of Chinese women and their will to persevere.

"Women have escaped from their cloistered lives and are working everywhere: at the front with the fighting men and the wounded; behind the lines ... far in the rear, in rural work, in hospitals, in war orphanages, in industrial and community services."[15]

Mayling participated with a closing message. If China had surrendered, she claimed, most of the Pacific would have been seized by the Japanese. She ended with one of her characteristic terse phrases: "The people of China are deafened by bombs, but they are anxiously listening for your reply."[16]

Tokyo's sharp reply to the Soong sisters questioned the family's true patriotism. An official Japanese spokesman wondered why the personal fortune of the so-called Soong Dynasty was not being tapped for the public welfare before appeals were made to America and other foreign lands for money. "The tremendous wealth they and their husbands and relatives have, and other members of the Chungking regime, are kept safe in banks in London and other cities abroad. I am led to credit these reports of great wealth, for all the photographs of this trio show them handsomely dressed in costly silks, doubtless wearing jades and diamonds, and also all are showing signs of being excellently nourished."[17]

Even the Bowl-of-Rice dinners in America were cited by Japanese propagandists as superfluous gatherings where people ate sparingly and turned over a dollar or two for overseas relief—cash that would have gone for multicourse Chinese cuisine.

As the war entered the beginning of its fourth year, Mayling acknowledged some $870,000 worth of medicines, surgical supplies and ambulances from the Medical Bureau, which had grown to chapters in 70 cities.

That fall Pearl Buck, author of the best-selling novel on Chinese rural life *The Good Earth*, joined an expanding list of notable Americans helping the bureau: First Lady Eleanor Roosevelt, industrialist Thomas J. Watson, Academy Award actress (and star of the film version of *The Good Earth*) Luise Rainer, lawyer-diplomat Myron C. Taylor, publisher DeWitt Wallace, and dozens of prominent socialites. Buck organized a new group, China Emergency Relief, as an affiliate of the bureau. "While our hearts are stirred by the bravery of the British," she said, "let us remember that on the other side of us for three long years the Chinese people, in the same cause of freedom, have shown the same bravery under bombing.... Famine and pestilence threaten millions who are helpless." [18]

The blockade of the Chinese coast limited incoming provisions for the country's interior. Only a "back door" route could alleviate supply problems. Construction of an overland truck road from Lashio, Burma, to Kunming, Yunnan Province, had received priority from Chiang in 1937. This highway connected with a railroad line to Rangoon, a regular port of call for ships with crucial cargo. This transport link could handle 100 or so three-ton trucks of essential supplies each day. Japan, of course, threatened to bomb the Burma Road if it were used for transport of any arms into China.[19]

Inland, the fierce summer air raids of 1940 intensified with three or four formations of 30 to 50 bombers loaded with incendiary bombs to drop on Chungking military and civilian areas.

A weary Mayling, tired from the many air raids and a post-op relapse, complained to Emma that writing seemed uncharacteristically difficult. Head and hand did not coordinate; she thought of one word and her hand wrote another. Sometimes her Chinese and English got mixed. Was she ready for an insane asylum? she wondered. Nature was sending her danger signals, she concluded.

The daily roar of enemy planes overhead compounded the mental and physical strain. One day, a bomb fell on her house, luckily only damaging the yard and breaking window panes. In that raid her friends suffered more, losing homes and possessions; even in the dugouts, clothes were blown off by the concussions. While struggling in longhand with her letter to New York, she witnessed the shooting down of an enemy bomber, and spotted four descending parachutes.

"The bombers are still circling overhead," she wrote. "They come in formation—in droves—looking like enormous black crows. Thud, thud, thud! They are dropping bombs now on the other side of the river. I cannot see the explosions as I am on the Huang-Shan side. My husband and I are living in the hills since our Chungking house is no longer habitable. The Japs know this house also, since that traitor Wang Ching-wei once visited us here, and told them of our whereabouts.... Heavens, how we lack planes here! We have enough trained pilots, but a deplorable scarcity of planes."[20]

The German invasion of Belgium and Holland and the fall of France jolted many Europeans and Americans out of complacency, and gave Emma much news to relay.

"There's not so much talk of our getting in the war," she pondered. "We feel totally unprepared, and it seems almost as though it might be over before we could get going. Generally, it strikes people that if Germany wins, then sooner or later we'll have to meet her ourselves. She'd come via South America, perhaps.... Everyone is depressed. At least in the last war there weren't radios with news broadcasts every hour or so from here and direct from Europe. You could relax between editions of the newspapers. But now, there is a continual clock watching for the next radio news. This, in isolationist America."[21]

Emma expressed bitterness over feelings of outrage by the average American with Nazi bombing and machine-gunning of civilians, and their loss of homes and worldly goods, while similar harm to Chinese held much less concern. "What makes me most bitter of all, however, is to think that none of this war need have come anywhere in the world if the democratic statesmen had not been so colossally stupid, and the ruling cliques immeasurably greedy. Now we will have to come to their rescue, I suppose, in order to protect ourselves."[22]

The Medical Bureau opened a building at the 1940 New York World's Fair, then in its second summer. The undertaking sold Chinese odds and ends amidst a well-positioned display of medical items shipped to China. Emma, because of her ongoing commitment to ABMAC, accepted a paying job there as executive vice president. As the Christmas holidays approached, she again supervised the packaging of 36,000 boxes of cards. Those sales at year-end would net some $20,000.

The 1940 presidential race between Roosevelt and Wendell Willkie vied for attention with the war in Europe and the Far East. The Republican nominee, chosen by convention delegates over party stalwarts Dewey, Taft and Vandenberg, faced an incumbent seeking an unprecedented third term, which in itself generated strong feelings against FDR. Willkie's selection by his party stemmed from well-orchestrated grass-roots enthusiasm for a non-political figure. To Emma, he seemed an intelligent, upright sort of individual, with first

1940 presidential candidate Wendell Willkie, novelist Pearl Buck and Chinese ambassador to the U.S. Hu Shi added luster to China Relief charitable gatherings in New York. (ABMAC Records, Rare Book and Manuscript Library, Columbia University.)

class business ability and a gift for clear speaking and writing. Yet he had no training in conducting foreign affairs, and no political experience. "But people are saying rearming is a business undertaking and needs a business man for its competent organizing," Emma pointed out, "and as the former, probably his views are similar to Roosevelt's.... Both parties have come out against our participation in the European war. ... it shows that both realize the country is dead against it at this time."[23]

But by mid–September Willkie's campaign slumped. The transfer of 50 aging U.S. destroyers to the British, in exchange for the right to take 99-year leases on their naval and air bases in the Western Hemisphere, proved widely acceptable. Willkie favored this move by FDR, a crucial measure to save the British fleet, and step to counteract an imminent invasion of Britain itself. By autumn the first peacetime compulsory military draft kept voters more focused on global issues, than on domestic matters. And more and more the Republican presidential runner shared Roosevelt's views on preparing the country for war.

In September voluntary army enlistments in New York swelled, with many recruits admitting the pact trading overage destroyers for bases led them to join up. And suddenly the war in China was back as a frequent topic on editorial pages, and received increasing attention from radio commentators and columnists. Everyone waited—for further overseas developments, and the outcome on election day. Emma's friends said they were voting for Willkie, but she was sure Roosevelt would win a third term.

FDR did beat his opponent, 27.2 million votes to 22.3 million. But Willkie did not fade from the mainstream. He had discovered new horizons. Now an internationalist from grappling with world issues, he'd travel widely—and soon into the life of Mayling.

A wave of patriotism arose that fall. More and more concerts and plays opened with the playing of "The Star-Spangled Banner." The flag's colors appeared as lapel ornaments, and flags stood inside banks and other office buildings. Greek and Italian shops displayed in their windows banners inscribed "God Bless America" or "We Thank God We Are Americans."

In her 54th letter to Mayling (since 1937), Emma spoke of a joke played on the unwary in New York. "You were asked if you'd like two free tickets to the opening of The Burma Road. Assuming it was a new play, you'd say yes, and then be directed to telephone such and such a number. If you did, it turned out to be the Japanese Consulate!"[24]

Mayling asked her 45-year-old spinster-friend what occupied her spare time—when she wasn't working for China relief activities. "I sometimes wonder myself," Emma replied in a long and revealing picture of what went on in New York. "I do have some leisure to read and think, and when I realize how much that means to me, I am full of concern to think of you without it. My Chinese work is roughly the equivalent of a full-time job, and a good deal of my reading is along the same lines. I read practically every new book on China that comes out here ... and 4 of the 7 magazines I take have to do with the Far East—the 5th is 'Foreign Affairs.' I have studied a good deal, off and on, and finished all the work for a Masters in Chinese studies, but have never gotten around to writing the thesis."

Turning to her social life, Emma called it "sketchy." She still lived on West 89th Street with her grandmother, age 89, "and one can't do much in her house."

She then mentioned her "excellent friends." Mandy Mandeville Ferris— who was with her in Peking for a time—and her husband Gil were the closest.

> Their suburban home is my second home, and I go there for gaiety and an entirely different atmosphere—yacht club, cocktail parties, chit-chat. A very fine composer [Bernard Wagenaar] and his wife [Irene] keep me in touch with musical affairs, a young Georgia girl of 23 [Carson McCullers] whose first novel is just out and getting off to a phenomenal start and her husband [Reeves] have now returned to town and I am much involved in their getting settled.
>
> That is one of the nice things about New York, all sorts of people get here sooner or later. Just this week, richer in this respect than most—Eunice [Higgins Calpin] and her husband [Raymond] dropped in unannounced one day on their way back by motor from the launching of the U.S.S. Washington in Philadelphia, an old bachelor cousin [Harry Peebles] from Chicago turned up whom I hadn't seen since on my way to China, and yesterday, also unannounced, a woman I had known in Peking dropped in with her new husband on their way from California to New Mexico by way of Maine. And so it goes.[25]

Nevertheless, Emma wished she lived in the country rather than the city, and would still rather take a sea voyage than stay put anywhere. She no longer expected to write any kind of novel, and seldom read one. The urge to write had greatly diminished.

> I have lived for years with old and sick people—Grandmother is the only one of the lot left now—but it has certainly not prematurely aged me—just this morning a young woman of 28 snorted when I said something that implied I was considerably older than she. I can get a tremendous kick out of lying in the sun on a sandy beach, a night club evening with a congenial man, a good job by a foreign correspondent anywhere in the world, first class symphony or popular music, unusual food and talk. I like hard work, but loathe monotony, routine and confinement. Sounds as though I were applying for a job! But you asked for it.[26]

Mayling came to realize Emma had become a true cosmopolitan.

16

Committed to Victory

Chiang Kai-shek and his brother-in-law, H.H. Kung, now vice premier and finance minister, predicted major military gains for China in 1941. American and British loans and material assistance brightened the envisioned road to ultimate victory. China had recaptured 89 towns during the prior year, although 66 cities and towns were lost to the Japanese. A new system of defense entailed completely obliterating traces of some 2,000 miles of roads for a 100-mile wide band facing the Japanese. This left no highways along which Japanese planes could bomb supplies, and the Japanese themselves could advance only as fast as they could build new roads and bridges. After they had gone ahead a bit, the Chinese cut in behind them and disrupted enemy supply lines.

Overall, as the year progressed, Chiang's army stood better equipped and trained through imports and supplies from the United States. And Roosevelt's New Year's address emphasized the importance of China's war of resistance against Japan.

Aircraft, particularly pursuit and interceptor planes, led the list of Chinese military needs. Observers pointed out that beefed-up air power in China not only would impair Japan's striking thrust but might nullify the fast developing threats to French Indo-China, Singapore, Burma and the Netherlands East Indies.

The Red Cross in its mission to bring relief supplies to China's interior worried about the transport hazards along the precarious Burma Road. An initial convoy of Red Cross trucks had crossed some 300 bridges, climbed to 8,000-foot heights, negotiated hairpin turns along cliff edges, and faced blinding monsoons. Scores of vehicles, wrecked and abandoned at the bottom of deep ravines from both accidents and air bombings, were soon proof of the risks of traveling on this supply route, which had been carved out of rocky mountainsides often by the light of torches made of straw soaked in oil.

Before the end of winter, strong sentiment to aid the Chinese brought together a high-level amalgamation of American fundraising groups and agencies, led for the most part by those Emma Mills called "the best people." In little more than three years, relief aid to China had grown from the small nucleus of Mayling's Wellesley classmates and their friends, and a handful of sympathetic Chinese in New York's Chinatown, to a joint national drive, and well-staffed assemblage. This new organization called United China Relief, Inc., spearheaded and chiefly financed by Henry Luce, merged seven agencies to coordinate appeals being made independently to serve medical, charitable, and educational needs in China. Formed by a group of distinguished bankers and industrialists, the umbrella organization, which embodied the American Bureau for Medical Aid to China, announced a campaign to raise $5 million by July 31. James G. Blaine, president of the Marine Midland Trust Company, accepted the chairmanship, emphasizing that "only by combining existing efforts in a truly nation-wide campaign for gifts can we hope to enlist the increased resources and support available to a united movement."[1] It did not represent a new appeal but a coordinated, strengthened one on a broader scale.

Among the United China Relief organizers-directors, Luce became the most vocal. In this role he and his wife Clare flew to China by Pan American clipper to make a first-hand study of conditions at the war front and of the most urgent needs of its people and Chiang's troops. Their five-day visit focused on medical relief work and foreign missionaries. As publisher of *Time* and *Life*, Luce had in mind how his magazines could build more interest in his embattled birthplace. In March 1941, *Life* published a photo essay by the photographer-and-reporter team Carl and Shelley Mydans, who had been sent to Chungking by Luce. Increased coverage of the war filled more pages and columns later that year. In the June 30 issue of *Life*, Mrs. Luce's own photos ran in a feature called "China: To the Mountains."

The Chiangs welcomed their notable American guests at a tea. An air raid had just ended, resulting in 40 dead, and many more wounded outside air-raid shelters. Luce heartlessly noted, "There is not much sympathy for the victims now because it is felt it is mostly their own fault for not going into the dugouts."[2]

Henry Luce described the Generalissimo as a "slim, wraithlike figure in khaki" who grunted a few words of greeting. As was her custom when meeting VIPs, Mayling wore a cheongsam, a traditional Chinese dress which clothed her almost from her ears and jet black hair to her ankles and emphasized her slimness and agility. Clare, anxious to observe the fighting front, asked Chiang to okay a personal military flight to the Sian battlefield, a risky undertaking. For the better part of two days the Luces flew in a small Beechcraft over the Szechwan plains and Tsinling Mountains, then traveled by land vehicles—even Mongolian ponies—to within eyesight of the enemy. Luce, much impressed by the Chinese army and its magnificent spirit of courage and determination, left Chungking as an even more solid ally of Chiang and his cause.[3]

By June Luce and his colleagues had raised $1 million for United China Relief. The campaign received a municipal boost from New York mayor LaGuardia's proclamation of China Week—highlighted by a colorful parade of 4,000 Chinese and American marchers, and speeches and appeals by Governor Herbert Lehman, Wendell Willkie and Chinese government officials. Eleanor Roosevelt acted for the distaff side of the White House when she personally bought for Mayling a summer dress of shantung at her favorite store, Arnold Constable on Fifth Avenue. Bolts of the same fabric, she explained, also were being cut and sold to aid Chinese relief. The Roosevelts' son James, en route to fill an assignment as military observer in Africa and the Near East, had visited the Chiangs that spring, and Eleanor now wanted to thank Mayling for their hospitality to the First Family's oldest son. While writing her enclosed message to Chungking, she said to store personnel, "I've sent dozens of notes to Mme. Chiang. Now I'm glad to be able to send her something."[4]

On June 18 United China Relief held a testimonial dinner in New York for the Generalissimo and Mayling. More than 1,600 people jammed the Waldorf-Astoria Hotel ballroom—up to that time the second largest group ever served there. "How many because of an interest in China, how many to hear their dear Clare [Boothe Luce] speak, of course, I can't tell," Emma remarked.[5] Mrs. Luce dramatically reminded her audience that a million Chinese soldiers had been killed, two million wounded, fifty million Chinese driven from their homes and forced to trek thousands of miles into the interior. "What dollars are to Britain, pennies are to China now."[6]

Emma wrote Mayling: "Wendell Willkie presided, but [former Ambassador to China] Nelson Johnson's brief, affectionate impression of the two of you brought the greatest applause of the evening.... This is the fourth or fifth big party United China Relief has put on for straight promotion." She added that the campaign had been extended to mid–October; it had fallen short of its $5-million goal. Money had been spent lavishly with inadequate returns, and a disheartened Emma believed that the first million received would have gone to the participating agencies, anyway.[7]

> Many of the key people running it came from Luce's magazines and are trained in advertising or promotion, and not at all in fund raising. The magazines and some members of its Board have gotten tremendous publicity out of it. Apparently China is at last achieving social standing.... Not that it would matter if the money were coming in fast enough. The executive director of United China Relief [B.A. Garside] has long been in the China field, and ... known as a dictatorial sort impossible to work with. There are cross currents of politics, and some deliberate sabotage of the participating agencies, and a strong tendency for this new group not to be a cooperation of existing groups, but simply a new group in the field in competition with them. They get small gifts from our regular donors, and so far have largely failed to get the large gifts from new sources that were promised.[8]

Emma's attendance at the tribute reflected a new turn of events in her life. She now had an "independent income." Grandmother De Long, the last of her generation, died quite suddenly at home in her 90th year on November 24, 1940, leaving Emma and her brother De Long Mills modest trust funds for life. After clearing out a half-century of furniture and artifacts from the family townhouse,

Henry and Clare Boothe Luce provided extensive coverage of the war in China in Time-Life publications. The Luces also played a leadership role in merging China support groups and contributing lump sums to the Chiangs' relief funds. (ABMAC Records, Rare Book and Manuscript Library, Columbia University.)

she found a small apartment in the Chelsea section of Manhattan. She thought of how simple it would have been, if to facilitate the move to 161 West 16th Street, a small bomb had fallen on the old dwelling on West 89th Street. Exhausted by consolidating furnishings into a one-bedroom dwelling and selling many pieces, she boarded a steamship for a month's vacation at Montego Bay, Jamaica. It was her first overseas holiday since visiting her brother's naval base in Panama in 1934.

Not long after her return, Chinese vice consul Cheng Pao-nan met with

Emma to talk about his new job representing ABMAC in Chungking. "It was at his instigation that I started these letters to you," Emma reminded Mayling. "I hope that it will be possible for you to talk with him, and that his presence in China will be as useful to you there as we expect it to be for our work here. He has talked to me of the possibility of my going over, too, now that I am no longer tied down here.... I could manage to live on a very nominal salary in China, but I don't at the moment see that I could be of any special use there. I do think there is a job ... here in fund raising, a job that is steadily growing in scope, and until I can see some definitely useful niche somewhere else, I'll stick to that. I still have all the resiliency and adaptability I ever had. ... any thoughts on the subject, let me know."[9]

Mayling quickly replied—albeit her first letter in nine months. She explained the long gap was not a waning of affection, merely an inability to stretch a day of wartime duties into something over 24 hours—"a feat that is beyond my powers." Besides, she had been in Hong Kong for four months, beginning in November of the prior year. There, she underwent treatment for chronic pain from the vertebrae dislocated in the overturned automobile accident en route to Shanghai early in the war.

A newspaper reported that Mme Chiang had canceled a lecture tour to the States. Fund-raisers there had cabled that she'd be worth ten army divisions to China if she came. But the general told her to cable back that she was worth 20 divisions to him in China, so she didn't go. Nevertheless, her passport would be ready. "I will be able to go at any time in the future. I am definitely planning an American trip as soon as the war is over."[10]

With American directness and surety, Mayling told Emma that Chinese military authorities were now confident that the tide toward victory had clearly turned in her country's favor. She expressed the belief that for Japan, speaking for her Axis partners as well as herself, to threaten war on the United States if any opposition was made to the plans of the aggressors, would have an effect precisely the reverse to that expected. "The Axis Powers evidently thought that they had only to threaten America with dire punishment unless they 'trembled and obeyed,' to borrow the arrogant phraseology employed by the Manchus, to fill Americans with terror."[11]

There was not a subject in the world on which Mayling would not speak with authority, at least in private conversation, recalled Ilona Ralf Sues, a journalist-publicist hired by her early in the war. Close-up to Madame Chiang, Sues described her as "pulsating, vibrating, dynamic ... the Fighter—for a decent government, for an efficient administration, for a modern China: a frail, delicate little lady pitting herself with fiery spirit and unbending will power against an age-old obsolete system, against mildewed tradition, against the almighty monster of corrupt officialdom. ... and challenging the world with the battle cry: 'China Will Rise Again.'"[12]

A passionate reformer, Mayling antagonized many. Her aides trembled when she flew into a dictatorial temper. She could fascinate and enthrall some interviewers and could dominate a crowd of courtiers, Sues remembered. "She had admirers but no true friends.... She did not talk with people, she talked at them.... She demanded blind obedience and broke anyone who dared think differently."[13]

Mayling neither cared about criticism nor minced her words in her role of interpreter of Western thought and purveyor of Western reactions to her husband. The military clique hated her for her influence upon their leader. They resented a woman's influence on their chief and her interference in state affairs—indeed, she was his "contact man" and "aide de camp."

Westerners chiefly read of Madame Chiang's striking attractiveness, Spartan puritanism, self-effacing modesty, exceptional ability, charm and smile, and, of course, her American education. More than merely an official hostess, she was depicted as her husband's trouble-shooter and English interpreter.

"He is her one overriding care," F. Tillman Durdin of the *New York Times* wrote from Chungking in 1941. "What he wants takes precedence over all her other cares. She sees that he gets his vitamins; and he sends her off for a rest in the country when she gets so overtired that her brain just bogs down and refuses to work." Above all, Westerners were reminded of her courage, her energy and her gift of daring.

"In her own country—and in America as well," Durdin concluded, "she has become the symbol of a militant, new, progressive China, unconquered in the face of attack by a ruthless, military foe many times more powerful."[14]

Apart from the extraordinary attributes, positive and negative, evidenced by the inner circle and purveyed to the outside world, more objective observers provided a picture of a fragile human being. An American official just back from Chungking spoke to Emma of a Mayling behind the so-called bamboo curtain.

> If she works one day, she must rest two. She still suffers from her automobile injury, her back and neck, and now she has toothaches no one can explain. She worries and cannot sleep, then takes something for it, and must get up again before she has completely slept it off.
>
> The Generalissimo has no such difficulties, sleeps like a lamb ... doesn't understand how high strung she is.[15]

This confidante thought Mayling needed someone to let her hair down with and talk things out. Emma, he believed, might be valuable in this role. Pearl Chen served as secretary, but she did not always show good judgment. Mayling was enthusiastic about coming to the States, but the Generalissimo promptly vetoed any such plan.

Mayling had not an instant's doubt that China would be victorious, though she had her bad moments. She and Chiang sometimes had to cheer each other up.

Mayling addressed Emma's cautious inquiry on a return to China, now that Grandmother neither held her back nor held the purse strings. Mayling described the poor living conditions in the Chinese capital, the bad food and accommodations, pointing out that many Chinese from America and Shanghai attempted to live there but had to give up because of rampant disease. There was a lack of water—with each available bucket of Yangtze River water costing $1.50 just for portage.

Air raids sometimes lasted over six hours, she explained.

> When some of the people could not bear the fetid suffocating air in the dugouts, and came out to catch a breath of air, suddenly the second wave of planes dropped flares in the heart of the city. The people tried to force their way [back] into the dugouts, and in the panic over 500 people were killed. Fires raged all night long. Such conditions will continue as they did last year, & the year before. Furthermore, there is not *one* single amusement place, or any sort of social life. Nothing but sheer, wearying, heartbreaking work between air raids. The heat, and the rain are not romantic.[16]

Mayling came to the conclusion—and the decision—that her closest friend in America should stay there. Work for China at home, Mayling emphasized. Moreover, she realized that Emma continued as a discreet conduit of information and gofer of sundry personal items. As such, she remained virtually irreplaceable.

> My own life is one of unremitting toil, but I feel I owe it to my country to persist in it even if I have to die at my post. But there is no reason why you should. Besides ... I speak and write Chinese whereas, for you, everything would be even harder since you have not been brought up by changing war conditions.[17]

Many Americans felt war was near for them. Maritime observers noticed an increasing number of navy ships being repainted in a camouflage color with above-deck bright metal areas covered with canvas. More and more cargo vessels were converted for navy use. The threat of "gasless Sundays" stemmed from an oil tanker shortage on the East Coast. A campaign in New York to recruit air raid wardens seemed part of a psychological buildup rather than practical necessity. City dwellers talked of moving heirloom furniture to the country for fear of bombings. In central and south China some 2,000 Americans faced growing harassment by Japanese military authorities, reportedly because of the freezing of all Axis assets in the United States. Another blow at Japan—a military mission to an increase lend-lease aid to the Chinese army—pointed toward the democracies' goal to defeat both the European Axis and Japan. America would now assist in procurement and delivery to China of military materials. General John Magruder headed the mission, joining in Chungking FDR appointee Owen Lattimore, an adviser to Chiang, and Flying Tigers commander Chennault.

China, in spite of intensive, damaging air raids, economic difficulties, clashes between the Koumintang and the Communist party troops, the separatist movement in South China, and a drain on the energy of the people caused by four years of hard wartime living, by and large remained committed to victory.

Mayling's personal thoughts on America's emerging role in the Far East carried some fears. Although encouraged by Washington's greater support, she said that in some quarters there were those not so sure that it would help China if America became an active belligerent.

> They fear that America's own requirements for munitions might curtail the assistance that is now being extended to us. But others think that, as America is now getting into her full stride in production, this fear is not justified. And it is also believed that there is very little danger of the Pacific Fleet being sent to the Atlantic in any event.[18]

A month later Mayling concluded that China "is now reaping the reward of her steadfastness and determination in the shape of much better defined diplomatic and material assistance from America and Britain. Whether Japan moves north or south, China will benefit."[19]

This would be her last letter to Emma for more than two years. Fast-changing developments in the Far East seemingly curtailed her correspondence. Besides, more and more Americans were arriving in Chungking, bringing news directly from the States. Emma's summaries—the so-called "straws in the wind" commentary—seemingly had lost much of their importance and value for China's First Lady. Mayling and the Chinese government commended Emma Mills' contribution to civilian relief—and her role as unofficial steadfast correspondent to Mme Chiang—by presenting her its Medal for Distinguished Service.

New York maintained its leadership in mustering donations. A radio appeal by former governor Alfred E. Smith to "adopt" war orphans by American grandfathers and grandmothers drew scores of members into an "Esteemed Grandparents Club."

A "Drink Tea for China Day" opened an intensive fall campaign for China relief. Chinese children at a number of city intersections hawked 10-cent drinks of iced tea from water coolers decorated with Chinese posters and flags. Packages of Mayling Tea, named expressly for Mme Chiang, sold for $1 a half-pound. Scores of women's organizations joined together to aid children in China. Each group received a scroll on which individual members might inscribe their names in return for a contribution of 25 cents. Each donation fed a Chinese child for a week; the scrolls were assembled in a Book of Life and sent to Mayling.

The outpouring of American help—especially in New York—brought a reciprocal gesture of thanks. Learning of the recent loss of its last remaining giant panda at the Bronx Zoo, Mayling initiated a search among Chinese hunters and farmers in west China for the rare and prized animals. During the summer and fall of 1941 the quest in the remote bamboo mountain forests intensified. By early October two cubs had been captured for Mayling's special gift—"with the hope that their cute antics will bring as much joy to the American children as American friendship has brought to our Chinese people."[20]

Earlier, in the 1930s, American explorer Ruth Harkness had captured a panda—her second prize catch—for the Chicago Zoo and named it Mei-Ling. Mayling felt miffed instead of honored. She insisted the creature be re-named O Lin; however, it publicly became known as Su-Sen, according to Harkness biographer Vicki Constantine Croke.

John Tee-Van, an ichthyologist at the Bronx Zoo, collected Mayling's unique gift in Chengtu, his destination from a long roundabout trip of nearly 35,000 miles via Rangoon and the Burma Road. The pandas, named Pan-dee and Pan-dah, were formally handed over by Mme Chiang at Chungking, and soon began an arduous journey by plane to Hong Kong, then Manila, where a ship carried this precious cargo via Hawaii to San Francisco, then by air to New York. Midway in the voyage to Honolulu, the Japanese bombed Pearl Harbor. Camouflaging of the ship started immediately, and the chief officer threatened to camouflage the pandas, as he asserted that their black and white coloration was entirely too conspicuous during airings on deck.

Pan-dee and Pan-dah joined the zoo on December 30, where they gave a great deal of wartime escapist pleasure. Mayling garnered much goodwill and praise for the capture and export of the rare animals, which even few Chinese had ever seen. John Tee-Van's skillful transport and handling of the cubs led to a promotion as executive secretary (and later director) of the New York Zoological Park.

When the two pandas began their well-guarded trek to America, the Far East stood on the brink of armed clashes beyond the Chinese mainland. Amendments to U.S. Neutrality Act, permitting arming of ships, became law in November. Japanese forces were massing in Indo-China for a possible move against Thailand. Threats by Tokyo against the Netherlands Indies and Singapore, even the American possession, the Philippines, grew. Canadian troops joined British forces at Hong Kong, and Americans were urged to leave Shanghai. The outcome of American-Japanese negotiations—talks that Toyko's special envoy in Washington termed "last proposals"—seemed dismal. Japan's premier demanded a purging of United States and British influence in the Orient. And on December 6 President Roosevelt strongly appealed to Emperor Hirohito for peace.

Ensconced in her West l6th Street apartment, Emma Mills turned on the radio for the 3 p.m. Sunday, December 7, broadcast of the New York Philharmonic, and was astounded to learn of the surprise Japanese bombing of Pearl Harbor.

> From then on, the afternoon was fantastic.... [Artur] Rubinstein's performance of the 2nd Brahms concerto broken into by repeated bulletins. Manila bombed—[then] denial from a radio correspondent speaking from Manila—the 'West Virginia'

reported sunk, Hull's indignation at the Japanese reply, so full of malicious fabrications ... all personnel recalled to Floyd Bennett and Mitchel [Air] Fields ... a broadcast from the news room of the White House with a background hum of voices, & a stutteringly excited broadcaster.[21]

The next day Congress declared a state of war with Japan, and China, after more than four years of conflict with Japan, officially made it a war. The European Axis, Germany and Italy, soon declared war on the United States. In the Far East Hong Kong fell to the Japanese, who bombed Manila in late December and invaded Burma.

A month later Emma recorded her observations of events immediately after the attack and the jelling of morale.

> By the 8th, it was evident that the Japanese had, characteristically, misunderstood our psychology so completely that no entrance into hostilities could have been more perfect for instantly uniting the whole country & killing once and for all the isolationist case.
>
> Of course, the Chinese were immediately delighted. They came to the ABMAC office Monday [December 8] with beaming faces. ... a day or two later, they began to realize many Americans can't tell them from Japanese, & there were stories of some being beaten up. They started wearing identity buttons, putting placards in their shop windows, & United China Relief photographed its Chinese staff for identification cards.
>
> On the 9th came the first air raid alarm.... The girl at the switchboard told me the upstairs office had heard over the radio in the publicity room that hostile planes were within 200 miles of New York.... A few minutes later, the sirens on the fire apparatus housed just back of us broke loose—there was no doubt of their intent.... Keep away from windows seemed all either of us could think of, so we went on with our work [the scare proved a false alarm] ... The next morning as I came out of the subway, a police car was tearing through the street with siren wide open, but that was part of a second false alarm.[22]

Emma Mills' large high-rise building posted notices in the halls and elevators on air raid procedures. All tenants were to go to the inside stairwells above the 5th and below the 10th floors in case of an alarm. The building was to serve as a shelter for the neighborhood, as well.

> I emphatically prefer to remain in my own apartment. My foyer is perfect for a blackout & removed from any windows in case of an actual raid. Everyone seems to take it for granted we'll have one—a "token raid" they suggest—but De Long [her brother, a Naval officer] voiced a decided no for the East coast though holds them possible on the West coast. Principally because of the difference in degrees of fanaticism between Germans & Japanese—he regards any raid as sure suicide for the raiders.[23]

17

The Common Battle and High Ideals

The premeditated and brutal attack by the Japanese on U.S. territory quickly expanded the war in Asia. Overnight, China gained Western allies. With American and British backing, Chiang became a key player not only in the Far East but a potential partner in the Declaration of the United Nations, affirming cooperation against the Axis and a proposal for a future world security organization. Just days after the bombing of Pearl Harbor, the Generalissimo sent an eloquent message to President Roosevelt, stressing their common battle in the Pacific to free the world from brute force and endless perfidy. Chiang held the president in high esteem because of his leadership in the world fight for freedom and the hope he would be the guiding spirit in the task of reconstruction.[1] FDR's portrait was the only picture of a foreigner hanging in his Chungking quarters.

More and more, Chiang leaned upon the advice of his wife. Her understanding of the West and its modus operandi provided inestimable input to his negotiations with, and messages to, the English-speaking world.

Mayling's own writings and speeches turned from admonishing the United States and other democracies in their pre–Pearl Harbor failure to come to the rescue of China to emphasizing her country's new role as a great power and its part in building a better world. Writing in the May 1942 issue of the *Atlantic Monthly*, she asked the question: "Cannot we in the new day whose dawn is nearing, strive together to gain supremacy in the peaceful arts of government and administration that will secure lasting happiness for the people of all races and thus create a world revitalized by new hopes and worshipping a more Christianlike ideal?"[2]

At every opportunity she reminded the West that China had been fighting alone, yet its battles were for America and the whole world. On a NBC May 31, 1942, "Army Hour" shortwave segment from Chungking, she interpreted a brief talk of the Generalissimo, who stressed the need for moral and material support. The first group of Chinese pilots had already graduated from training at Luke Field in Phoenix. He pushed for planes and guns—with a Churchillian phrase, "tools for the job."

A forceful personage in her own right, Mayling became the interpreter of China to the Western world—a bridge between her native land and the Allies.

Positioned as the chief spokesperson for China's plight and aspirations, Mayling on most occasions translated Chiang's words and interpreted the conversations of others from English (or French) into Chinese. With her husband's limited knowledge of foreign languages (except Japanese), she could recast statements and discussions to convey a different meaning, slight or otherwise. It was much debated whether or not the general understood English and to what extent. Undeniably the war brought many Americans to his side, and exposed him to English words and expressions.

An American G.I., Syd Greenberg, believed the Generalissimo understood more than he let on, but declined to speak English. Assigned to the Chinese army as a photographer in 1944, Tech Sergeant Greenberg on a flight with Chiang to inspect troop training centers explained in English the intricacies of his Leica camera. "He spoke some pigeon [sic] English, but didn't want anyone to know it. I used my tortured Mandarin to relate my experience in the Salween River campaign in Burma with General Wei Li-huang, and Chiang replied in Chinese that he understood."[3]

Emma Mills once recalled Chiang's knowledge of English during a Taipei visit to the presidential residence. "He spoke practically accentless English to Mayling's police dog, which didn't understand Chinese.

"'Come here,' and the dog obeyed.

"'Sit down.' The dog sat beside him.

"'Bark!' The dog whoofed.

"'Eat,' and the dog ate."[4]

Mayling's own public words increasingly turned to the solidarity of women in wartime, and a unity of mind and purpose of women of all nations to perform their duties. "The overthrow of the Axis is the key to women's emancipation." She pointed to the value of spiritual strength—a firm faith, robust spirit, and high resolve—to achieve victory over the forces of aggression.

"In war service and social work we ought especially to develop our spiritual strength, employing it in stimulating morale at the front and influencing the tenor of social life. Victory," she predicted in a speech to mark International Women's Day in March 1942, "will mean an unprecedented elevation of the status of women in society."[5] Perhaps only Mayling's icon of stateswomanship, Eleanor Roosevelt, could have equaled her words to promulgate this hoped-for role of women in a postwar milieu.

Mayling envisioned equality for Chinese women in their sacrifice for homeland. The choice between being "pampered dolls" or equality was theirs, she exclaimed to a large gathering in Chungking. Her challenge purportedly led women in the audience to give wedding rings and other jewelry to provide means to fight the war, and pledge that they would raise a million Chinese dollars.

Early in 1942 Chiang Kai-shek joined a unified command in the Southwest Pacific as Allied supreme commander in China. As the Japanese invaded Burma, Thailand and Indo-China, and threatened British-controlled India, he played a part in campaign strategy in what became known as the China-Burma-India (CBI) theatre of operations. In his new role, Chiang exercised his muscle by beating back Japanese troops at the Hunan provincial capital of Changsha and penetrating enemy defenses around Ichang on the Yangtze River, the farthest point of Japanese land thrust toward Chungking.

In 1942 the Japanese army blocked off the Burma Road supply route. The United States counteracted by starting to build a 500-mile northern spur from Ledo, India, to Lashio, Burma, where it eventually connected with the upper segment of Chiang's initial highway. Airlifted supplies over the Hump kept armies at the front on the job.

Money from the United States and Britain to strengthen China's military effectiveness trickled in. Congress approved a half-billion-dollar loan. British aid added fifty million pounds. Behind the financial and political bargaining in Washington stood T.V. Soong, now China's foreign minister. Chiang insisted that T.V. get the money with no interest, no terms of repayment and no conditions for its use. It augmented the hundreds of millions in Lend-Lease goods already pouring into China.[6] It proved to be the tip of a munificent iceberg in cash, provisions, cargo trucks and artifacts. A grand piano for Mayling even received priority. Cut in two for weight reasons for cargo plane delivery at Kunming in Yunnan province, the instrument met a sad fate. When the overloaded aircraft developed engine trouble flying over Burma, its crew pushed the two sections of the piano out the cargo doors.[7]

With Japan's move into Burma a reality, the Chiangs decided to take their first trip outside of China. Neighboring India with a huge population and strategic territory needed to be courted as a solid ally. An unofficial and secret visit (initially, it seems) by plane became common knowledge when the Chiangs reached New Delhi. A news flash announced their extraordinary journey—an opportunity for Pandit Nehru, India's leader, to repay the hospitality of the Chiangs on his visit to the Chinese capital in 1939. Nehru had been chiefly responsible for sending an Indian medical mission to China, and its doctors merged themselves fully with their neighbor's war of liberation.

Mayling addressed the women of India at a conference in New Delhi, noting that China's enemy was now their enemy. "The Japanese are already at your door. ... who knows what will happen when they strike India? They will say to you: 'We come to liberate you.' But that is a lie.... The spirit of the new China is one for all and all for one. We are unified by suffering, and victory will crown our efforts."[8]

Her remarks extended a neighborly hand to the leaders of India to join the crusade in a bedarkened hour. Describing the people of India as China's brothers, she called the two countries pillars supporting the economic and industrial edifice of Asia. The message registered strongly with the millions of Indians seeking to toss aside the yoke of British territorial dominion. The credo of Asia for Asians would come about by actions of wartime allies, not through Japanese invasion and occupation. Full cooperation in the British government war efforts meant ultimate independence for India, now a training base for China's air force and crack infantry.[9] It served as a depot of supplies for Chiang, and was acknowledged as the key land and air link between China and her allies.

Mayling's words on China's fight against Japan clearly resonated in New Delhi and beyond. Borrowing the memorable words of American patriot Nathan Hale, she proclaimed, "We prefer death to slavery!"[10]

On his flight back to Kunming, Chiang learned of a worsening military situation in Burma. Upon landing in China, he boarded a plane to Lashio in northern Burma to confer with British general Archibald Wavell and U.S. general Joseph Stilwell, Chiang's newly appointed chief of staff (and commander of such Chinese forces as Chiang chose to place under him) as well as commanding general of American forces in the CBI theater. Alerted to the meeting, Japanese bombers attempted to annihilate one or more of the three leaders, but were unsuccessful. An air raid several weeks later did come very close to doing bodily harm to the Chiangs. On this second trip by Chiang to Burma—this time accompanied by Mayling—they found themselves unprotected in a garden in the Burmese summer capital, Maymyo. Enemy aircraft bombs struck as close as 50 yards.

Reporting on CBI for *Life* that spring, Clare Luce hitched a ride to Maymyo with General Stilwell, in line for a pictorial build-up. Luce, a familiar figure on foreign war fronts, hardly surprised the Chiangs, whose mission remained focused on getting any and all means to help China. Above all, the impatient and often cantankerous Stilwell's prime aim in early 1942 was to keep the Japanese out of India, and open and protect life-giving supply lines.

The Chiangs' return to Kunming became one of the more dangerous flights. Air intelligence reported Japanese pursuit planes in the area; the Generalissimo's pilot ordered passengers to don parachutes. Dressed in a Chinese long gown, Mayling refused to put on the uncomfortable gear. Besides, there were only four parachutes for some 20 people. When that fact became known, Mayling's personal maid panicked. Mayling soothed her by explaining that if they were forced to jump from the plane, the maid was to put her arms tightly around Madame Chiang. Together, they'd bail out together using just one parachute. The dutiful maid, however, replied: "A parachute is meant for one. I would not do anything to endanger your life, Madame." An hour or so later, the aircraft flew out of the danger zone when a squadron of Chinese fighters appeared to guide the Chiangs safely to their air base.

The influx of government money from Washington lessened the urgency, yet hardly the need, for private support to the citizenry of China. Nevertheless, the United Relief Fund geared up for a $7,000,000 campaign for 1942, more than double the prior year's goal. There was talk of an amalgamation of the Chinese relief agency with their Russian and British counterparts. Emma Mills, now working just two and a half days a week with ABMAC, began to look for employment closer to the war effort, perhaps in Washington. The arch enemy in the Pacific enveloped the minds of the general public. Emma noticed words to that effect written in chalk on a neighborhood building: "We dry clean Japs—with a knife. P.S. With a gun, too." And scrawled in the dust on the back of a truck: "We haul dead Japs for fertilizer."

Mayling's intensified commitment to the advancement of women, her efforts to aid the plight of orphans and widows, and support of the air force that she built with American help endeared her to the West. A heroic and illustrious figure, she brought a keen understanding and appreciation of the East to those beyond China's borders. "Full realization of the significance of China's epic fight began to dawn ... when the powers themselves felt the shattering impact of Japan's might and began to ask what secret weapon it could have been that enabled China to remain undefeated," wrote Mayling in a by-line article in the *New York Times Magazine*.

> Accustomed to view war in terms of material equipment, in the beginning they failed to understand that our weapon was the spiritual heritage of the Chinese race. It is also incomprehensible to us why the West for so long swallowed insults, indignities and face-slapping with a mien meek and mild on the plea that it was unprepared for war.... In fact, no nation could have been less prepared than we, for China had still not recovered from the wounds of decades of civil strife.[11]

America's academic institutions, in particular, listened to Mayling's message. They prided themselves on the fact that her learning and leadership skills and humanitarian thrust stemmed from an education on its shores. That spring colleges and national scholarly societies conferred honors in absentia. The social science honor society Pi Gamma Mu awarded a special membership and key to Mayling (and General Douglas MacArthur). The citation noted her cheerful and courageous counsel to her people in their sorrows and successes; her participation in the intellectual and spiritual renaissance of a nation; her blending of thought of East and West.

Stetson University in Florida cited her work in literary, social and Christian endeavors. Goucher College conveyed a Doctor of Laws, received on her behalf by China's ambassador Hu Shih. Mayling's alma mater added to her honors, with a Doctor of Laws degree for accepting the "obligations of her privileges" and assuming it "a privilege to fulfill the obligations of her position." Hu Shih, Wellesley commencement speaker that June, again accepted. He spoke of her American education and understanding, and appreciation of the American ways of life that had made her an important force for the development of democratic institutions in China.

"We are especially thankful to Wellesley for having given us Mayling Soong, who, by her personal charm, untiring energy, intense patriotism, has made for herself an exalted place among the great women of our generation."[12]

Moreover, the college established the Mayling Soong Foundation to encourage an interest and understanding by students in the Far East. Mayling and her class members contributed generously to the fund which would award scholarships, and present lectures and exhibits on Oriental subjects.

To mark the 25th reunion of '17, nearly 1,000 alumnae representing a score or more classes gathered at a luncheon in New York to listen to a broadcast of Mayling from China. "I have faith that from the crucifixion experienced in this war, the democracies will learn the lesson that prevention is better than cure; that it is better to prevent wars than win wars. But war can only be prevented if the world society is so constituted that all races are given equal opportunity to develop their native genius, not hampered but aided by stronger and more advanced races."[13] Wellesley graduation week events raised some $5,000 toward relief work. Groups in other parts of the country made similar contributions, as did 80 members of '17 celebrating Alumnae Day on campus.

Fluent in the history of America and China, Madame Chiang regularly reminded Westerners of the commercial inroads of foreign powers into China, beginning in the mid–19th century. She spoke of the establishment of large, self-governing compounds, in such treaty ports as Shanghai and Canton, in violation of China's sovereign rights, and the shrouding of them under a thin veil of foreign settlements and concessions. The West instituted

> the vicious legal device known as extraterritoriality, which removed foreigners from the jurisdiction of Chinese courts. Nor did the West keep its hands off our material resources. The richest of our mines passed under foreign control. Foreigners administered our customs, salt revenues, railways, in fact, took over the management of virtually all public utilities, while even the control of foreign exchange was vested in them.[14]

Mayling having pointed out this prevailing abnormality—this inferiority status—to the Allies in the midst of growing friendship, they listened, then acted. The United States and Britain abrogated the long-standing extraterritorial treaties—seemingly the last impediment to China's status of equality and progress in the family of nations. In October 1942 an announcement of this long-sought change reached the Chiangs. The relinquishment of special territorial rights was formalized in early 1943, but not implemented for all practical purposes until the conclusion of the war when the old system of foreign imperial privilege had no place in an emerging new China.

Chungking garnered international press attention during the first year of America's participation in the war, and never more so than when President Roosevelt sent one of the country's most winsome and sure-footed statesmen on a 31,000-mile fact-finding tour through Egypt, the Middle East and Russia, and ending in China. Wendell Willkie, defeated in the presidential race of 1940, nonetheless had forged a genuine friendship with Roosevelt, and accepted the goodwill assignment as personal emissary from the White House to understand the problems of world leaders as well as the attitude of the man on the street, and determine the industrial and technical needs of countries fighting the Axis. Furthermore, the 49-day trip demonstrated the unity that existed in U.S. foreign policy and the conduct of the war.

Roosevelt ruled that no women—including Mrs. Willkie—would be passengers in the wide-ranging journey taken in a converted army bomber manned by a six-member crew.

Upon reaching Chungking, Mayling and the Generalissimo pulled out all the ceremonial stops to welcome Willkie, who served as a leader of various China relief campaigns in New York. Talks and protocol calls were high on the agenda, with increased aid to China an ever-present topic for the Chiangs. The country's future recovery needs and potential role in the United Nations frequently came up in conversations. At an elaborately staged reception and dinner given in his honor, Mayling and Kai-shek praised Willkie as "a farsighted statesman of high ideals."

With his engaging manner, Willkie charmed the Chinese with his vigorous approach to Chinese-American friendship. "I came to China not through what used to be called the treaty ports," he said, "but through great, wealthy provinces to the west of here. I've worked and lived in the West of America and I know from experience the kind of aggressive self-confidence which is developed in pioneer regions by men who are not afraid to take chances—in pursuit of something in which they believe. Prediction is not my business, but I would be prepared to take a substantial bet that the confident and aggressive spirit I have seen in Sinkiang, in Kansu and Szechwan is not likely to be stopped by floods, earthquakes or by the Japanese."[15]

At the conclusion of his remarks, many in the audience joined a well orchestrated public celebration and procession to accompany Willkie to his guest house. The well-coached swarms shouted his name in friendship as he traveled about Chungking to banquets and military reviews, and the local press devoted much space to his triumphal arrival.

Willkie's agenda focused on several lengthy sessions with Chou En-lai, Communist leader and a member of the People's Political Council in Chungking. At Willkie's urging, the English-speaking Chou received an invitation to a dinner in the American's honor—the first time Chou had been entertained by the official family of China; for Willkie, it was an outward sign of a united front between the Nationalists and Communists.

One afternoon Mayling gave a special tea party in his honor. A chorus of young war orphans sang, after which Willkie picked up a large cake and handed it to the children. Bending down, he kissed one of the girls while the guests applauded. "Madame Chiang Kai-shek and I are going to howl and howl for the right kind of world when this war is over so that all nations can be free and seek their own just aspirations." In response, Mayling described him as "the embodiment of warmth and spontaneity of a free world society of free nations."[16]

Mutual admiration between the bright, entrancing 45-year-old First Lady and the plain-spoken, ruggedly handsome American took hold, in private meetings as well as in public venues. The two seemed smitten with each other, and she found him, in her words, "a very disturbing influence." Chiang biographer Jonathan Fenby has written of this and other behind-the-scenes encounters between Mayling and the clandestine womanizer.[17]

One evening, while a dinner at the Kungs' compound got underway, Willkie asked his traveling companion from the Office of War Information, the publisher Gardner Cowles, to replace him on the receiving line. Willkie then disappeared—as did Mayling. When the party ended well past midnight, Cowles went back to the guest house. Not long after, the Generalissimo strode in with his bodyguards. They asked where Willkie was, but Cowles did not know. Chiang searched the quarters, and left.

Willkie, with a smile expressing sensual triumph, arrived back at his guest house at 4 a.m., and gave Cowles an enthusiastic, even adolescent, account of the night spent with his alluring hostess. To cap it off, and to Cowles' chagrin, he added, "I've invited Mayling to return with me to America on our plane." "You're a goddam fool," Cowles shouted. He then told of Chiang's late night search for the errant guest of honor. Cowles and Willkie, however, agreed that Mayling's beguiling and sexy personal attractiveness far exceeded her advanced notices. "Be careful and discreet, Wendell. You can't fly into Washington and be greeted by your wife with Mayling on your arm. And if you're thinking of running for the Presidency again, landing in the capital with Madame Chiang at your side would be a serious mistake."

The spreading scuttlebutt of the duo's liaisons settled upon Mayling the tantalizing tagline of the Dragon Lady—an appellation that stemmed from a slinky Oriental archetype in a popular wartime comic strip and radio serial called *Terry and the Pirates*. Its hero was partly modeled on the China adventures of the Flying Tigers. (That fall Hollywood released *Flying Tigers*, its screen tribute, starring "tough as nails" squadron leader John Wayne in his first war movie.)

Cowles' secret memoir described a startling skirmish with Mayling the morning after. At breakfast Willkie, with second thoughts on his invitation, asked his friend to tell her she could *not* accompany him to the United States. When Cowles delivered the message, Mayling expressed her rage by scratching her long fingernails down his cheeks. The facial marks, he noted, were so deep that for a week they remained visible.

Before his departure, Willkie told H.H. Kung that Mayling had the brains and persuasiveness and moral force to help educate America about China—the perfect ambassador, he emphasized, and he would see to it that FDR gave her all the planes and weaponry China wanted.

Cowles soon learned that Willkie and Madame Chiang had concocted a bizarre scheme to "rule the world." If he got elected president in 1944—with the financial backing from U.S. funds to China in American bank accounts—she would lead a coup in China to oust the Generalissimo and even her political ambitious brother T. V. Soong from controlling posts. "I'd rule the Orient, and you, Wendell, would rule the western world." Cowles considered the proposal absolutely crazy. Yet he was so "mesmerized by clearly one of the most formidable women of the time that I would not have dismissed anything she said."[18]

On the day of departure Mayling accompanied Willkie to the airport, and the two embraced and kissed. Earlier, they had met privately for an hour, adding to the anxiety of Cowles and other aides.[19]

But foremost in Mayling's mind that October day was her determination to see Wendell Willkie again—and he, her. She immediately made plans to return before year's end to the country she had known so well in her youth.

18

Homecoming

Before Wendell Willkie boarded his plane to return home, he made one last pitch to Finance Minister H.H. Kung for a visit by Mayling to America. She would gain inestimable goodwill and understanding for China and its struggling people, he said, and personally deliver the message of the need for increased aid to her husband's government and armed forces. Japan, he added, remained strong and determined to rule the Far East and control its destiny.

"Madame is the perfect ambassador," Willkie insisted. "With wit and charm, a generous and understanding heart, a gracious and beautiful manner and appearance, and a burning conviction, she is just what we need as a visitor."[1] His words seemed to describe what he sought as the ideal companion apart from the diplomatic role he envisioned for her.

T.V. Soong, ensconced in Washington to keep Chiang's China solvent by currying favor of administration officials, took umbrage over the idea of his sister in town to woo America—and with almost no holds barred. Soong had staked out China's major ally as his quarry and dreaded the thought of any interference, even familial. An irritated T.V. soon took off for Chungking, and out of his sister's way.

The Generalissimo apparently required greater persuasion. He often said he did not want his wife to go to America. She stood at his side as chief personal adviser and dutiful go-between. Mayling, however, spoke of health problems. The after-effects of her automobile accident five years earlier still caused back pains. Moreover, she pointed to her painful skin inflammation known as urticaria; its source, said her doctor, was chronic nervous tension. Apparently, within the Soong family, it was a hereditary ailment as well. Her appetite was nearly destroyed and sleep almost impossible for long periods. Chiang feared stomach cancer as its cause, and relented on opposing his wife's long journey. Doctors in America, he concluded, could best diagnosis and treat her maladies. Mayling's medical conditions acted as a cover for the trip.

Her aches and pains—and angst—had been part of her life since the beginning of the war. Domestic friction in the Chiang household added to her ills. The Generalissimo, it seems, had reverted to his old ways of bringing into a marriage a concubine or two. Apparently, he secretly re-coupled with his second wife, Ch'en Chieh-ju. Chiang had summoned her back to China from a long exile. Soon there was talk that he had gotten her pregnant. Marital spats between the Chiangs cracked the mirror of harmonious domesticity. The Generalissimo could hardly protest Mayling's departure and indeterminate sojourn abroad. Privately, he may have even welcomed a sabbatical from an overbearing and increasingly flirtatious wife. Mayling began gathering an extensive and eye-catching wardrobe for the overseas homecoming.[2]

Upon return from his widely reported global odyssey, Willkie summarized his observations in a coast-to-coast broadcast on October 26. His comments stressed the necessity of strengthening ties to China. It provided an overture to the main attraction about to wing its way to an eager and receptive public.

In late November 1942 a Boeing 307 Stratoliner landed at an airbase near Chungking. The craft, leased from TWA, had been flown from the States by a former bush pilot named Cornell Shelton to pick up an unidentified passenger. The airstrip that chilly morning quickly filled with clusters of automobiles carrying several dozen military officers, both American and Chinese. A handful of attendants and nurses smoothed the transfer of the mysterious traveler from an ambulance. A stretcher bearing a woman was maneuvered into the plane. The pilot and crew immediately recognized the special "cargo"— Madame Chiang Kai-shek. Her 18-year-old niece Jeannette Kung stood nearby waiting to board the plane for a flight over the Hump to India and Africa, then across the South Atlantic. Mayling did not exchange a word with pilot Shelton, and he was ordered not to speak to her or anyone else about the long and secretive undertaking.

Landing at Morrison Field near Palm Beach, Florida, Mayling and her entourage stayed overnight, and the next morning changed planes. Shelton remained as pilot of a C-54 in the last leg of the trip, ending at Mitchel Field on Long Island. Thereafter, she insisted on Shelton as her pilot whenever she ventured beyond China. She later loaned him several hundred thousand dollars to set up a company to manufacture passenger seats for airplanes. The Kungs would hold the financial reins but Mayling kept a 50 percent interest in the Florida-based operations.

The Chinese government offices apparently had no advance knowledge of Madame Chiang's overseas trip. From the plane, she proceeded directly under a fictitious name to the Harkness Pavilion of New York's Columbia Presbyterian Medical Center. The only news about her arrival came in a purposely vague announcement on November 27 from the White House. A brief summary of her need for treatment for chronic discomfort from the 1937 auto injury was released, but the location of her hospitalization remained top secret. The White House, however, noted that Mme Chiang would be a guest of the Roosevelts in Washington after completing the course of treatment.[3] Mayling's aides provided no indication of the duration of the First Lady's well orchestrated visit to America. Her homecoming after a 25-year absence brought her to an America again at war as it had been on her departure for China in 1917.

Cloistered behind a tightly closed medical curtain, Mayling heeded an accelerating clamor for public appearances, for, indeed, she realized that she had become one of the most celebrated women in the world. Only Eleanor Roosevelt gained permission to see her. They talked for an hour. "Although she seemed tired and delicate," Mrs. Roosevelt revealed, "she said she already felt better. She makes a great impression on one of a strong character and a pleasant one."[4] The solicitous First Lady concluded the visit with the desire to take care of Mayling as if she had been her own daughter. The Roosevelts would later discovered the Madame to be a difficult "daughter" and houseguest.

Mayling made satisfactory progress as a hospital patient, and no cancer or serious organic condition existed. Doctors, however, relieved her sinusitis and extracted several wisdom teeth. Until the end of the year she remained at the Harkness Pavilion, taking over the entire 12th floor and being well protected from countless well-wishers and the press who sought interviews. Mail reached 1,000 letters a day, swamping her aides. Nephew Louis Kung, acting as her secretary-general, set up a staff to handle the correspondence, and he personally supervised all of her contact with Washington and the public. Wendell Willkie, who had planted the seed to bring about Mme Chiang's journey, managed to enter the inner sanctum of the Chinese officialdom surrounding Mayling. Emma Mills, too, stood ready to be of any service in any way at all, but made no direct attempt to contact her close friend. She knew Mayling in due time would take the initiative to bring them together.

Requests for Madame Chiang to speak to American organizations and at pro–China rallies poured in. She had predicted such an avalanche. Upon her recovery, there was no way she could easily refuse many of these invitations, and certainly not the one from the leaders of the U.S. Congress.

Shortly after the start of the new year, Mayling moved out of the medical center for a bit of country life at FDR's Hyde Park, New York, estate. This interval provided a week of solitude for Mayling to prepare drafts of her forthcoming address to Congress. The Roosevelt staff kept chiefly to their own agendas, but jumped when Mayling gave orders. One day *The Good Earth* author Pearl Buck, at home in Bucks County, Pennsylvania, received an urgent call on behalf of Madame Chiang. "Please come to Hyde Park immediately," the caller demanded. On arrival Buck found herself embarrassingly unexpected. Mayling had actually wanted her absent traveling companion-secretary, Pearl Chen!

Mayling arrived by train in Washington on February 17, 1943, accompanied for the White House visit by Jeannette and Louis Kung (on leave of absence from Harvard). Her luggage contained numerous silk sheets for her personal use. She made it clear: they had to be changed several times a day

A guest at the White House, Madame Chiang had long admired First Lady Eleanor Roosevelt as a role model. The February 1943 visit gave Mayling many opportunities to urge the President to aid her government with money and military supplies, and to consider it a Big Four Allies partner. (Copyright Washington Post, reprinted by permission of the DC Public Library.)

because of her delicate skin condition, irritated by ordinary cotton cloth. Mayling summoned a White House maid or butler, not by the usual buzzer or bell, but by the clap of her hands in traditional Oriental manner. And she insisted on having meals served in her quarters for her two nurses and the Kungs. Jeannette made a lasting impression on the Roosevelts. She looked and dressed like a young Oriental man. Only when White House valets unpacked her suitcase did they discover she was a woman. Completely fooled, too, at first, FDR greeted her as "my boy." Unfriendly to her hosts, Jeannette tried to impress them and their dinner guests by reminding them she was a direct descendant of Confucius. Both Kungs broke White House rules. They especially disliked having to clear private visitors to see their aunt. Ushers there, however, kept a physician from New York waiting because the Kungs gave no advanced notice of a meeting.

During her ten-day visit Mayling periodically dined with the Roosevelts. On one occasion the president asked how she and the general would deal with a wartime strike of coal miners. Mayling replied with a gesture. She drew a long lacquered nail across her throat. The move made her answer clear to all those at the table. Eleanor Roosevelt later wrote that Mayling theoretically knew exactly what democracy should be. However, it was not so easy for her to carry it out in practice. Mrs. Roosevelt realized that she and Mayling were "worlds apart in our conception of the duties and obligations of the individuals in a democracy today, perhaps also in our conception of what the future organization of the world should be when the equality of man is a primary aim."[5]

One evening at the White House, Mayling made a heartfelt gesture for Mrs. Roosevelt's solicitous care and hospitality. Wearing an emerald jade pendant that had belonged to her mother, Mayling unpinned the jewel and handed it to Eleanor.

Mrs. Roosevelt noted the reactions of men with whom Mayling talked. "They found her charming, intelligent and fascinating, but they were all a little afraid of her, because she could be a cool-headed statesman when she was fighting for something she deemed necessary for China and to her husband's regime; the little velvet hand and the low, gentle voice disguised a determination that could be as hard as steel."[6] Through it all, the message of increased support became louder and louder. Even for FDR it was becoming tedious, albeit effective.

To gain deeper support for her country, and greater focus on the Asian war zone, Mayling had welcomed the invitation to address Congress, the only private "citizen" to do so and the second woman—Queen Wilhelmina of the Netherlands had been the first. At noon on February 18 Mayling arrived on Capitol Hill amidst a protective flank of policemen, detectives and Secret Service and entered the packed Senate chamber for a brief extemporaneous talk prior to a major address in the House of Representatives. Wearing a long side-split Oriental dress of black highlighted by buttons of small diamonds and jade, and a bejeweled pin of aviation wings of the Chinese air force, she imparted an aura of exotic glamour to the legislative chamber.

For the senators she noted the long friendship between China and the United States, and the great many similarities between her people and Americans. "I feel that if the Chinese people could speak to you in your own tongue, or if you could understand our tongue, they would tell you that basically and fundamentally we are fighting for the same cause, that we have identity of ideals, that the Four Freedoms [of speech and expression, of worship, from want and from fear] which your President proclaimed to the world resound throughout our vast land as the gong of freedom, the gong of freedom of the United Nations, and the death-knell of the aggressors."

Mayling drew upon her education in America—formative years when she learned the language "of your hearts. So coming here today I feel that I am also coming home." Toward the end of the talk she gestured sparingly but effectively and folded her slender hands and pressed them quietly but firmly against the rostrum where she stood.

Mayling closed her remarks with an ancient Chinese story of a Buddhist temple monk who, day after day, rubbed a brick against a stone. Asked by a young prior who sat nearby in an attitude of prayer, endlessly murmuring "Amita-Buddha," why the elder tried the impossible to make a mirror out of a brick, he replied, "Yes, it is just as impossible for you to acquire grace by doing nothing except chanting."

Mayling explained the significance of the story. "My friends, I feel that it is necessary for us not only to have ideals and to proclaim that we have them, it is necessary that we act to implement them."[7]

Walking over to the House side of the Capitol, she recognized a man she knew, and suddenly stretched out her hand. "Why Malcolm, how glad I am to see you here." He was Malcolm Ainsworth, the son of the president of Wesleyan College when she lived in his home as a young student. "How is your mother?" she asked. Upon her introduction by Speaker Sam Rayburn, Mayling leaned over and whispered, "I'm being blinded by the newsreel camera lights and the glare in my eyes makes it impossible to read my speech." He, in turn, asked the press to switch off the powerful kleig lights.

Her carefully prepared remarks in the House of Representatives reached beyond the members of Congress; they were spoken over a multi-network radio hookup. The country heard her praise fighting men in far-flung areas called upon, day after day, to perform routine duties and prepare for possible enemy action.

"It has been said, and I find it true from personal experience, that it is easier to risk one's life on the battlefield than it is to perform customary humble and humdrum duties which, however, are just as necessary to winning the war."

Mayling commended all those in the military, those true patriots "possessing the morale and physical stamina to perform faithfully and conscientiously the daily tasks so that in the sum total the weakest link is the strongest." She called America both a cauldron of democracy and an incubator of democratic principles. Americans of diverse ethnic backgrounds and nationalities, she noted, were devoted to the same high purpose. "This increased my belief and faith that devotion to common principles eliminates differences in race and that identity of ideals is the strongest possible solvent for racial dissimilarities."

She read without glasses in a concise voice without any accent. The combination of her words, her calm assurance and her stage presence mesmerized the Congress.

Introduced by Speaker of the House Sam Rayburn (at right) Mayling delivered a moving account of her people's struggle and needs. Congressional members responded in force, sending massive amounts of aid to her homeland. (Copyright Washington Post, reprinted by permission of the DC Public Library.)

Madame Chiang made no mention of the Generalissimo in his struggle to unite China and drive out the Japanese. But she spoke in some length of her people's ordeal against an enemy of great military might that had failed to bring China to her knees. In closing Mayling called for Congress to devote itself to the creation of a post-war world, and through the United Nations to help bring about "the liberation of man's spirit in every part of the world."[8]

Tumultuous applause echoed throughout the House chamber. Mayling smiled, then shook hands with Speaker Rayburn. She left the hall for a Senate Foreign Relations luncheon—of chicken à la king on toast—presided over by committee chairman Senator John Connally, who sat between her and Eleanor Roosevelt. The corridors of Congress buzzed with praise over Madame Chiang's words. Recently elected Representative Clare Luce of Connecticut called it the proudest and most humble speech from the lips of a statesman. Other legislators described it as "superb" and "wonderful." Edith Nourse Rogers of Massachusetts spoke for the majority of her fellow House members: "Everyone who heard her logical and moving appeal will demand more help for China.... Her reminder that our country and hers have an unbroken history of friendship prompts us to be worthy of that friendship and to do our utmost to furnish China with the means of driving out the cruel aggressor which has ravished her land."[9] Mrs. Roosevelt, too, praised her speech on Capitol Hill as beautifully delivered with a very remarkable expression of her concept of democracy.

Mayling had succeeded beyond her most fervent hopes in boosting aid to China. She had cast a spell over Congress and held it in the palm of her small hand.

The next day, at an unprecedented presidential press conference for both men and women, 172 reporters gathered about FDR and Madame Chiang as they discussed the problems of increasing aid to the Chinese fighting front. At one point in the session, with an engaging smile, she said that the president had solved so many problems and come through so many crises with flying colors that she was certain she could safely leave to him the problem of working out ways and means to increase the flow of aid. Roosevelt pointed to the logistics of bringing supplies to China, but shipments, he explained, would increase as fast as possible.

The president conceded that if he were a member of the Chinese government he would want to ask: How soon and how can aid be speeded up? His answer was that America would do it as fast as the Lord would let them and with as much speed as the country could bring to bear on the problem.

In a jocular mood, Mayling endorsed what the president had said and added the observation, "The Lord helps those who help themselves."

A reporter asked if her trip was a personal or an official mission. "Personal," she replied, thereupon the inquirer observed that her speech to Congress had made such an impression that "it might percolate into official mentalities." The reporters and FDR laughed. Mayling smiled and said that was something for the reporter to judge. A follow-up question probed further. "If the President requested, would she remain in Washington as a liaison officer with Congress?"

"I do not think the President needs me or any one else."[10]

Both the press and the public, as well as government officials, clamored to see and hear this outspoken and bewitching First Lady. On February 23 Mrs. Roosevelt and her houseguest held a press conference of newspaper women. Mayling again stressed the urgency of arms to China—ammunition, planes, gasoline. As for food, she declared that her country was capable of producing enough without outside help. When the subject turned to equal rights for women, Mayling answered without qualification: "I have never known brains to have any sex."

She urged women to give more thought to the responsibilities involved in equality than to privileges. "Since man expected women to share responsibilities," she added, "it was up to them to give women equal rights." She even suggested that women sit at the peace table because "statesmen had thus far failed to make and maintain peace."[11]

This poised and intellectual emissary, the press agreed, was never caught off guard, always saying the right thing convincingly. Mayling once jested that she preferred to face Japanese guns to reporters' pencils.

On February 22 Mme Chiang's hosts accompanied her to Arlington Cemetery where she placed a wreath on the tomb of the Unknown Soldier while a military band played the Chinese national anthem. From there the presidential car headed for historic Mount Vernon. Mayling and Mrs. Roosevelt concluded the tour by honoring George and Martha Washington with wreaths at their tomb.

A month before Mayling's visit to the nation's capital, Emma Mills received her not-unexpected phone call. On Saturday morning, January 23, while studying for a basic course in engineering—the latest foray into higher learning, and this time to fit herself for factory work tied in with war production—the telephone rang.

> After I had identified myself, a second woman spoke and wanted to know if I didn't recognize her voice. It was a minute or two before I realized it was Mayling. She asked me up to Harkness to take lunch with her.
> There was a large policeman just inside the entrance to the building. I don't know that he was there on her account. I asked at the desk for "Mme. Liu," as instructed, & the fussy old man gulped visibly. Before he got around to doing anything about it, a man appeared & we were introduced. He said his name was Callahan, a bodyguard—he'd take me right up.[12]

After a brief wait in a small reception room, a young nurse came to escort Emma to Mayling's suite. The two reached out to each other in a warm enthusiastic greeting. Their last meeting in China, faraway in time and distance, suddenly seemed less so as the longtime friends settled into a leisurely chat over lunch.

After her week at the White House, Mayling had returned to New York. She made her initial public address there on a breezy March 1 at City Hall Plaza. The talk reinforced the role she held for the future China. Before Congress, she had stressed the urgency to supply armaments and the will of her people to resist invaders. Now she emphasized the common cause with America beyond the final victory. "If we thought that we were fighting only for China, to be very frank with you," she pointed out at the welcoming ceremonies, "China would not be the China of today, but would have been a conquered China."

In his greeting Mayor Fiorello LaGuardia cited the bravery and courage of the Chinese people. "If our West Coast is completely secure in 1943, it is because your country has been holding the line since 1937. Few of the great nations are entirely guiltless, but let me make up for the past by assuring the independence of China fully and completely for the future."[13]

From the steps of city hall to the streets of Chinatown and to the stage of Carnegie Hall, Madame Chiang faced multitudes of New Yorkers who vied to see this leader of war-weary China and applaud her message. At a mass rally largely organized by United China Relief, in Madison Square Garden, Wendell Willkie introduced her. "We speak of her wit and charm, and her beauty," he asserted, "but you miss the point of her if you think of her only as an angel — though she is one, an avenging angel because she moves with a purpose and a mind."

New York governor Thomas E. Dewey and other regional governors vowed that defense plants in their states would bring forth the armaments China desperately needed.

At Carnegie Hall, the Chinese community honored Mayling. She spoke in classic Mandarin. Many of her all–Chinese audience could understand little of what she said because they used the vernacular Cantonese. Those that did were reminded to be proud of being Chinese—they showed what kind of people they were by the fight against Japan. The thought and feeling of her ad-libbed remarks animated her. She let go the rostrum to which she seemed to cling, and soon walked back and forth, casting out her declaration earnestly, sometimes angrily, at the audience. Mayling ended her round of engagements at a reception given by Consul General Yu Tsune-chi at the Waldorf-Astoria Hotel, her base of operations.

Before the end of the four days there, her physicians ruled out shaking hands and prescribed as much quiet rest as feasible between appearances. The next stop of her agenda—eagerly anticipated for years—had all the earmarks of a full blown homecoming.

Arriving on the snow-covered campus of Wellesley from nearby Boston's South Station, the college's most illustrious graduate enjoyed a nostalgic evening in the midst of 80 classmates of 1917. She remembered countless first names, crying out to school friends as they literally gathered at her feet. Only Emma Mills and one or two others had she seen since graduation. Many journeyed hundreds of miles in spite of gas rationing and train travel difficulties to share the homecoming with the only Oriental student they had known in their youth some 25 years past. In her honor, they all drank tea out of the Chinese cups given by Mayling to each classmate at the 20th reunion.

Her return had its informal sightseeing and banter over the remembrance of things past. But the four-day visit called for a speech to the student body—an event before 2,200 undergraduates, faculty, trustees, townspeople and distinguished guests, including Massachusetts governor Leverett Saltonstall. Madame Chiang's emotion almost overwhelmed her. "Strong emotion often tends to make one inarticulate," she began. "It is not easy for me, therefore, adequately to express my feelings today as I stand in your midst."

Her voice trembled and her hands shook. She gripped the sides of the podium, and swayed, appearing close to fainting. Her face drained of color. A nurse stepped to her side, and held smelling salts under her nose. The move revived her, and Mayling continued her speech. A lengthy address, it encompassed a review of women through the ages who had helped build civilization in a world dominated by men. She stressed the struggle by her sex to gain higher education and suffrage.

> With the riches of the ages within your grasp, with the wide field of specialized branches of knowledge to be had at your will, with the maturity of mind to be gained in your contacts with your professors and advisers, you should be aware of machine-made processes of thinking. Do not be afraid to strike out and explore the fertile realm of your own minds and let them lead you in your conclusions to what they will so long as you are true and honest to yourselves.... Stern days are still ahead. Yet within these very portals is the cenote of learning. Here your strength could be reinforced.[14]

The audience of enthralled students and academics responded with deafening applause. The festivities continued with ceremonies initiating the scholarly guest of honor into Phi Beta Kappa, and a gathering at her sorority, Tau Zeta Epsilon. At nightfall an outdoor serenade of college songs by sorority sisters and their friends provided a fitting ending to the day.

Mayling relished a lengthy stroll over the campus, noting the changes of a quarter-century. Her dorm, Wood Cottage, had long since succumbed to expansion of the stone buildings that stood out against a background of clear blue sky. Arm in arm, Lt. Commander Mildred McAfee in the uniform of the WAVES, and on leave as college president, and Mayling walked up and down the wooded paths, stopping to point out some well-remembered landmark or vista. They entered the library where the teenage foreign student had pored over her books. When Mayling returned to her campus suite at Tower Court (where mounted machine guns on an adjoining rooftop reinforced her security), she remarked it was a homecoming she could never forget. Wellesley represented one of the happiest times of her life. It had always seemed like home, and would continue to be that forever.

While in the Boston area, Mayling agreed to be honored by city fathers in Symphony Hall. Mayor Maurice Tobin quickly organized a celebration, with a presentation of an honorary citizen scroll and a check for $88,000 from the Greater Boston United War Fund for war orphans. Governor Saltonstall introduced Mayling as "one of the most wonderful women in the world and the most charming." She responded briefly with thanks, not having the time nor energy to compose her usual expanded and erudite remarks.

Mayling returned to New York for several days' rest before boarding her private car for the long journey west. Chicago had requested that she make a stop. And the city's sizable Chinese population rolled out the red carpet as did Mayor Edward Kelly. Many downtown buildings and store windows added colorful flags, bunting and signs of welcome. Upon her arrival, she received a large silver key to the city. In Chicago her hosts were taking no chances with

A special highlight of Mayling's seven-month 1942–43 sojourn in America: a return to Wellesley and reunion with dozens of classmates. On a brisk late winter walking tour, guided by President Mildred McAfee, China's First Lady wore slacks—attire until then unacceptable for students. Her stylish appearance broke down the skirts-only rule on campus. (Courtesy of Wellesley College Archives.)

her personal safety, a major concern. The city formed a special guard of 74 police men and women.

Madame Chiang received the press at her Drake Hotel suite, met the parents of eight of Chicago's Flying Tigers, greeted a wide spectrum of notables—among them, publisher William Allen White, baseball commissioner Judge Kenesaw Mountain Landis, American Federation of Musicians president James C. Petrillo, University of Chicago president Robert Hutchins—and accepted from the daughter of Cyrus McCormick, founder of International Harvester Company, a gift of $100,000 to be used by her and the Generalissimo in any way they saw fit. Other checks for war relief totaled nearly $70,000. The climax to a very productive stopover brought together 23,000 people at Chicago Stadium to hear this woman who had been the center of tremendous interest and curiosity, even adulation.

She pulled out all the stops in her remarks, beginning with a recap of early American history, and noting the importance of the Pilgrims' Mayflower Compact, and the covenants and ideals that crystallized in the Declaration of Independence. She then turned to the present, bringing in parallels to her homeland.

"Though our two countries have widely varied backgrounds, histories, cultures, and traditions, both recognize the inherent ability of the individual as an individual with powers to sway, to contribute to, and to help mold the destiny of a nation." Looking to China and its leader, she added,

> The land where "the barefoot boy with cheeks of tan" may become the highest executive also declaims that here indeed a man may become what he wills himself to be.
> With firmness and perseverance I stress again that to insure peace and prosperity for all peoples, war, that acme of human folly, should not be permitted to recur. Only with concerted vigilance and action by the United Nations and later, by others who will have gained the wisdom of adhering to the principles of "live and let live," can this world be rendered perdurable for peace.

Mayling, indeed, was at ease with the writings of Jefferson, William James and Confucius.[15]

The last leg of her cross-country journey focused on California and its large Chinese communities. As her special railroad car passed through large and small towns, people eagerly waited for the train to come by and hoped to catch a glimpse of the almost legendary lady from China. Occasionally, Mayling stepped out onto the observation platform on the end car. More often, the wife of a Chinese Embassy official or a secretary or a maid caught a breath of air on the platform. When spotted, groups of people, especially children, shouted, "There she is! There she is!"—not knowing that the woman seen on the train was, in essence, a stand-in.

The train made brief stops at Omaha, Cheyenne and Ogden. Many an hour, day and night, Mayling worked on the speeches she was to make in San Francisco and Los Angeles. Railroad officials said she was the "easiest passenger they had ever taken care of." Her only request was that the menu for her party exclude sea food and veal, and that no great amount of rationed foods be bought.[16]

With the largest Chinese population in America, and the largest contributors—$5 million—to the Nationalist treasury in the battle against Japan, San Francisco greeted its wartime heroine with gala parades through Chinatown and at city hall. Chinese and American flags flew on every available pole and staff. "I never dreamed there were so many Chinese children here," Mayling said as she smiled and waved her handkerchief to the throngs of youngsters on sidewalks. The festive mood left her breathless ... yet far from speechless. With tears in her eyes and in a voice choked with emotion and fatigue, she accepted a key to the city from Mayor Angelo Rossi. "As I look out at San Francisco's beautiful Civic Center, my mind flies back to the modern Civic Center we were just building in Shanghai before the war. It is in ruins now. But China, like the mythical Phoenix, always arises anew from the ashes. And I pledge that the China which will rise again will be a great China and a friend of America."[17]

A regal banquet for 1,300 high ranking Chinese and American guests in the Palace Hotel preceded the following day's chief speaking event at the Civic Auditorium. Several thousand would-be ticketholders were turned away once the 10,000-seat building could hold no more. Governor Earl Warren introduced the guest of honor, strikingly attired in a black velvet Chinese-style gown, trimmed with gold braid. Mayling spoke of the diverse geographical vastness of her homeland and the United States, their threats by outside evil forces, the ideals of justice and freedom for which each were fighting, and the need for both countries to win the peace and avert future war. "We of the United Nations have a greater aim before us—the advancement of mankind—toward which voluntary service should be our deepest pride and vicarious pain our highest decoration."

In San Francisco she was reunited with her youngest brother, 37-year-old T.A. Soong. Enamored of America and high finance, he had opted for a life in banking on the West Coast, where the Soongs maintained a stronghold of investments.

Mayling largely devoted the fourth and fifth days to her own compatriots who referred to her as "Missimo," a play on the Generalissimo's title. In the city where Sun Yat-sen had lived in the early 1900s, she placed a wreath at the foot of an imposing statue in his likeness. She stopped at the Chinese Six Companies building to greet delegates representing most of the Chinese settlements in the Western states.

She urged the Chinese community to buy U.S. war bonds. "In buying war bonds you are helping win the war for America and China." Mayling might easily have succumbed to the temptation of begging for aid. Her clear message of help stayed above mere drumbeating.

She headed for southern California for the conclusion of her six-week trek. Accompanied by the ubiquitous unsmiling nephew, Louis Kung, she stepped from the Southern Pacific train at Los Angeles, met Mayor Fletcher Bowron and citizens' committee representatives, and proceeded downtown for the traditional welcoming parade. Mayor Bowron proclaimed "Mme. Chiang Kaishek Day," and noted that when General James Doolittle and his men bombed Tokyo, "it was said in jest that the planes came from Shangri-la, and it was only after he had returned to the United States that we learned the planes which bombed Tokyo were made here."

A movie fan (and onetime municipal censor in Shanghai), Mayling enraptured a galaxy of stars at a motion picture industry reception. Some 75 screen notables attended, ranging from Shirley Temple and Mary Pickford to James Cagney and Bing Crosby. Like visiting royalty, she received a select group of producers, directors and writers, shepherded by actor and humorist Robert Benchley. Mayling stole the show. As each of the Hollywood icons were introduced to her she made a remark or comment that clearly revealed a keen knowledge of film world activities and gossip. Shortly before the tribute, Dr. Wellington Koo, Chinese ambassador to Great Britain, appeared at her suite to discuss a possible trip to England.

At the final celebration in Los Angeles, an afternoon audience of 30,000 filled the Hollywood Bowl. In front of the outdoor shell an enormous stage had been erected to hold the Los Angeles Symphony Orchestra, military bands and detachments, and the huge cast of a special pageant on the history of China, mounted by David O. Selznick, chairman of the local branch of China War Relief and producer of *Gone with the Wind*, and narrated by Walter Huston. When Mayling rode into the amphitheater in an open car with eight smart-looking Chinese cadets walking beside it, an instant roar resounded, from the Bowl box seats to the upper benches.

Mayling's lengthy speech first gave an overview of the attacks on Nanking and Hankow, and the final retreat inland to Chungking, and the struggle to build air power to combat Japanese fighter planes. She praised President Roosevelt for his foresight, statesmanship and moral courage. "We take pride in the fact that, amid all the stern and never-ending demands of war, we are preparing for a just and permanent peace and for the strenuous world building that lies before us. You, too, are taking similar steps and, like us, you are as determined."[18]

Mayling might have ended her American tour in April in Los Angeles. But suffering from a cold and sore throat and exhausted from the continuous round of engagements and speeches, she decided to recuperate in New York. Moreover, she carried an invitation to address Parliament in Ottawa, Canada in early June. Back East, she made it known a return visit to the White House was in order. British prime minister Churchill already had stayed there five times within 18 months. Why not the First Lady of China! How could the president refuse in the wake of her praise for the country's leader? According to high Washington officials, Roosevelt was anxious to get her out of the country. (Yet still a third visit to the executive mansion rounded out her agenda in June!) Her coziness with the Roosevelts annoyed Willkie, who nurtured plans to run again for the presidency in 1944, and "rule" the postwar world with his Asian lover. Willkie, at one of their trysts, told her that next visit to the White House would find a different administration there, and she replied quickly, "Not at all! It will be just the same. My next visit will find the same President, for I am going back next May!"[19]

Emma Mills, in part, would piece together the backstage story of Mayling from firsthand chitchat. Living on her own for some two years, Emma often entertained friends without the meddling and criticism of elderly and staid family members. On Sunday, April 18, she served dinner for three women guests. "They get along well together, & we laughed considerably," she noted. "All have traveled a good deal in Europe, all have lived in Greenwich Village. I enjoyed getting the meal, as I always do, setting the table, playing hostess. It was Sunday morning for dowsing the plants in the bath tub & digging up the earth around them, too. So I didn't get back to studying my calculus till evening & haven't read the paper yet."[20]

Phone calls from staff volunteers soon updated her on frustrations and reorganizations at United China Relief. That agency had failed to send a representative to the American Bureau for Medical Aid to China board meeting to substantiate their charges of misappropriation of bureau funds overseas. The wrangling between groups would continue to accelerate, she surmised.

Emma was relieved to receive a call from a weary-sounding Mayling.

"I cannot sleep," she complained. "I thought of you, and wondered which of my speeches on the tour did you like best? I finished writing the one delivered in Los Angeles only an hour and a half before I gave it. And didn't have time to get my hair properly done. I looked like a walking corpse in the newsreels and pictures taken there."[21]

The next day Emma joined Mayling at Bear Mountain State Park, some 30 miles north on the Hudson River. A Secret Service guard met her at the train station.

Mayling had settled into the manager's house at the park while the rest of her party stayed at the inn. "I thoroughly enjoy the privacy here—and the price—only $7 per day," she exclaimed. "They tried to find a house for me, but the only possibility was one for $6,000 for six weeks. I refused to be gouged. I hated the Waldorf; the corridors were neither day nor night for me, and, oh, the bill!"

Her food at Bear Mountain, she explained, was prepared at the inn by a Swiss chief and brought over to her quarters. "I want my Chinese cook to learn from him."

Earlier in the year Mayling had entrusted Emma with a special task. She sought to have Chinese silk, lavishly embroidered with dragons and flowers, and brought from Chungking, made into 14 cocktail jackets as mementos for American friends. To do the job it took two weeks of intensive tailoring by a skilled acquaintance of Emma at Columbia University. At Bear Mountain Mayling fussed over the jackets, liking every one of them so much that she decided to keep several for herself. Emma had the choice of one from the remaining batch.[22]

As the conversation turned from clothes to love affairs, Mayling sat down before a mirror and began rubbing various creams on her face. Wendell Willkie, she revealed, had been with her the day before. It having been a rainy afternoon, they resorted to gin rummy, playing for $10 a game with winnings to war orphans. He won steadily. "I tried everything to distract him," she explained, "teased him about kissing the ballerina in Moscow, and kissing Chinese babies, but to no avail. After he had won seven games straight, I threw the cards in his face and quit."

Mayling showed Emma a telegram she'd received from him that morning. "Angels don't throw cards in their partner's face," it read, "and they pay their debts." Willkie had called her "an avenging angel," in his introduction at Madison Square Garden, and those words stuck.

Mayling quickly responded to his telegram; she sent an official war orphan gift receipt for the money she lost, but without any comment.

Apparently, their secret trysts had been going on since her arrival in New York. The subject of love affairs startled her trusty confidante. "Emma, you've had much more experience with them. How did you feel when you broke one off?"

A bemused Emma made no reply.

Mayling then related an amusing tale of a Wellesley chum seen in Los Angeles. Ruth Charlton, she said, appeared plumper than ever, with much make-up, artificial eyelashes and clothes of extreme style. This middle-aged classmate told her she spent all her time keeping herself beautiful for her husband. Mayling retorted, "Why waste all your time for one man?" Charlton then asked her if she were going home soon, and thought she had better plan an early return to the Generalissimo. A puzzled Mayling asked why. Charlton thought Mayling's remark expressed a belief in extramarital affairs.

"What a fool," Mayling snorted. "It never occurred to Ruth I meant humanity in general."

And she added plaintively, "What could I get away with, surrounded by eight Secret Service guards, and with a day or night nurse always nearby?"

Emma learned that she had decided not to go to England. "I don't think my reception would be as cordial as in America. Therefore, it would be a more wearing experience and nerve wracking. My wallops against Churchill in the Chicago speech [she took offense at his wanting a two-year wait until pursuing an all-out war against Japan] probably would work against me in London."

As the afternoon of chitchat came to an end, Emma showed Mayling a letter from fellow alumna Ruth Adams. Mayling read it, then tossed it back. "I wouldn't have expected such a poorly written letter from a Phi Beta Kappa classmate." With a shade of disillusion and superiority in her voice, she added, "I suppose our class are mostly New England housewives after all."[23]

Before Emma's departure, Mayling organized a hike around the lake at Bear Mountain. Accompanied by two Secret Service men, they walked swiftly over the two-mile trail. A guard beside Emma murmured, "You'd think Madame was in training."

In late June Mayling again sent for Emma. Highly pleased with her trip to Canada as a guest of the governor general, she believed the country had given her a bigger welcome than would have her nemesis Churchill. "My hosts were charming and cordial—best of the English are hard to beat." When told by Emma that she had missed the broadcast of her speech there, she had a secretary bring a written transcript to the room and read it aloud herself.

"How do you think it compares with the other talks? Which one did you like best?"

Emma was more interested to hear that Mayling had put in practically what she had said about the Canadian war effort following a recent trip to Ontario. In effect, the Canadians, Emma had explained, were dissatisfied over their relatively small part in the war.

Mayling then spoke of Henry Luce's visit and his tremendous support, both in terms of money and publicity. A personal appeal to *Time* subscribers to give $5 had brought in a quarter of a million dollars for China relief, and the magazine placed Mayling on its March 1, 1943, cover. But she scolded him severely for professing to be trying to help China with one hand and printing, with the other, stories that implied that it was Chinese custom to eat babies in famine times, and that all Chinese women have syphilis.

"He's confused in his thinking and not as intelligent as his wife."

Emma lost no opportunity to warn her against both of them. "They're a sinister pair."

Mayling served tea and toast with strawberry jam, then proudly showed her rare, finely bound editions of Shakespeare and Plutarch, and a set of the *Yale Chronicles*, a gift from financier—and ladies' man—Bernard Baruch.[24]

Mayling left for Chungking laden with a trunkful of gifts and awards: the National Social Sciences Institute gold medal, a *Churchman* magazine commendation, a Hobart-William Smith Colleges honorary degree, a New York Southern Society medallion, and numerous other mementos and prizes. A special accolade came from Wesleyan College in Macon. The school had invited her to receive a degree. It was a homecoming replete with memories of her early days as a very young student. She shared the podium with Mrs. W.N. Ainsworth, widow of the Wesleyan president of Mayling's day, who placed the hood signifying the honorary Doctor of Law on Mayling's shoulders. The college conferred similar honors in absentia on sisters Ailing and Chingling.

On June 28 T.V. Soong casually told Washington reporters of his sister's pending departure for home. In fact, she secretly had already left for China by way of Brazil.

At their last get-together, Mayling sounded "iffy" about seeing her old pal again; in Emma's mind it meant they'd be casual about their goodbyes.

Not since the triumphant tour of Revolutionary War patriot Lafayette in the 1820s had a foreigner held the attention of so many Americans. The First Lady of China captured the interest of people, day after day, for months. In the midst of a global war for Americans on far-flung fronts, Mayling inspired the country with words of thanks and hope. She proclaimed the fundamental principles that were at stake in the battle against enemy aggression, and looked beyond to the day when the democracies would insure a just and lasting peace.

The country had read of her remarkable leadership and Herculean efforts in behalf of Chinese refugees, wounded soldiers and war orphans, and of her steadfast courage on visits to battlefields and during bombings. Her roots in the United States, where she had received her education and absorbed a deep understanding of the West, its language, and its commitment to individual freedom and concern for the welfare of the common man, led people to respond.

"Her clear intelligence, sincerity of purpose and ardent faith in spiritual values," observed industrialist Thomas J. Watson, at the conclusion of her visit, "have gone straight to the American heart." And he added, "The wife of China's Generalissimo has set an historic example of the tremendous influence which women can exert and the important part which they can play in the betterment through public service and the promotion of international understanding and friendship."[25]

The more immediate thrust of her extended visit aimed at aid for the struggling, poorly equipped Chinese army. Her urgent pleas for planes, heavy arms and gasoline brought an encouraging response from the White House and Congress. Upon his return to Washington from China that winter, T.V. Soong reinforced his sister's petition for immediate succor.

Her influence affected policy-making on Capitol Hill. She conveyed her frustrations over second-class treatment of her people. She successfully convinced Washington to repeal the Exclusion Act barring Chinese immigration. An obvious injustice to a strong ally, the ban, once lifted in late 1943, strengthened U.S.–China relations and further elevated Mayling's role beyond that of a charismatic overseas fundraiser.

Besides, Mayling's monetary appeals helped to extend the Lend-Lease program at home beyond its initial two-year projection. She gained a hefty commitment of ten percent for China of all Lend-Lease aid. And into her pocket went hundreds of thousands of dollars for personal relief work. Countless individuals and groups turned over checks as large as $100,000 (from the International Ladies' Garment Workers' Union) and as modest as $2 (a donation from 20 school children in upstate New York). A handful of sympathetic Americans even sold family heirlooms and gave the proceeds directly to Mayling's war chest.

The First Lady's beauty, charm and clothes attracted particular notice, even heroine worship. Her wardrobe—usually a modification of the traditional dress of Chinese women for her own comfort and style—never failed to be reported in coverage of her public appearances. She understood clothes as did an actress—for effect, as props. At Madison Square Garden she wore a black dress with gold trimmings, and with green earrings and black gloves; at Wellesley, a floor-length gown of blue velvet (the College color); in Chicago, a Chinese gown of black velvet, edged in ruby red sequins, which were matched by rings, flower brooch and earrings of rubies and diamonds. "Her hair has the breath of a wave, her nails are painted a light, bright red, and she wears high-heeled American platform shoes," wrote *Vogue*, which photographed her in a full-length brilliant blue gown with traditional high-neck Chinese collar.[26]

At Wellesley their trailblazing alum made a most unorthodox fashion statement. On her campus walk with President McAfee—in a military uniform as commandant of the WAVES—Mayling wore a beaver coat, a turban—and slacks! Pants on its most prominent graduate quickly led the faculty to end its ban on trousers. And McAfee concurred, "Anyone who can look as smart as Madame Chiang in slacks may wear them."[27]

Separated from China and the seat of government for more than seven months, Mayling undoubtedly wondered what challenges she would face in both the political and domestic spheres. Nonetheless, the outpouring of increased material aid and the resulting sense of kinship between the United States and China offset her long, and possibly self-indulgent, absence from home. Notwithstanding, China's emissary now faced a struggle toward final victory and abiding harmony—and that would take more than cogent words.

19

Table Talk

Emma Mills had welcomed the opportunity to be with Mayling at length, after a hiatus of nearly two decades. Those periodic visits gave Emma's life a buzz and scope. Since Mayling's departure for China, matters had dulled. Having completed the 30-week basic engineering course at Columbia, Emma voiced an extreme restlessness over life in general. Everywhere she looked more and more women were actively participating in war-related work; many had replaced men in homefront jobs. She was conscious of those of her sex operating elevators, driving taxis, directing traffic, punching tickets on railroad trains. She reacted by investigating an overseas Red Cross job.

The woman who interviewed her in Washington seemed impressed. But regulations set 45 as the age limit.

"Are you sure you're 48?" the interviewer queried the still young-looking applicant. "You even don't look 40. I'll check how adamant the Red Cross intends to be on this score." Further interviews remained on hold until that question was settled. Before leaving Washington, Emma dined with a friend working at the army map section. Her assignment consisted of handling the transfer of Chinese army staff maps and geographical terms into English usage, a task Emma envied. Turned down by the Red Cross, she continued her job quest at intervals all summer in 1943.[1]

In late August the Columbia placement office sent her off to an interview on campus. In the science building she met with a chemist in charge of a special top-secret project. Few details were revealed about this war-connected undertaking. Was it splitting the atom that had brought Columbia into the news two or three years earlier? she wondered. Or uncovering some new source of energy? Even her interviewer couldn't take her inside the restricted part of the building without a special pass. He explained that Emma's job would be principally washing equipment, sweeping up, running errands. Having been an executive, could she take orders from striplings? he asked. "Some of the laboratories need a woman's touch. The cleaning up must be done with judgment. Frankly, it is an experiment taking anyone from your 'age group.' Are you willing to be a guinea pig?"[2]

Emma agreed to take the comparatively low-level assignment in the chemical research laboratories. Her workday stretched from 8:30 to 6 in the evening. "The place is certainly not well organized," she noted after two months on the job. "Some of the workers are loafers, and I'm not using such brains as I have at all. Read the paper each day & about a book a week while on the job—but I suppose I can count that in place of primping and gossip.... The trip up is easy, a good lunch available at Baxter Hall—which is now my main meal of the day—everyone agreeable to work with. I am using my hands & am not tied to a desk all day, & there's the pleasant outlook onto the campus."[3]

Emma's work entailed 48 hours a week, leaving little time for seeing friends and writing letters. Even her overseas correspondence with Mayling suffered for many months, into early 1944. In January she wrote her of a trustees' meeting of the Mayling Soong Foundation at Wellesley. The faculty, it seems, hadn't stirred themselves sufficiently to include Chinese studies in the curriculum. "I'm going to be a gadfly on the subject," she reported, with a postscript that the faculty chairman had asked for suggestions for the China program. Emma described meeting the first Far Eastern Mayling Soong scholar, Chandralehka Pandit, a niece of the Indian leader, Nehru—"a real find and we will be miraculously fortunate if we can keep up to such a standard." Emma concluded that the American girls in the college "must learn at least a little concerning the Chinese fifth of humankind. I am also concerned about a long range program to raise funds for the Foundation."[4]

The second half of the year 1943 had left Madame Chiang with very little time or energy to resume contact with her American friends. Upon her return to Chungking, she had received a spirited welcome from 100,000 or so people gathered in the main square. A celebration organized by the New China Life Movement, it hailed her role in bringing more help from America to China. "The American people," she reported, "are beginning to feel the full impact of the war, realizing more realistically what war means." Individually, she added: "I got an enormous spiritual lift from their spontaneous goodwill."[5] Furthermore, Mayling revealed that her overseas pilot, Captain Shelton, on the return flight encountered bad weather over Burma and tried to get a radio bearing on some friendly airfield. Signals seemed to be from an American base in Assam, India, and he started in that direction. But becoming suspicious, Shelton quickly changed direction. Afterward, he learned the signals came from an airfield occupied by the Japanese. Upon arrival in Chungking, Mayling as a gesture of thanks for safe travel decorated Shelton and his crew with the Chinese Standard of the Clouds medal.

Friendship with the United States firmly in place, Mayling concentrated on better relations with her British ally. Churchill had been outraged over the Chiangs' push for India's independence from Britain. "I'm not Prime Minister to preside over the dismantling of the British Empire," he had exclaimed. Churchill viewed the Far East as a secondary battle field; Germany, he stressed, was the primary enemy. American military forces would have to wait until Hitler surrendered before full-scale participation of British troops in the Pacific. This Germany-first strategy annoyed the Generalissimo, although the Allies' plans to defeat Japan were falling into place at least on paper. Lord Louis Mountbatten headed the new Southeast Asia Command Operations; in October he flew from India to China to confer with the Chiangs and American and Chinese military chiefs. Indeed, Churchill and Roosevelt stood together on most issues.

During her long absence from Chungking, her husband dallied in his drive against the Japanese invaders. China grew more fragmented and chaotic, and peace with the Communists remained elusive. Moreover, Chiang blockaded the Communists' armies in their northwestern stronghold. Nonetheless, the troops of General Mao Tse-tung seemingly engaged the Japanese more than the central government, and his guerrillas overall proved more effective fighters. A frustrated General Stilwell in the difficult job of supervising Lend-Lease supplies tried to ensure such equipment was not secreted for future use against the Communists by Chiang, a formidable task that generally lacked success. The Generalissimo looked ahead, knowing one day after war's end he'd have to face the challenge of communism which grew in strength, especially in rural areas.

In August Lin Sen, the aged figurehead chairman of China, died. Chiang was appointed to fill that post and was formally inaugurated on October 10. Roosevelt had promised Mayling during her White House visit that her country would be one of the Big Four and a party to plans in pursuit of the global war. It was as chairman/president that Chiang officially received an invitation to attend a top-level conference with Roosevelt and Churchill in Cairo a month later. There, for the first time, the Allied leaders met the Generalissimo, representative of an allied country of some 450 million people. As interpreter for her husband, the multilingual Mayling sat at the conference table at the Mena House Hotel in the shadow of the ancient pyramids. She was given to state, "If you allow me, gentlemen, I shall present before you the Generalissimo's exact thoughts." Mrs. Roosevelt had wanted to accompany the president, but he closed the door on distaff attendance. When she learned of Mayling's presence—and that of Churchill's daughter Sarah—the piqued First Lady quietly but quickly wired her displeasure.

One on one, Chiang struck his global counterparts as insular, stubborn and petulant. Yet the Allies had to keep him in the forefront of the war effort, and thus well supplied with military information and support. Mountbatten spoke of operations in Burma aimed at opening up air and overland supply routes. Chiang, of course, agreed with such proposals; without them he insisted his army would languish, perhaps vanish. A military assault in northern Burma, it was thought, required an Allied force of tens of thousands of men. Britain and the United States considered a seaborne invasion of south Burma only if scarce landing craft could be allocated. The preexisting needs for such equipment and manpower in Europe would soon lead to broken promises, and gave the Generalissimo an excuse for chronic inaction. None of his divisions engaged in battle any more than they had to be. And he routinely threatened a separate peace with Japan unless his demands were met.

Mayling made a vivid and lasting impression at Cairo. Her feminine charms beguiled many. Virtually co-equal in representing, if not governing China, she played her part well. "In a clinging black dress with a slit up the side, displaying a shapely pair of legs," writes Roosevelt biographer Ted Morgan, Madame was "a personality in which sexual allure and ambition mingled to achieve her ends."[6]

The first meeting of the Chiangs with Churchill revealed the prime minister's less than cordial feelings toward the Chinese couple. He greeted Mayling, quickly adding: "Well, Madame, I suppose you think I am a scoundrel, a blackguard, an imperialist, out to grab more colonies, and unwilling to part with what we have got." Her reply did little to calm troubled waters. "Why are you so sure what I think of you?"[7]

The four days of talks formulated an agreement to pursue the unconditional surrender of Japan. All Pacific islands seized by the Japanese would be returned to their rightful owners. The aggressor would be expelled from Manchuria, Formosa and the Pescadores, and all other Chinese territories taken by violence and force—and greed. The Soviet Union, which declined to attend, had already agreed to enter the war against Japan once Germany met defeat.

The Chiangs persuaded Churchill and Roosevelt to resist calling the war in Asia a secondary or second class battleground. With the war in Europe advanced far enough toward victory, the Anglo-American delegates agreed to press the war as hard in the East as on the European continent. The Cairo summit brought the Chiangs to the highest level of prestige and power both at home and abroad. But this soon dissipated in the last year or so of the Pacific war, because of internal missteps and outside re-examination of their role as a favored wartime ally.

Stilwell, impatient with Chinese politics, strived to increase the effectiveness of American aid and to improve the fighting capability of Chiang's army. Tens of millions of dollars in supplies never reached the front lines. The Generalissimo hoarded weaponry for the day when he'd have to turn back the Communist troops of Mao in a possible civil conflict. A big slice of Lend-Lease supplies fell off the books into the hands of scheming warlords, corrupt military officers and disloyal black marketers who behind the lines often bartered goods directly with the Japanese. A cunning Chiang believed, and rightly so, that America would totally defeat Japan no matter what he did or did not do on the battlefield. Stilwell, tagged "Vinegar Joe" because of his bluntness and acid wit, saw through this smoke screen of inactivity. Stilwell insisted that Chiang allow him to train Communist forces for the Burma campaign. Chiang refused, and, in turn, described him to Roosevelt as a liability and pressed for his recall.

Within the money-driven Soong family itself, there arose friction and disagreement. Chiang frequently floundered at the center of shifting allegiance among his wife's brothers and sisters. Although the dynastic titles and perks endured in one form or another, more and more they became a facade as an arrogant Chiang and his long-standing militant backers wrestled influence, if not control, from the Soongs and Kungs. Finance chief H.H. Kung had done little to stem rampant inflation and famine. As taxes became increasingly difficult to collect, he resorted to merely printing tons of money to keep the economy from total collapse. And he insisted on maintaining a formal exchange rate with the American dollar at 20 to 1, though the black market rate ranged as high as 800 to 1. T.V. Soong, out of his job as foreign minister yet installed as leader of the Executive Yuan, seethed with contempt for his inept and unsophisticated brother-in-laws who seemed to be leading China in no clear direction. When the clan's lone wolf, Mme Sun, indicated a wish to travel to the United States to investigate diversions of Lend-Lease funds at their source, and apparently participate in an anniversary program commemorating the death of her husband, her family warned of real danger. Her safety could not be guaranteed; in fact, her life might be in jeopardy. She remained in China. Brothers T.L. and T.A. Soong, settled comfortably in the States, tended to overseas accounts, carefully avoiding family squabbles and notoriety. Above all, Mme Kung, long in control of much of the clan's investments, realized the war soon would end, and now chiefly focused on their private fortunes.[8]

Mayling struggled to remain on good terms with all her siblings and their spouses. Living with her husband was another matter. Accepted at the Allies conference table as one of the Big Four, Chiang increasingly resented his wife's influence in foreign matters, not to mention her role as his key interpreter in summit talks. Whispers of a split between the Chiangs grew louder. The Communists fed to the press stories of a bitter rift. A possible divorce seemed on the horizon.

At a gathering of cabinet members and several Americans at the Chiangs' summer residence on July 5, 1944, Chiang denied he had had irregular relations with another woman or a child out of wedlock. His record was an open book, he added, and anyone could check on his every movement. As a Christian, he pointed out, he had kept the Commandments. Mme Chiang at the same time spoke along essentially the same line.

"Every time Madame Chiang had made a visit to Hong Kong during the [early] war period, the story of a break-up of her marriage had been broadcast by the government's ill-wishers," Vice Minister of Information Hollington Tong later recalled. Mayling's travels outside China added to the attacks on her private life. Official denials did little to quell humiliating hearsay.[9]

The domestic and family schisms aggravated Mayling's vulnerable nervousness. Illness returned in an even more serious stage than in 1942. Painful skin maladies reappeared. Nervous eye strain added to her indisposition, keeping her from reading and writing. "During the Cairo Conference," she explained to Emma, "I had a particularly thin time as it was necessary to dilate the pupils of my eyes and I can assure you that is not conducive to comfort." Turning to matters on the battlefield, Mayling had a brighter outlook—"brighter than it has been for some time, though it would not be well to be over-optimistic ... our troops in Burma have been acquitting themselves as to win world praise."[10]

Emma wondered how much of her illness was due to frustration in the political sphere—"an inability to make headway against the illiberal clique that now seems in control?" She also noted that Brooks Atkinson in the *Times* had a more hopeful dispatch. "He says that the present Japanese drive toward Loyang is unifying the Chinese and strengthening democratic tendencies as renewed Japanese aggression always does."[11]

China was certainly having a very bad press. But people, Emma thought, saw it as a reaction to over adulation of Mayling and China in 1943, plus the impressions brought back by army and navy men. She noted that the State Department couldn't be accused of ever having been specially pro–Chinese. Closer to home, her Wellesley classmates felt so uncertain about Mayling and the state of affairs in China that they voiced unwillingness to do much about their fund for her war orphans. United China Relief support similarly slumped.

Mayling mustered little enthusiasm to welcome Vice President Henry Wallace to Chungking in June 1944. Apparently Roosevelt sent him to China to get him out of the way during pre–Democratic Convention maneuvering; the president had plans to drop the increasingly left-leaning veep from the ticket that summer. The Wallace mission largely focused on dealing with the Chinese Communists, recognized by many in Washington as a stronger and more reliable fighting force against the Japanese than Chiang's men. Wallace convinced the Generalissimo to permit official U.S. observers to go to the Communists' stronghold in Yenan. As a tradeoff, Washington, Chiang insisted, must replace the uncooperative Stilwell. Wallace reported to Roosevelt: "Chiang, at best, a short-term investment. It is not believed that he has the intelligence or political strength to run post-war China. The leaders of post-war China will be brought forward by evolution or revolution, and it now seems more likely the latter."[12]

Wallace initially endeared himself to Mayling by bringing a cargo container full of books, educational films, technical data, scientific instruments, even grass seed and animal forage—a cultural relations gift for Chinese universities and agricultural centers unable to obtain such items since 1941. Nonetheless, Wallace's affinity with the Communists in rural China alienated Mayling. By the time his mission ended, she had started to pack for another overseas trip—her second in less than two years. And once she left Chungking, there was no one to speak up strongly in Stilwell's behalf.

Mme Chiang's American doctor, Cmdr. Frank Harrington, urged a rest cure away from the strain of public life and the intensive summer heat of Chungking. There, she had been living with the Kungs, and avoiding Chiang and the limelight. Her chronic skin rash and insomnia added to inactivity. She left China in utmost secrecy, accompanied by Ailing and nephew Louis Kung. The Kungs had been shifting personal funds to South America, where investments in mineral deposits, banks and shipping offered strong growth opportunities. The sisters flew to Brazil, where they moved into a villa on the island of Broccio near Rio. Mayling's plans remained open-ended. Although her health slowly improved, her medical advisers suggested treatment in the States. By early September the New York papers reported her presence in the city, and once again at the Harkness Pavilion medical center. The 5,000-mile air trip was made in a specially outfitted presidential C-54 transport loaned by Roosevelt.

A month in the hospital improved Mayling's state of health. She then settled in as a houseguest of the Kungs at River Oaks, their 17-room leased English Tudor mansion on the Hudson at Riverdale in the Bronx. The secluded dwelling at 4904 Independence Avenue adjoined the estate of conductor Arturo Toscanini. H.H. Kung, out of his post as finance minister, yet saving face as special delegate to the international economic conference at Bretton Woods in New Hampshire, enjoyed a sort of an extended exile in New York.[13]

Mayling's indefinite stay in America again fueled talk of a breakup of her marriage. British newspapers published reports of a pending divorce and a move to Miami. The press also referred to Chiang's second wife, Ch'en Chieh-ju, and her return to his household as well as to rumors of a pregnancy. The Chinese Embassy and Chinese News Service issued denials of a marital split; Dr. Kung called Mayling's establishment of a Miami residence a "falsehood," but avoided mention of any separation.

That fall Mayling lost her intimate political ally. Wendell Willkie sought the 1944 Republican Party nomination earlier that year, but at the outset quickly failed to win delegates, and bowed out of the presidential race. New York governor Tom Dewey ran against FDR, who won a fourth term in November. Shortly after Mayling arrived in New York, Willkie's health failed, and he required hospitalization. On October 8, 1944, he died of a heart attack at age 52.

An old China hand with recognized ties to that country's hierarchy and needs, Emma Mills encountered an ongoing outpouring of rumors and gossip as well as bits of well-based information and insider stories from friends and acquaintances with an affinity to matters Chinese. She carefully weighed what she heard, be it first-hand or otherwise, and often duly noted it in her journal for 1944:

> H.H. Kung's adherents are taking charge of the Bank of China, and he has succeeded in liquidating China Defense Supplies. ... a newly returned American army officer said Kung was taking 10 to 20% of the total national income of China.

Mayling is strongly under the influence of Mrs. Kung. I wish she had almost anyone else with her in Rio. And the weird Jeannette and rather gross young nephew are along as well. Mayling probably chose Brazil not just for her health but in order to raise relief funds in South America. The first rumors had been she was seeking a Brazilian divorce because she "couldn't take it."

Directors of the China Institute in New York are having trouble with Henry Luce. He gave the money for its new building and expected to run the show to suit himself.

Helen Stevens at United China Relief believes Mayling is done politically in China & and may not go back.

Director of Medical Relief Corps in China Dr. Robert Lim thinks it is most unlikely that Chiang is involved with any other woman. Says he gave up drinking and smoking 15 or 20 years ago & had led an austere life since.

No one can be sure such things will not happen or have not, but regard it as extremely doubtful in this case.[14]

Employed at the well-guarded Columbia campus lab for nearly a year at a salary now upped ten percent to $165 a month, Emma continued to complain over the lack of time-filling assignments and threatened to resign. The Army Corps of Engineers project—later revealed as part of the Manhattan Project to develop an atomic bomb—seemed close to shutting down and relocating primarily to Los Alamos, New Mexico. Her supervisor urged her to stick it out, reminding her she had the makings of a good technician.

How old, or rather, how young, does he think I am? she wondered. Well, Carl, the very blond glass blower & thirtyish, makes eyes at me. And came along today just as I was reading how Mme. Gorloge seduced Ferdinand, in "Death on the Installment Plan," & started reading over my shoulder. There was nothing to do but tell him I was reading a very naughty book, & close it.

I was reminded again of Ma, as I so often am when reading French novels. Some of her less lovely traits seem characteristic of them. Much of the attitude towards money running all through Balzac. The concentration on a small family group with suspicion & terror at the rest of the world. Celine made me think of her in depicting his father—that extreme willingness to believe the worst of his son & lack of any feeling of psychological responsibility for or understanding of children.[15]

In New York Mayling focused on regaining her health—and perhaps repairing from long range her troubled marriage. In stark contrast to her earlier visit to the States, she ruled out public appearances and press interviews. Emma would become one of the very few outsiders to gain entry to her sanctum sanctorum. She left an unusual account of their extended time together.

The day after landing in the city she called Emma, complaining she was miserable, "suffering the tortures of the damned," and could eat almost nothing and sleep only in the morning. She asked Emma to dinner the following day, and to pack an overnight bag. Her niece was going away; she could have her room at the medical center.

By the next afternoon the city shook from the brunt of a major hurricane. Stronger winds and heavier rains were predicted. Emma dialed the hospital to leave a message that she didn't think she could make the trip far uptown. Mayling's aide, Dorothy Garvey, returned her call. "Madame has had a wretched day and been looking forward so much to your coming." Foul weather notwithstanding, Emma made her way uptown, arriving soaked to the skin.

A steak dinner was served in Mayling's four-room suite. As usual, she ate fast and impatiently. Her skin condition had spread to almost every inch of her body. Constant itching made her very nervous. One doctor recommended a coat of tar, covered with powder, which made her more uncomfortable. "If they can't help me here, I will go somewhere else."

Mayling again brought up the subject of Emma's love life—a topic that seemed to intrigue her, albeit an uneventful, nondescript area for her middle-aged chum. Talk over the so-called troubled marriage of the Chiangs had reached Mayling. "She admitted she had never been in love herself, but spoke of her husband in a natural, easy manner. Once again she said she could be completely herself with me." Emma concluded that there was nothing to all the chatter of her being supplanted with her husband by former wives or sixteen-year-old beauties.[16]

Sexual encounters and sex appeal dominated the long conversation—as it often would that autumn. "Emma, more than anything, I always wanted perfect beauty—more than brains or money."

"Who has such 'perfect beauty?'"

"Mrs. Luce. But she's losing it now."

Emma thought her remarks about not caring for great wealth nonsense, for whoever was paying the bills allowed her everything she wanted.

Mayling related a sexually intriguing tale from her last visit to New York. Joe Kennedy, a notorious womanizer, had given up his apartment at the Waldorf for her staff, so she consented to meet him at Henry Luce's request. When he stopped at her suite, the conversation turned to lemon meringue pie. He claimed he knew of someone who could make a better one than her cook. A few days later a pie arrived from Kennedy, and a request to see her again. She invited him to come and have a piece with her.

While eating the pie, Mayling remarked that one thing she hadn't had in years was an ice cream soda. Kennedy suggested that they go right out and have one. Instead, she sent her nurse to buy two strawberry sodas. While waiting for her return, he brought up the subject of sex appeal. "You have more than any woman I've ever met."

"You really mean charm," she replied, trying to pass it off.

"No, Clare Luce has charm, but doesn't stir me in the least. What did you think has been the cause of all the enthusiasm about you? Why, sex appeal, of course."

Eventually, Mayling got rid of Joe Kennedy, and refused his additional requests to call, and didn't answer his goodbye telegram.

Afterwards, Mayling remembered that Kennedy had gotten on very well with Queen Elizabeth while ambassador to England. But then, she added, perhaps that was only diplomacy on the queen's part, when they wanted the help of the U.S. so badly.[17]

During the four hours of girl talk, Emma mentioned she would be 50 in two days. Mayling insisted they celebrate. So on the 16th of September, an impromptu cocktail party transpired with martinis in medicine glasses served by a nurse. Mayling had a gift from Brazil: a large green purse of alligator lined with chamois. In the midst of the celebration Emma caught a glimpse of visiting Ailing Kung, her son Louis, and H.H. Kung himself. "It was absolutely a duty call, brief on terms of intimacy & yet didn't quite ring true—perhaps I made them feel a little self-conscious. H.H. began by mistaking me for Elizabeth Moore [sister of Henry Luce]."[18]

Emma concluded that the Kung nephew and niece had too much power over their aunt. And Mayling, was too easy-going in regard to her staff. "A very complex person—some childish vanity.... She lacks normal companionship and recreation."

That fall, Emma, bored with little to do at the lab, left her job there with the Manhattan Project. "I shall very soon begin to be living on capital," she recorded. She now had more time for Mayling and for shopping but less to spend. However, wartime shortages persisted. Sugar, bacon, cigarettes were impossible to find. Cake chocolate, scarce. Scotch, non-existent. She commented on food and fuel in a letter to her brother serving as skipper of an aircraft tender in the South Pacific. "Almost never any meat, except cold cuts ... and the snowstorms and manpower shortages have slowed freight movements of some fruits and vegetables. Just to complete the home front picture, the coal shortage has brought about a new dim-out. Candles in store windows, and no more electric signs. ... some people have said their apartments have run out of coal a few days at a time."[19]

In February 1945 ABMAC asked her back for temporary work. That preceded a brief stint as a $75-a-week freelance researcher for textile importer and Chinaphile Alfred Kohlberg and his personal campaign to alert America to the infiltration of communism in the media and left-wing sympathizers in such organizations as the Institute of Pacific Relations. And a paying houseguest contributed to Emma's household expenses.

By April Mayling had recovered sufficiently to go out in public—put on some weight, looked much better and was less nervous. She made frequent calls to Emma, often at odd hours of the day or night—to come up to the Kungs' house in Riverdale for supper or lunch. After eating dinner one Saturday, they drove to Broadway with two Secret Service men to see the movie *The Affairs of Susan* at the Rivoli, entering through an exit door to loge seats.

Mayling naively believed her presence had been anonymous, but Emma overheard the manager's aside to an usher. "Mme Chiang Kai-shek!" in an awestruck voice.

A cluster of college chums surround Mayling following a luncheon in the mid–1940s at classmate Rosella Pretzfelder's home in Garden City, Long Island. Emma Mills, at left; "big sister" Dickey Lightner, in white hat. (Courtesy of Jane Lightner Meads.)

A romantic comedy, the film centered around an actress (Joan Fontaine) who kept four men on tenterhooks, changing her personality to suit each beau. Intrigued by its title, Mayling possibly identified with the enticing Susan.

That week she also ventured to the circus at Madison Square Garden, liking the horses and seals the best. Next she decided to visit the Bronx Zoo to observe the pandas she had sent over in appreciation of the support by New York to China relief. The grounds swarmed with Sunday visitors, and Mayling and Emma, and her driver, amah and nurse dodged around them as through shepherding a very valuable or fragile prize stock. When they arrived at the panda cage, both bears were asleep. The retinue stood in the crowd a few minutes, then made a rapid return to their car. On the way back to Riverdale, they stopped for ice cream sodas.

The war in Europe ended a month later, on May 8, 1945. Mayling thought of making a state visit to England that fall. Restless, with her energy level much improved, she decided to learn how to drive an automobile. Taught by her Secret Service guards, she made the grade, and found it very relaxing at the wheel, even in heavy traffic. It gave her the most wonderful sense of freedom to be able to step into a car and feel she might go off anywhere. At midnight several weeks later she phoned Emma. Might she come to her apartment with some birthday fruit cake (from Mayling's 48th)? In part it was an excuse to drive the Packard limousine. After an hour or so at Emma's, she called their Wellesley dorm mate Dickey Lightner in New Jersey to ask if they might briefly stop by. Mayling again drove, with a Secret Service man beside her. She joked about piloting a plane next. Her outings around Manhattan and into the country—including a ride to see Eleanor Roosevelt at Hyde Park and an inspection visit to the state prison for women in Westchester to gather information useful in the management of China's prisons—occupied several hours on two separate days.

"On the whole she is completely at ease in her driving," Emma observed. "And finds it relaxing. I think contact with the Secret Service men while she was learning has been good for her. A very simple, natural contact with ordinary people, & in a field where she took directions from them. She knows all their personal histories now & thinks of them as individuals. I told her a really expert driver always cusses out other cars on the road."[20]

The sudden death of Roosevelt, the Allied victory over Germany, and the machinations of Russia, along with a joint appeal by Truman, Churchill and Chiang to Japan to surrender, or face complete destruction, aroused Mayling to look beyond the end of the war in the Pacific and on peacetime matters as they concerned China. A summons to Emma one night virtually took her to Mayling's bedside that summer.

Emma had just turned off her bedroom light on July 16, 1945, when the phone rang. "Where have you been?" asked Mayling. "I have something for you to do. I'll be right down to pick you up. Pack a bag."

A little past eleven, Mayling pulled up to Seventh Avenue and 16th Street. And off they sped to Riverdale, where she had been writing an article on the approaching peace. "You have to go over it with me right now. You've got to tell me whether it would be intelligible to the man in the street."

Emma concluded the piece contained too much quoting of authority and citing of forgotten historical incidents. "It reads as if you were writing a college theme. And there are too frequent over-elaborate sentences."

"I suppose writing Chinese has affected my English style," Mayling observed.

They labored over the text well past 2 a.m., trying to simplify, sharpen, rearrange. When Mayling woke early the next afternoon, they soon were at it again, going over the revised version, which was further tightened. "I didn't even suggest omitting 'illation of illogic' or 'gurge' as I could see she was very fond of them and after all, a mere dip into a dictionary would explain them."

With the article finished, Mayling relaxed by driving up the Taconic State Parkway toward Peekskill, and largely discussing Wellesley. Both noted the engagement of its president, Mildred McAfee. Mayling wondered if it weren't a mistake to try matrimony at the advanced age of 45, and then said there might still be a chance for Emma—which was revenge, thought Emma, for her remark the day before that if Mayling could learn to drive she guessed I could, too.

Ten days later Mayling called again. A second article for a Sunday *New York Herald Tribune* supplement was ready for editing. Off went Emma by subway and bus for another long session at the typewriter. From time to time Mayling referred in scorn to its utter simplicity and called it journalese. Emma reminded her that sometimes the greatest thoughts were clothed in the simplest language, and she did all she could to prune and clarify. "She has a Chinese weakness for using pairs of words with identical meanings, as 'hearth & home,' for example," Emma observed. "We get on very well, she takes my criticism in very good humor and accepts or rejects my suggestions quickly. Almost always we end up by agreeing we've made a change for the better, and, of course, her final decision is final."[21]

The following day, the two started still a third article, "China after the War—What?" presumably for *Life* magazine. At one point in her writings Mayling groaned, "It sounds just like Mrs. Roosevelt's stuff."

The Kungs and their two sons, Louis and David, were very much in evidence throughout the house, and had visitors of their own. Occasionally they collared Mayling to discuss—behind closed doors—political bombshells: the dropping of Dr. Kung as governor of the Central Bank of China and T.V. Soong's ousting as foreign minister soon after his attendance at the San Francisco United Nations World Security Conference. Curious at to what his sister-in-law had put into her article, Kung asked to read it. He insisted that she cut a section on the growth of public opinion in China—a subject he evidently viewed as democratic "dynamite." After this confab with Kung, Mayling looked stricken, with dark circles under her eyes.

While reading the Sunday papers the next morning, Mayling commented on the news that Elliott Roosevelt was being released from the army, and said what a trial he must be to the family. Emma took up that remark, and tried to show her that the affairs of the Roosevelt family were sometimes used for political purposes—a son's deed to reflect on the father, etc.—and just so had the rumors of her troubles with her husband been deliberately circulated as part of a campaign against the Kuomintang administration. Mayling didn't see any parallel.

"W.H. Donald told me to issue a denial, but I refused. They have always had such stories circulated about us, ever since our marriage. People ought to realize they could not always be true. Time will show when I return to China that they have been untrue this time."[22]

Emma judged her as thoroughly Chinese in her inability to see the importance of public relations, as it was known in America.

Over the many months of Mayling-Emma conversations, Mayling made virtually no reference to communications from her husband—until late July 1945, when she spoke of a letter brought over by Chiang's nephew. The Generalissimo, writing on the anniversary of her leaving China for Brazil, spoke of his loneliness. She also referred to recent cables urging her return, adding reluctantly she thought she might have to go back at short notice before the summer heat of Chungking let up.

Mayling wondered how women managed to do their own housework, especially in hot weather, and pointed out that it took quite a lot of someone's time just to pick up after her. "You don't spill powder or drop clothes all over a room," Emma pointed out, "if you have to pick up after yourself." Emma surmised that to most Wellesley classmates Mayling's life would, for much of the time, seem duller than theirs—at any rate, the life she was leading now. "Miss Garvey told me that she dislikes new faces about her, à propos of the failure of the typist to take her dictation satisfactorily."[23]

Mayling had wanted to see Wellesley classmates that summer. A number visited Riverdale. But when they began to bring their husbands, daughters and *their* spouses or fiancés, she sputtered how exhausting such get-togethers had become. Emma, too, felt drained from visits. "It's a different world there," she deduced.

> I drink too much tea, smoke too much, feel an impact from her dynamic personality all the 24 hours of the day. I love being with her, but a visit leaves me quite limp, whereas I return from most of my excursions with renewed energy. All week I have been waiting for her to send for me again, as she said she soon would. Bought a couple of dresses in preparation, & have been practicing the Chinese patriotic songs on the piano, as she asked me to. The last evening, while we were waiting for dinner to be brought upstairs, I tried them out & she sat beside me playing the melody with her right hand.[24]

At one of Emma's last stopovers at Riverdale, Mayling handed her a personal check for $1,000. Emma protested, but Mayling explained, "I'll be so far away soon and some day you may need money in a hurry. I worry you live alone, and what you would do in case of sudden illness or accident." Emma reassured her. "I have good friends nearby who'll help. I consider this check a credit and will not touch it except in great emergency."

By August the world waited for the Japanese to admit defeat and surrender. The tremendous news of the dropping of the first atomic bomb on Hiroshima, and two days later a second one on Nagasaki, along with Russian entry into the war with an attack on Manchuria, signaled the end of the conflict in the Far East. As to the bomb development, which Emma peripherally had worked on, she felt appalled by its implications. She remembered that some of the Columbia men had been splitting atoms and playing around with heavy water, but didn't put it in terms of a bomb. "Uranium was not supposed to be mentioned, but occasionally some one forgot to call it by the designated symbol."[25]

On August 14, 1945, New York celebrated the Japanese surrender. Frequent radio bulletins led up to the early evening official announcement that the war finally was over. Immediately boat whistles and automobile horns started a jubilant din, joined by paper showers from windows and rooftops. The next day Emma celebrated by walking to Chinatown where colorful ritualistic dragons led spontaneous parades. Residents on fire escapes and in windows waved Chinese and American flags and cheered the thousand or more people on foot. Over at Times Square, Mayling had driven her car down into the huge boisterous throng. So many had been drinking and kept getting in front of the car that she had to stop. The American to Chinatown, thought Emma, the Chinese to Times Square.

As the chief representative of China in America, Mayling opened her door to newspaper, radio and newsreel interviewers, eager for her words on the victory in Asia. "Unless we implement and maintain in action the professed ideals for which we of the United Nations entered this war, all the bloodshed and sacrifice of our loved ones will be of no avail," she stated. Using parts of the text of the article on peace she had written just a week before, she said the foundation of peace is faith—spiritual faith. "Unless we have faith, peace will not be possible. The San Francisco Charter is only a blueprint.... It has to be implemented with action. And that takes time ... and there will be many obstacles."[26]

Mayling already had been summoned back to Chungking by the Generalissimo. An army transport plane stood ready to fly her back from Washington.

"I don't feel ready to go, Emma. But my husband needs me in the coming crisis with the Communists. I hope and pray the country can avoid armed conflict and achieve national unity. I will miss you. And might never see you again. The Communists might 'get' me."

Several Wellesley friends told Emma that she should return with her; Mayling needs you, they pointed out. Emma weighed the pros and cons.

> Does she even want me? She certainly needs some one to be completely herself with, but I wonder if the good that would be wouldn't be offset by the harm of my being a "foreigner." Mayling is already considered, with a good deal of justification, too American. I have no desire to get even indirectly involved in intrigues and politics, and while I can be adaptable and pliant enough to follow along with her, the time comes when I need to get out from under & be myself, with my own humdrum life, but my own.[27]

Mayling never raised the idea of bringing Emma back to China. The Kungs, no doubt, felt this American confidante had been exerting a subtle yet increasing influence over China's First Lady. An in-house foreigner with a possible "back door" to the Chinese government through Mme Chiang did not sit well at all with this powerful, all-controlling family.

20

Victory Without Peace

The Generalissimo, soon after his wife's return to Chungking, outlined his program for a strong united China. Although the Communist disturbances occupied much of his time, he spoke of unprecedented plans to turn the country into the model democratic state of the Far East. As such he foresaw the abolishment of press censorship so that his people might have freedom of speech. Moreover, he mentioned a law to facilitate the rise of political parties—another right denied to the Chinese under his standing order. The democratization of China, he summarized in an article aimed at American readers, would follow the principles of his mentor Sun Yat-sen, the George Washington of China.

And it made clear that America more than any other nation had the ability and means to carry China to the status of first-class modern power. Chiang looked to the United States to help stabilize the currency and build up agriculture, industry and education. Not overlooked was his army. He expressed the hope that Americans would provide continued help to upgrade and strengthen the Nationalist army.[1]

Chiang's troops and Mao's forces remained at loggerheads. So far, the Generalissimo had failed to honor his pledge to Roosevelt and Churchill at Cairo that he'd settle his differences with the Communists. The role of the Soviet Union in the Far East worried many. Moscow initially stated that it had lost interest in the Chinese Reds and sought to improve relations with the Nationalists. In the last weeks of the war when atomic bombs were dropped on Japanese cities, Russia declared war on Japan and quickly invaded mineral-rich Manchuria. Weeks later Russia and China signed a treaty by which Stalin recognized the Chiang regime as the legitimate government of China, and agreed to refrain from meddling in its domestic and political matters. On the very day Mayling was reunited with her husband, she attended a dinner given by him for Soviet ambassador Appolio Petrov to celebrate the conclusion of the Sino-Soviet agreement.

With Russian troops in Manchuria, according to the terms of the Allies' secret agreement at Yalta in 1945 (of which Chiang had no knowledge), the treaty gave the Soviets ample time to hand over Japanese-captured arms to Mao, and strip the region of its industrial plants and machinery and ship it home as war booty.

More and more Americans were becoming communist-conscious as Russia and its satellites flexed their muscles. Emma expressed serious concern over her country's eagerness to bring home GIs from overseas and forget all about the war. She called it naiveté to believe that once war was won in a military sense it was going to stay won in every other sense as well. Many returning soldiers and Red Cross workers from China were not favorably impressed with Chiang, partly because of clever Communist propaganda that downplayed the Nationalists' ability to unify and govern. Moreover, Emma voiced uneasiness over the pro–Communist lecturers right at home under the very aegis of the Mayling Soong Foundation on the Wellesley campus. "One is Miriam Farley of the Institute of Pacific Relations staff, and the other Lawrence Rosinger of the Foreign Policy Association. He was in some of my classes at Columbia & has never been near the Far East. William C. Johnstone ... is at least an academic person." Besides, she concluded, these guests fell far short of the caliber of good speakers regardless of political views.[2]

Early vestiges of the Communist probe appeared on Emma's doorstep. Two unannounced FBI agents came to inquire about Alfred Kohlberg, her employer earlier that year, and Dr. Maurice William, a New York dentist and student of Marxism—both very active in ABMAC and other Chinese interactions. Were they paid agents of the Chinese government? She explained that Kohlberg's investigations into pro–Chinese communist activities stemmed from a visit to Chungking in 1943. Emma thought he had given up on curbing the spread of communism overseas and become more interested in communism in America. The more vocal of the two young FBI agents admitted he knew little of the background on the China matter—which was typical of the times. Could he come back again to talk more?

Emma agreed, and at the second encounter was duly impressed by his intelligence. "We got quite chummy, and I gather they are equally vigilant on the other side of the question."[3]

All in all, she had remained pessimistic as the year of Allied victory neared an end. Nevertheless, a bright area of her life emerged from trading in the stock market. Since the settlement of her grandmother's estate, she received enough proceeds to invest on a small scale. She now read *The Wall Street Journal* religiously, and her choice of holdings paid off in short order. One hundred shares of Anchor Post, bought in March 1945 at $4 a share, had tripled when sold in December at $12, a profit of some $700. The pressure for a full-time job lessened. Instead, she became absorbed in going through family papers, and in particular, editing a mid–19th century maritime diary kept by a grandson of New York governor and U.S. vice president Daniel D. Tompkins.[4]

Immersed in reading and research, she bought 13 books at a Macy's sale one day. "Oh, dear!" she exclaimed. "It is certainly fortunate, however, my weakness is not alcohol."

The First Couple of China traveled to Chinese cities to assess the war damage inflicted by the occupying Japanese, and to bolster the central government's role and call upon all Chinese to work for the regeneration of their country. In Shanghai, not seen in nine years, Mayling accompanied Chiang to the home inherited from her mother, finding it still livable. Mme Chiang made a special flight to Changchun, capital of Manchuria, where Russian troops remained. As a token of goodwill, she distributed 30,000 boxes of candy for the occupation army to "sweeten Chinese-Soviet relations." At a military ceremony there, an optimistic Mayling praised Stalin both as a statesman and strategist. "With the victory of World War II and with your handing over Manchuria to China, the relations of our two countries are bound to be manifestly friendlier than ever."[5]

Emma began a new series of letters to Mayling—more gossipy and fretful than the wartime missives. "I have been feeling very much at loose ends since you left, but things usually solve themselves for me one way or another. Meanwhile, I worry over the state of the world, enjoy quite a lot of company, and take out my constructive instincts in some really quite ambitious experiments in cooking, of all things."[6]

Mayling's replies were few and far between. The first upon her return was a cable asking Emma to contact Dr. Frank Co Tui, vice president of the American Bureau for Medical Aid to China, and get him on a plane to China as early as possible because the Chinese war minister needed medical treatment. Emma received the message as it was to be kept an "unofficial" visit. In spite of Mayling's request for priority, Co Tui experienced three or four days of delays in his journey from the West Coast through Hawaii, Guam and Manila to Shanghai.

ABMAC again had its eye on Emma. By spring of 1946 the organization brought her back to plan a medical conference. When that ended she stayed on as a "buffer and smoother over," earning $70 a week. That June when executive director Helen Stevens went on vacation, and later in the year traveled to China, Emma occupied her office, handling incoming mail, signing every check, and "going through the proper motions."[7]

The bureau's fellowship training program—its single most important and long-lasting contribution to Chinese medical education—engaged Emma and many on staff. The plan focused on training fellows to become better teachers from a semester or two at medical institutions in the United States. Also, ABMAC began sending over American medical specialists to participate in research and instruction. One of Emma's tasks involved the placing qualified individuals—as well as discouraging unsuited applicants wanting to go to China. One particular day they included a group of seniors at Skidmore College and a high school teacher who had worked in a steel mill during the war.

Other projects promoted public health demonstration centers and studies to improve the nutritional content of rice. But income from fund drives soon fell as the U.S. public lacked interest in supporting reconstruction in China, chiefly in the light of reports about government corruption.

Personnel matters often fell in her lap, as she noted in her journal. "Mr. Scanlon slid into the chair by my desk again today. This time it was about— ——, who's supposed to be doing a publicity job for us in China at this point. Did I think she was really 100%—? I couldn't get what he was driving at. He explained—'a little pink perhaps?' He'd just happened to notice on her record she'd once worked for one of those Spanish outfits, & a labor union. She's a great hulking woman who hasn't quite made the grade & drinks too much from loneliness & feels sorry for herself, & I told him as much, each promising strict secrecy as to the other's revelations."[8]

Outside the office, Emma joined a committee for a new group called the American-China Policy Association, an outgrowth of Alfred Kohlberg's anti–Chinese Communist crusade. Feedback from China indicated that Communists were playing "Moscow's game" and hence were "up to no good." The Generalissimo, it seemed, was surrounded by a self-seeking group of reactionaries who even clipped all adverse comment from the newspapers he was allowed to see. And Chinese farmers had told one ABMAC supporter that they didn't want their children to be educated for then they would become officials and hence corrupt. They preferred them to be poor farmers, illiterate, but honest.[9]

The American Bureau for Medical Aid to China named Emma Mills Executive Secretary in 1948, recognizing a decade of pioneer service as volunteer and staff member at its New York headquarters. (Mills–DeLong collection.)

China offered both opportunity and challenge for medical personnel. Many high-ranking visitors often endeavored to meet with Mme Chiang. But frequently she was away from Nanking, the restored capital, and on the road. On June 12, 1946, she wrote: "The last few months have been nothing but travel, travel, travel and then more travel. We have just come back from my second visit to Manchuria. It is strange that, in spite of all these years of air travel, I have never become immune to air sickness. Just imagine, about a year ago I was in New York and we were having such fun together and here I am in Nanking in the thick of things. (May I claim credit for myself for not dragging in our old Latin tag, *mutatis mutandis*?) The Generalissimo and I hope to go to Kuling sometime this summer but everything depends upon the developments in the political world." She made no reference to repeated rumors, published and unpublished, that the Chiangs were coming for a visit to the United States.[10]

Emma remained decidedly realistic over the international scene. The Russians were not getting out of Manchuria as agreed and were putting pressure on Nanking for economic concessions. Moreover, Chinese Communists demanded a hand there. "It is all so much what I have expected; I am oppressed by a feeling of dread, indignation, helplessness—will another world war start there again? Former Ambassador to Russia Joseph E. Davies has said today the Russians had every moral right to try to find out about the atomic bomb by espionage in Canada! A radio report stated that they had 200 known agents in Montreal alone."[11]

A trusted friend of China, Emma and other China hands expressed concern over the reactionary Nationalist government and the need for some real measure of reform which would cut the ground from under the feet of the opposing side. New blood was needed among the leaders, Emma pointed out to Mayling. "We feel no confidence whatever in the outcome of large scale fighting, that has been tried before, and there are too many complicating factors involved now. I have stripped this of all qualifying acknowledgments of difficulties, etc., and pass it on for what it is worth, but I think it is a fair boiling down of a fairly widespread point of view, from people who have long terms of service in China, some of whom are very recently returned. Some Chinese even share it."[12]

The staunchly independent Soong sister, Mme Sun Yat-sen, quietly out of politics and concentrating on relief work from her house in Shanghai, called for formation of a coalition government of Nationalists and Communists, and declared that the presence of American military forces in China had become a detriment rather than a boon to order. She asked the United States to think twice about making loans to a one-party government in which Chiang was president and her brother, T.V. Soong, premier. Her stepson, Sun Fo, chairman of the Legislative Yuan, urged a similar coalition and a drastic overhauling of the Chiang regime.[13]

In a rare meeting, possibly the last with Mayling, Chingling in late 1947 asked what the bottom line was for a settlement between warring factions.

Although the war had been over for more than a year, Emma noticed ongoing shortages of sugar and butter. Ration coupons for shoes, however, were no longer required. But there were few decent shoes to buy. Even some restaurants lacked meat to serve. Nonetheless, Emma entertained frequently and capped the year with a New Year's Eve party, gathering 15 local Chinese friends and ABMAC fellows in her small living room. Before the midnight banquet, the guests played Chinese records, but were most enthusiastic over Emma's set of Chinese dominos.

In 1947 the Communist paranoia intensified at home and abroad. A cold war existed with a so-called iron curtain between eastern and western Europe. In Washington a Central Intelligence Agency (CIA)—apart from the FBI and State Department—was established to gather and analyze foreign intelligence for the president. The new Taft-Hartley Labor Management Relations Act required union leaders to disclaim any connection with communism.

In China the Truman administration struggled to reconcile combative dissidence and attain a united and democratic country. In November 1945 the president had asked Army Chief of Staff George C. Marshall to leave at once for Chungking to stave off a threatened civil war. As special envoy, he grappled with the task for more than a year. A coalition government and a melding of Chiang's and Mao's troops remained out of reach. Neither side believed such a government was possible to share. Washington, however, made it clear—without unity there would be no significant future U.S. help; since V-J Day total grants and credits already had bordered on two billion dollars. The China bloc—chiefly Republican and partisan—managed to lift an embargo on arms, believing increased firepower would defeat the Soviet-backed Chinese Communists without American combat units.

Through ABMAC programs Emma Mills heard of lax discipline within the Chinese army. "One of our fellows [Chinese assigned to the United States] has failed to answer what he has been doing since the school was closed the 23th of May. Another told Harvard authorities he had administrative responsibility for the 100 Chinese medical officers in the U.S. as he was the senior officer here—all pure fiction. A third, a woman, but not our responsibility, has refused to return to China this month as instructed. Another angle, although 80% of the Chinese national budget is said to go for the army, Dr. Robert Lim has written us that a medical major general is now receiving one-third the pay of a coolie."[14]

More disturbing words reached Emma. Nationalist "thought police" activities led to arrests for mere mention of the words "masses" or "labor movement." Corruption charges, too, rocked the very core of Chiang's government. His Soong and Kung relatives and their "privileged corporations," it was charged by the central executive committee of the Kuomintang, had mismanaged foreign currency funds. It was alleged that the family, chiefly T.V. Soong, obtained more than their allowed quotas of foreign exchange in amounts as large as tens of millions of dollars and imported luxury goods that others were barred from handling. Members of these special corporations utilized diplomatic passports to facilitate transactions. The questionable deals of Mayling's brothers and a nephew cast a shadow over her international luster, which had gradually dimmed since her American homecoming in 1942–43. Support of her civilian relief activities by the U.S. public slumped; at ABMAC where she still served as honorary chairman donations dropped off significantly.

In 1948 the Generalissimo requested immediate stepped-up aid in the conflict against the Communist army. He pressed for three billion dollars for the next three years, plus military manpower. He also hinted that an invitation to the White House would be most welcome. The Chiangs, meanwhile, staked their hopes for a large U.S. commitment on a Republican electoral sweep that November. With Gov. Thomas Dewey in the White House and Republican control of the House and Senate, the Nationalists believed money would pour into Nanking. The stunning victory of Truman at the voting booth, however, upset predictions and strategy.

Just days after Truman's triumphal mandate from the American people, Mayling packed her bags for Washington to appeal personally to the "China Lobby" for more and faster aid to China. No official invitation was forthcoming. In a radio broadcast from Nanking, she alerted Americans of her departure — claiming certain organizations had invited her and that requests had been coming in from many quarters for her to speak on the "life-and-death struggle against communism." The Chinese Embassy prepared for her arrival.[15]

Several days later she landed in San Francisco, where a military air transport had been sent to carry her to Washington. A State Department assistant chief of protocol greeted her, but the White House made no welcoming gesture other than supplying aircraft. Unruffled, she proceeded from National Airport to the Leesburg, Virginia, estate of George Marshall, now secretary of state. His wife had been Mayling's guest in Chunking in 1946, and she remembered Mrs. Marshall's open invitation to visit their country home some 35 miles outside the city. She settled in for what was announced as a short stay.

Hat in hand, Mayling took on the assignment to enlist the support of her adopted country in China's military and economic struggle. First stop was Walter Reed Hospital where Marshall was undergoing a physical check-up — and within days, a kidney operation. A courtesy call, it turned into a three-hour business session. "I am encouraged," she remarked as she emerged from the medical center. "I would like to know anybody who has seen and talked with General Marshall and does not come away encouraged."[16]

Mayling's mission spun its wheels in the days ahead. A hoped-for invitation to address Congress failed to materialize. Moreover, the Joint Congressional Committee on Foreign Economic Co-operation voted not to ask her to a hearing. Similarly, the Senate Foreign Relations Committee made no gesture to listen to her eleventh-hour plea for aid. Surprised and disappointed, she cooled her heels in Leesburg.

Finally, her country's ambassador in Washington, Wellington Koo, secured a place on President Truman's calendar some ten days after knocking on his door. The president agreed to see Mayling and Mrs. Marshall at an afternoon tea at which she would try to state her case. It was her second visit to the Truman White House; just before leaving the States at the close of the war in 1945, they had chatted briefly. The Trumans' tea party on December 10 was just that. The president avoided serious talk. For Mayling, it became a lost opportunity through no fault of her own.

At the end of the month, Acting Secretary of State Robert A. Lovett revealed that she called upon him in a non-scheduled interview. But, he noted, she brought no new proposals. For all intents and purposes, Mayling's trip had failed. Yet she was unwilling to go back to China, and thus settled down in the Washington house of T.V. Soong.[17]

Before moving out of the Marshalls' estate, Mayling wrote to Emma to acknowledge flowers sent there by ABMAC. Commenting on Emma's words that she was keeping her fingers crossed on the success of her mission, Mayling replied: "Were you the praying type, you might have tried something in that line. It might be a good thing for you if you were that type. Do you agree with me?

"Of course you will have a chance to see me. You could not escape it if you wanted to, and probably in dear old New York, where I will have to go for a checkup with Dr. John Loeb, as soon as my work is finished in Washington. Meanwhile, behave yourself."[18]

By the end of 1948, the Communists controlled Manchuria and most of China north of the Yangtze. Every day the Reds were pushing back the Nationalists troops. Many of Chiang's men were going over to the winning side or merely waiting till the enemy got ready to annihilate them. Others, lacking offensive spirit and no real leadership, were drawn into cities, then defected.

Mao laid down conditions for peace, ranging from annulment of the constitution (the Communists had refused to participate in the 1946 constitutional convention called by Chiang) to a system of land reform. In effect, a call for unconditional surrender. The proposed settlement hit directly at the heart of the Nationalist government. War criminals had to be punished, and at the top of the list of 45 such individuals stood Chiang and Mayling. It left her in no hurry to return to China and the side of her husband.

Her quest for aid deemed a failure, she even had lost the favor of her early boosters. Eleanor Roosevelt's cutting but truthful remark that Mayling "can talk beautifully about democracy, but does not know how to live democracy" ended their friendship. Henry Luce's Far East thrust had chiefly turned to culture with greater support of the China Institute in New York. Willkie and Roosevelt were gone; the China bloc in Congress, eloquent but politically stymied.

George Marshall, gracious host to China's First Lady, had washed his hands of Chiang, and moved on into the post of secretary of defense in 1949, replaced in the State Department by Dean Acheson, whose wife Alice

Stanley had graduated from Wellesley with Mayling, but was never close. The tight-knit college crowd overall remained loyal and responsive—and filled Mayling's empty hours in New York.

Settled in at the Kung residence in Riverdale, Mayling began her late night calls to Emma. At two a.m. one morning, she asked: "Are you awake?"

Emma replied: "I am now!"

"Too many people and interruptions here in Riverdale. I need quiet time. Would you set out your typewriter so I can come to your apartment and work?"

She also asked her to arrange a luncheon for the Wellesley circle. It took numerous phone calls for Emma to pull the reunion together. Some 25 gathered at Dickey Lightner's Ridgewood, New Jersey, home. Afterwards, Mayling took a dozen to New York's spring flower show and to dinner. Emma again was on call. Before the year ended Mayling would join Emma for a half-dozen lunches or dinners, and several overnights, at her modest 16th Street apartment.

By July, exhausted from office duties and running errands for Mayling, Emma departed for a long vacation on Barton Lake in northern Vermont with two unmarried sisters she had known since childhood. Pre-breakfast swims invigorated this city dweller. "It is the perfect moment of each day, and all else is part of a slow diminuendo. The pine woods are fragrant, the water invigorating, drying yourself standing on a rock against the sun-warmed wall delicious. And nude swimming is always preferable; it's hard to say exactly why."[19]

In the afternoons there were blueberries to pick from bushes covering the ground like carpet. Throughout the day, walks and naps, reading and knitting, and visits from friends and their friends. But after a week, Emma wrote: "I've been depressed the past three days and definitely under-stimulated, for a change. Am not sure whether fatigue is catching up with me or I'm falling into the aimlessness of the rest of the household. Perhaps even, to a certain degree, into the habit of irritability.

"By mid-afternoon," she later continued, "I begin to feel bored, and by dinner time, melancholy. This sort of inactive, isolated vacation does not do for me any more. My personality really has changed the past year or two."

Events in China continued foremost in her mind. She finished reading General Chennault's *Way of a Fighter*—"it certainly does no credit to many of our military or our policy makers." A long-expected State Department White Paper on China stirred her. The report, prepared in part in 1947 by General Albert Wedemeyer, successor to Stilwell as commander of U.S. forces in China, but suppressed by Marshall for two years because of the fear it would hasten disintegration of the situation in China and aid the cause of the Reds, blamed the debacle on Nationalist (and Chiang) maladministration, corruption and lack of leadership.[20] "This will make an incredible chapter in our history when all the records are available. The only thing I could think of to do to help has been to put a word or two on China in such letters as I have written."[21]

A surprise awaited her in New York: new bedroom drapes and bedspread.

A handwritten noted explained the change. Mayling and her secretary-companion Miss Garvey had played "house" for a weekend at the apartment, and ended up replacing window drapes and bed cover.

"It took us two solid evenings to get the rod in. Gosh! We ought to charge you overtime! Also if you find your desk drawers mussed up, it is because we tried to find a screw driver, an awl and a hammer for tools. You have nothing! Where do you keep your tool box? I hope you like the bed cover. You ought to. It is purported to be George Washington's favorite!"

Mayling pointed to butter, eggs and bacon and vegetables in the refrigerator, before signing the note "The Neat Housemother." In a PS, some orderly kitchen advice: "You should never leave the dish spray on the stove. The heat will melt the rubber. Also shake it out well after using, otherwise the water collects in the compartment for the detergent."[22]

Back at the ABMAC office after three peaceful weeks in the country, the hardest part of the first day was getting used to the traffic noise from Broadway and 58th Street and a nearby fire house. With all the windows open on a hot August morning, it was deafening. And with dirt from outside that Emma wiped off her desk several times. "Busy enough, and ended with almost a headache, but I'll be hardened in a day or two."

First order of business: preparation for a television debate on the topic "Should We Give Military Aid to China," chiefly between the bureau's president Magnus Gregersen for the affirmative and Nathaniel Peffer, professor of international relations at Columbia, on the negative side. A large map was needed for the TV program. Emma scurried about the city for an all-inclusive one. The American Geographical Society had only an out-of-date map of Asia. Finally, a small one in the office sufficed once Emma and Allen Lau, assistant executive director and her trusted aide, marked out the Communist occupied areas and mounted it. On the telecast "each side made one or two good points and one or two blunders. But Gregersen was obviously sincere and Peffer, sarcastic, as usual, which showed in his face as well as approach. The increase of these China programs is most encouraging."[23]

But old China hands faced growing disillusionment, and feared a pullout on the mainland. Talk of the inevitable closing down of ABMAC spread. Would the bureau be able to utilize their funds for fellowships in a Communist China, she wondered?

The Generalissimo already had moved his government's official reserves of 400 million dollars to the off-shore island known as Formosa, along with many of its prized museum treasures from Peking. Some 300,000 of his most loyal troops were deployed on this outpost. On October 1, 1949, in Peking, Mao proclaimed the People's Republic. From its capital, Chingling Sun pledged her allegiance to the Communist government. Its clear mission—agrarian reform—attracted many to its flag. In the final weeks of 1949 Chiang and his son and political heir, Chiang Ching-kuo, would flee with remnants of the Kuomintang to Formosa.[24]

The eloquent and forceful Mayling rarely broke her silence during her third lengthy sojourn in the States. The number of speeches and interviews were very few in comparison to her ongoing wartime public visibility. The sweeping successes of the Communists, however, aroused her desire to speak out. In a September talk with Hearst Newspapers correspondent David Sentner, she defended her husband as a selfless leader who had been smeared in a global campaign by the Communists. "The Communists have been unable to attack his integrity so they have used the device of charging he is surrounded by corruption. No matter what they say about the Generalissimo they cannot say he ever stopped fighting Communism or has sold out to Russia."[25]

Mayling proceeded to list the three groups in the smear campaign: the Communist Party and its affiliated fronts; synthetic liberals or reactionaries; and diplomats who sponsored a pro–Soviet or pro–Chinese Communist policy. The world conspiracy against Chiang and his government had begun almost 20 years earlier, she explained. With a dig at the Marshall Plan for the recovery of Europe not being extended to Asia, the forthright First Lady submitted, "To ignore what is happening in the Far East while fighting Communism in Europe is like treating one limb of a sick man while neglecting the rest of his body."

Mayling planned a return to China. "I believe the Generalissimo needs me. I will go where he goes." But at that point Chiang was on the run, from one city to another in China. Where would she fly to?

With the mainland utterly lost, Mayling made plans to leave America for her new home. On January 8, 1950, she gave a farewell talk over the NBC network from Riverdale. "In a few days I shall be returning to China. Not to Nanking, Chungking, Shanghai or Canton. Not to the soil of the mainland. I shall return to my people on the island of Formosa, the fortress of our hopes, the citadel of our battle against an alien power which is ravaging our country."

A spirited valedictory, it stressed the dedication to fight for freedom. "We are not defeated.... As long as a breath remains in us, and with faith in the Almighty, we shall continue the struggle. Not a day, not an hour, will pass which will not be devoted to our struggle for freedom. We shall fight fire with fire. Unremittingly and with the tenacity of life, we shall fight and bleed the enemy."

In closing she touched upon the lack of tangible aid. "At such a time, no pleading can be with dignity.... It is either in your mind and your will to aid China in her struggle for liberty, or you have abandoned liberty.

"We stand with empty but willing hands. We stand humble, tired, crying for peace and rest, even more than for rice and bread.... With or without help, China shall fight for liberty. Alone it will take longer and cost more lives. With help our gains will be swifter. But free we shall be."[26]

Two days later Mme Chiang was airborne on the first leg of her flight to Formosa—and aboard commercial airliners. Declining to hold a press conference, her only words at departure from New York were "Thank you and God bless you." At the new capital, Taipei, she sprung into First Lady mode. Appealing for military and technical advisers to aid the Nationalists' ongoing fight against Communism, she, however, ruled out armed troops from the United States. "It should not be necessary to have to ask someone who is a real friend for help. If they are your friends that wouldn't be necessary."²⁷

A visit to tiny Quemoy Island, the gateway for an expected Communist invasion of Formosa, buoyed thousands of troops and residents there. Just months before, the Nationalists had fought off a determined Communist bid to take the island. A reputed, yet questionable, 15,000 enemy soldiers had been killed or captured. Mayling distributed food, cigarettes and Bibles to those defending Chiang's free China. Few countries could point to a First Lady with greater initiative, energy and outreach.

Once more Emma submitted her resignation from the Medical Bureau, and again it was refused. The ABMAC Board asked her to stay on in a new position as executive secretary, replacing Executive Director Helen Stevens. She canceled her plans to take a slow freighter to England; instead she ended up on a fast plane to China.

In April ABMAC sent her on a 16-day inspection tour of health care services and medical facilities on the former Japanese-held Formosa (renamed Taiwan by the Chinese). Emma visited hospitals, rural health stations, nursing schools and medical colleges. They included the National Defense Medical Center and

In January 1950 Madame Chiang ended a lengthy, and largely unsuccessful, period of mustering U.S. support for her husband's military campaign against mainland communist takeover. She delivered a farewell talk on radio, declaring Formosa to be "the fortress of our hopes, the citadel of our battle against an alien power." (Mills–DeLong collection.)

the Taiwan School of Nursing and Midwifery. She made note, too, of other aspects of life on the semi-tropical island with its seven million people—transportation (mostly bicycles), food (similar to mainland fare), education (one of the highest literacy rates in the Far East), general morale (excellent). As the bureau's representative, she especially observed the fine cooperation between the native Taiwanese and the newly arrived Chinese—at least in the medical field.

Emma Mills's return to the Far East after 25 years brought comparison with the medical profession of 1920s China. "When I left Peking there was to all intents and purposes no Chinese medical profession.... I didn't realize how amazing the progress has been during the interval, in spite of war, civil war and enemy occupation.... The same with the military.... The Chinese soldier was a scarecrow, the camps a mess. This time I went into all sorts of military establishments, announced and unannounced. Everything was neat and orderly."[28]

Excursions to mainland China remained out of bounds. The United States did not recognize the People's Republic. Besides, as an unofficial guest of the Nationalist government, and to a degree of Mayling and the Generalissimo, any travel there even by an American citizen-tourist—even an old China hand—would be out of line.

Emma and Mayling re-connected several times in Taipei, and Chiang joined them briefly one day. "I'm telling everyone to whom I mention the episode at all that he is both handsomer and more genial than I had expected from his pictures," she told Mayling.[29]

Emma's report to ABMAC on the Taiwan tour generated both a publicity and fundraising plan and speaking dates, along with a special appeal letter to the Class of '17. In her talks to medical missionaries, Wellesley Clubs and community service groups—averaging one a week that summer—Emma stressed Taiwan as a place to launch propaganda to the mainland and a focal point for the hopes of regaining the mainland, especially as predicted conditions there deteriorated.

As an authority on Taiwan and celebrity of sorts among old China hands, ABMAC asked Emma to personally sign its latest appeal letter, a mailing numbering in the thousands. Then, in June Senators William F. Knowland, Paul Douglas and Alexander H. Smith asked to see her in their rethinking of a policy change toward the Chiang regime. Equally significant, the State Department head of the Far Eastern section, Dean Rusk, responded favorably to an interview request by bureau director and Congressman Walter Judd.

"Rusk said practically nothing and was poker-faced throughout, but did ask to see my written report on Taiwan.... Both Judd and Senator Smith told me they thought a change in policy was definitely in the wind, but State had to find a face-saving formula. They also considered Rusk a great improvement and put some faith in him."[30]

Emma helped plant the seed for the Truman administration's re-analysis of relations, particularly basic economic and support programs. Mayling admired her comprehensive reporting gift and keen diplomatic skill. Indeed, it brought the subject of Taiwan to the forefront in certain influential Washington circles.

21

Frequent Flyers

On June 25, 1950, Stalinist North Korean forces invaded South Korea at the 38th parallel line of division and headed for its capital, Seoul. The Korean peninsula, divided into U.S. and Soviet zones for the final assault on Japan in 1945, burst into a full-scale war as the UN Security Council authorized use of force to restore peace. U.S. troops quickly landed, bearing the brunt of this three-year conflict.

The war immediately changed America's policy toward Formosa from a sharply restrictive stance to an involved, protective program. President Truman isolated the Nationalists' island with the Seventh Fleet, and insisted Chiang refrain from air and sea attacks on the mainland. This cessation doomed guerrilla resistance there. Shipments of arms and ammunition followed, as did some $300 million in fortress-building military aid to Chiang, plus military advisers—a stark contrast to the cutoff of help a mere six months earlier.

Chiang responded to the UN call for concerted action in Korea by an offer of three ground divisions. U.S. commanders vetoed the gesture, fearing a full-scale Chinese Communist countermove.

Mayling reminded America that Formosa was more important than ever to the whole democratic world. Free China stood as an Asian fortress against communism, she pointed out, and foreign aid would make a consequential difference in the course of all free peoples against all communists. "If there is to be freedom anywhere, there must be freedom everywhere."

In 1951 newspaper correspondent Marguerite Higgins interviewed the Generalissimo. She concluded that "whatever may have been the failings in the past of the men around him, Chiang here in Formosa is personally regarded as a man of integrity and dedication."[1]

Mayling and the Generalissimo, who would be re-elected to five more terms as president, settled into an official residence in Shinlin, a northern suburb of Taipei. Set against green hills amid lush gardens backed by a protective forest of evergreens and palms, the heavily guarded dwelling centered around a reception area–living room that contained many overstuffed chairs and divans and teakwood tables. At a meeting there in 1972, Mayling told this author that some of these furnishings came from her family house in Shanghai. Chiang especially had wished to replace the well-worn Japanese-style pieces, filling the room with familiar Chinese articles.[2]

Mayling's watercolors—landscapes of her native land—hung prominently on the walls. Mayling took much pride in her new pastime, displaying an artistic aptitude far greater than that of most amateurs. She gave a number of such paintings as gifts to friends, and published several portfolios of her brush works. Emma initially deemed them as having "no originality," yet one would occupy conspicuous wall space in her Manhattan bedroom. Others called her work nondescript, without any memorable style.[3]

In 1952 a depressed and listless Mayling returned again for a lengthy stay in New York. The painful inflammation of her skin resulting from protracted nervous tension necessitated overseas treatment. And virtually all her Soong and Kung family lived in the States. Often a guest of the Kungs, who had acquired a 36-acre estate, "Hillcrest," on Feeks Lane in Locust Valley on the North Shore of Long Island, she unfailingly put Emma on call to do errands or arrange gatherings with the old school network—chiefly in March 1953 for a well-publicized visit and address at Wellesley just before her return home. It had been a decade since Mayling's last campus visit, and she insisted on bringing a dozen or so college friends with her by plane from New York. Emma, as she had in the past, helped write her campus speech.

> How she loves long words and parallel phrases! I suggested cutting down on the past and stressing present achievements on Formosa, as both less likely to run into old prejudices, & give her a chance to fresher material. I insisted she cut a nasty reference to the British—not by name, but unmistable. Mayling protested, but I told her she could say what she pleased at home, but here she was a guest & couldn't embarrass our government.... I rewrote the beginning, putting in some reference to the college.... How they'll love it. But I longed to simplify some of those tortured phrases.[4]

On the day of Mayling's talk, Alumnae Hall quickly filled, with many students sitting on the floor, with an overflow listening from a public address system in the ballroom underneath. She spoke very slowly and distinctly in a low voice.

"Some of the tortured phrases remained, but people were apparently almost hypnotized by her unusual choice of words."[5]

Later during a tour of the campus, Mayling and President Margaret Clapp sat down on a bench twice for a smoke, and the students flocked around. Emma spoke up: "Miss Clapp, I have a better opinion of the college now that they have a President who smokes." Mayling, it seems, played a role in making smoking in public more acceptable—even permissible—at Wellesley, as she had in changing the dress code to allow slacks in the 1940s.[6]

As a thank-you gift for her hospitality at Wellesley, Emma, Mildred Green,

Mills' travels to the Far East accelerated in her latter years. Her itinerary usually included visits with her Chinese friends at the National Defense Medical Center and Veterans General Hospital on Taiwan. (Mills–DeLong collection.)

Cornelia Van Arnam and Rose Pretzfelder bought Mayling a traveling clock—a reliable timepiece she had been looking for since her last trip.

Emma had left ABMAC not long after her tour of Formosa in 1950, citing staff jealousy and office politics. Probably her health played a part, too. Within a month or so, doctors had removed most of her thyroid, leaving her voice so impaired that sometimes she whispered, sometimes croaked, and sometimes barely spoke at all. A full recovery took nearly two years; speech therapy—even singing lessons—helped significantly.

She remained determined to find a way to go on with work for China—to the point of investigating living in Taiwan (which Mayling advised against because of meager pay scales). Meanwhile, the China Institute in New York hired her for six months to prepare a survey of some 6,000 recently arrived Chinese professionals and students in need of financial help or jobs in the United States. A project assistant, Helen Erickson, looked upon Emma as "unconventional"—an urban-raised young woman with many advantages and family prominence yet toiling in workaday jobs. When a young Chinese acquaintance in Taiwan, Irene Shao, asked her help to come to America to further a career as a physical therapist, Emma arranged for a visa—and proceeded to pay her tuition at Sargent College of Health and Rehabilitation Sciences in Boston. Moreover, in the early 1950s a former staff member she had known at ABMAC, and who had taken a job with the Chinese delegation at the United Nations, suggested that she and Emma share a two-bedroom apartment in her 16th Street building. Once larger quarters on the 15th floor were found the young and attractive Lilyan Chao Foo brought Emma into a whirl of UN diplomatic social engagements. These living arrangements continued for several years until Shanghai-raised Lilyan married the recently widowed minister-counsellor, and soon-to-be ambassador, Chen Chih-mai, who would serve in Australia, Japan and at the Vatican.

While Mayling's trips to New York, ostensibly for medical checkups, became more frequent in the 1950s and 1960s, Emma's flights to the Far East also accelerated. Shortly after volunteering at a Manhattan-based foundation for raising funds for scholarships, teaching supplies and equipment for the True Light Middle School, which had 19th-century missionary roots in Canton that spread to Hong Kong during the war, she traveled there at her expense to the new campus. It would be the first of a half-dozen visits to the flourishing private girls' school, with side trips to Taiwan to enjoy the company of Mayling and friends at the National Defense Medical Center and its School of Nursing.

Avid anti-communist Alfred Kohlberg again recruited Emma to his latest project in November 1953, this time, the Committee of One Million, a volunteer endeavor to help maintain a firm American stand against any concession to Communist China which would jeopardize U.S. security and dishonor commitments to allies in Asia and throughout the world. Chiefly, the group wrote letters and lobbied against the admission of the mainland to the UN. With this aim, Emma and others enthusiastically sought endorsements by members of Congress, along with various high-profile organizations and individuals, and gathered their signatures backing the status quo to keep Taiwan in the world body.

The workaday world, now unnecessary in Emma's life, seemed ages away. A typical day gave her the solitude and freedom she had long sought. She loved the morning, waking up with the feeling that the most wonderful things could happen. She fixed breakfast—usually toasted rye bread, half a grapefruit, and Twining's breakfast tea, which she drank while perusing the stock market news in a daily newspaper. Then a cigarette. Dressed about nine. Next, read all the paper before going to her desk, and usually there was time to write in her journal. Odds and ends of housework until lunchtime.

"Content, for the most part, in the evenings," she recorded, "but sometimes in the afternoons feel restless or slightly futile. Usually go out. I love this apartment & enjoy doing or buying things for it. Like other people to enjoy it, too."[7]

The summer months were filled with visits to classmates and various friends—in northern Michigan; Ontario, Canada; Vermont; Martha's Vineyard; the North Fork of Long Island. Plus weekends in New Jersey, Westchester and Connecticut. A jolly guest, a fascinating storyteller, all her hosts agreed.

Mayling, invited to receive an honorary degree from the University of Michigan in 1958, combined the overseas sojourn with a medical checkup. Catching the Asian flu as it spread across much of the world that winter, she again felt the need for a physical exam from her New York doctors—for in fact her neuro-dermatitis had again flared up. Her address on July 10 at Ann Arbor warned against Cold War disarmament by the free world, noting that it would leave it open to communist domination. Over the next five months she crisscrossed the country defining and interpreting the threat of communism in speeches at meetings and conclaves of the American Bar Association in Los Angeles, the American Legion and its auxiliary in Chicago and the Naval War College in Newport, Rhode Island.

To Washington's National Press Club: "In reality, the danger today is not a hot war; the danger is the outcome of the soft tactic which the Russians have used so far with such skill."

Before the All-American Conference to Combat Communism, Indianapolis: "Communism in action today under the direction of the Kremlin is opportunism wedded to decit and nurtured in violence."

At the American Farm Bureau Federation gathering in Boston: "We have made Taiwan a lighthouse of freedom and a living symbol of courage and adversity not only to the hundreds of millions of our own countrymen on the mainland, but also to other peoples throughout Asia."

The full text of these speeches, published in Taiwan in 1959, was distributed by the Nationalist government.[8]

Apart from public appearances, Mayling developed a new interest—collecting antique and vintage furniture. She poked about Manhattan's Third Avenue shops for French collectors' pieces to furnish the country place of the Kungs. Usually she spoke pidgin English to shield her identity. Miss Garvey then would return to close the sale. On one such outing, the shopkeeper said Mayling looked very much like Mme Chiang Kai-shek. Miss Garvey agreed. "Many people think so, but not if you saw them together. Besides, I believe Mme. Chiang speaks better English."[9]

That winter, when Emma helped to dismantle the contents of the apartment of an old family retainer and companion of her mother, Amelia Clarke, Mayling insisted on seeing the place. Enamored of the bedroom pieces there— especially Emma's mother's bed with its decorative Chinese footboard—she asked: "Did your mother die in it?" "No," replied Emma, "no one had. But she gave birth in it." Emma realized what was back of the question because then she wouldn't worry about any of their ghosts coming back to haunt her. Mayling insisted on acquiring everything that Emma didn't want, and so the bed in which she was born, and a few matching pieces were tagged for delivery to the Kungs' Long Island house. Emma attached no special significance to her buying of furniture, calling it a whim, a way of amusing herself. Yet the association with Emma's family mattered greatly. "It comes full circle that the bed especially should go to my first Chinese friend. Since she lost many of her own family things on the mainland, these associations mean much to her."[10]

Close friends of Emma occasionally expressed annoyance that she virtually "hugged" Mme Chiang all to herself—and never had them meet her. Others criticized Emma for turning down invitations or canceling engagements when "her friend" was in the city. Her college roommate complained, "If I were only Chinese maybe you would spend some time with me." Emma agreed, describing it as being "socially immobilized" when waiting for an expected call from Mayling. A few journalist-pals wondered if she confided in her venerable school chum. Emma explained she was a combination of girlhood friend, court jester and errand girl, and let it go at that. Journalist and old China hand Irene Kuhn thought it a pity.

"I certainly don't want to get mixed up in gossip and rumors," Emma pointed out, "particularly of a political nature, what with all the Kungs."

Irene agreed and remarked that those family members had certainly caused much ill-will and trouble.

When a possible meeting with Mayling came into a conversation, Emma politely dismissed the idea. Had it never occurred to them, thought Emma, Mme Chiang had no desire to meet more people than she absolutely had to.

Emma put up the best defense she could. "They have no conception ... of all the pressures there are upon her, all the demands on anyone in a similar position."[11]

Speeches and interviews occupied much time. "I'm scheduled to appear on TV's *Meet the Press*. And I have several more speeches to national audiences—and have to research and write a different one for each occasion," she told Emma in a hurried phone call in 1958. I wish, thought Emma, she'd make those talks simpler, with shorter sentences, fewer highfalutin words.

The *Meet the Press* interview on September 21 revealed a tired-looking Mayling who spoke with deliberation—and fatigue—yet handled the questions adroitly.[12]

Several days afterwards, Emma's phone rang. Mayling, in bed with inflammation of back and shoulder muscles from a draft in the TV studio, summoned her uptown for lunch with school friends. Before the others arrived, Emma brought up the question of the Taiwan Straits Quemoy Island crisis with mainland China. "The Nationalists' opportunity of counting on a comeback attempt over the situation is foolhearty. The idea of America getting involved over the off-shore islands isn't popular." "I know it," Mayling admitted.[13]

In December 1958 she spoke to the national convention of the Farm Bureau in Boston. A brief visit to Wellesley followed. There, Mayling presented a set of her paintings to the new art center, which she termed "too modernistic." "I knew no one there. So much has changed. And I don't like the new addition to the library—it doesn't harmonize with its surroundings."[14]

Emma spent more time with her than any other U.S. visit—dozens of meals, gossipy evenings and overnights. Together, they watched television, often a movie. "As the amusingly old movie *42nd Street* went along, two or three times Mayling picked up her long Chinese gown and danced gaily around the room, imitating the steps, improvising a few wriggles & knicks of her own.... It was wonderful to see her in such good spirits."[15]

Mayling expressed a growing concern about Emma's future financial security. She was taken unaware when out of the blue Mayling offered her a job. "My nephew David owns a small factory in Miami which makes seats for airplanes. There is a general manager who does most of the selling, and a Chinese vice-president who is also treasurer. But they need another vice-president for follow-up. Would you take it? It pays $800 a month."

David Kung joined in to explain the set-up. The company had just received a million-dollar order from Trans-Canada airline. "The seats are not only very comfortable," he boasted, "but can be folded back against the fuselage in five minutes if the load is to be freight."

"This is quite out of my experience," explained Emma. "I'm not sure I could take office routine again, and after all, I'll be 65 in a few months, and that is usually considered retirement age."

"David, tell her again what the salary is." Both assumed her answer would be yes. "You can keep your apartment here in the city, but you'd have to have a car in Miami. If I could learn to drive one, you can, too. I'd do the job myself, if I were staying here. And I'll visit you there on my next trip. You should go with David and look over the place."[16]

Salubrious Miami Beach attracted Mayling. Broadcasting and publishing executive George B. Storer, a major anti-communist supporter of Chiang, warmly welcomed her and the Kungs to the hospitable city in the 1950s. Mayor Kenneth Oka and his wife entertained these VIP Chinese sojourners, too.

Emma thought about the business offer, acknowledging it was tempting and exciting. Perhaps if she were ten years younger and convinced she'd make a success of it. Yet, she feared complications. It could sometimes become very awkward to mix friendship and business relationships. "And I value her friendship very much indeed."

Several more laid-back occasions surprisingly revealed Mayling's thoughts about marriage. When talk in typical Chinese matchmaker fashion turned to finding a husband for her companion-secretary, Dorothy Garvey, a college chum stated rather smugly, "Every woman really wants to get married." Mayling strongly disagreed. "If I had my life to live again, I wouldn't marry, but see what I could do on my own."[17]

Mayling and Emma met frequently in Taipei or New York following the Nationalists' retreat to Taiwan. ABMAC continued its work there with health and social agencies, although Emma played an unofficial role while Mayling remained honorary chairman. (Mills–DeLong collection.)

Mayling, once more absent from Chiang for a lengthy spell, had divulged a bit of her real feeling toward domesticity and life with the Generalissimo.

In early 1960 Emma made the first of two around-the-world trips with European stopovers in Copenhagen, London and Paris, where this writer briefly joined her. Stock trading generated sufficient funds for first-class global travel. Indeed, success in buying and selling on Wall Street impressed friends to the degree that they often consulted her on their choice of stock investments. Even Mayling asked Emma to set up an account and handle transactions.

When the two met at the presidential residence in Taipei that year, Mayling invited her upstairs on the day of Emma's departure. She expected a check for deposit in Mayling's U.S. investment account. To her surprise, she was handed over ten $100 bills—a personal gift. Because of customs regulations, Emma later stuck the cash into an inner pocket of her purse, deciding the best procedure was simply to forget it was there.

Emma never quite gave up the idea of having more time in Taiwan, wishing it were somehow practical to spend half of each year overseas. "I know they spoil me badly—why?" she asked in her journal. "And yet in addition deep down somehow there is an empathy between the place, the people I know there & myself. And I am always stimulated and excited ... there is so much going on and being accomplished. The island itself is very beautiful, too; it would be fascinating to learn more about the natural history of it."[18]

Mayling's devotion to Wellesley and her classmates never faltered. For their 45th reunion in 1962 she unknowingly generated a bit of campus controversy.

Unable to attend, she, nonetheless, wished to be remembered, and thus sent from Taiwan 150 large handwoven bags with an embroidered Nationalist flag on one side. Upon receiving the shipment, the Alumnae Office alerted '17's reunion chairman. Doesn't she realize the bags would be controversial? The Chinese flag would constitute a visible endorsement of Chiang's government by Wellesley! Cooler heads prevailed. The college backed down, allowing the class to carry them in the reunion parade. Classmate Alice Acheson—wife of Truman's former secretary of state—however, was overheard to remark "anybody who wants can have this trash; I'm certainly not going to take it home."[19]

Mayling's health—always a concern—worried Emma, especially word of a gallstone operation at Taiwan Veterans' General Hospital, performed by Dr. George Humphreys, ABMAC officer and a professor of surgery, who flew out from New York to lead a team of five doctors in the OR. Recovery was so complete that in 1965 Mayling undertook an unofficial U.S. visit—and indefinite stay—to see family and special friends and make a few speeches. It began with a news conference in San Francisco at which she advocated quick destruction of Communist China's nuclear installations. These words expanded into a full-fledged campaign, more official than not, to urge bombing of mainland atomic sites. Quoting Churchill, she clearly stated: "Give us the tools and we shall finish the job." Wearing a traditional ankle-length *chi-pao* with the silver wings of the Nationalist air force on her left shoulder, she spoke to various organizations and TV audiences, notably again to *Meet the Press* viewers (October 31, 1965). Encouraged by public reaction to her main message, she settled in Washington with an entourage of eleven retainers and military aides, and leased a house belonging to realtor Leo Bernstein, a block or so from the residence of Secretary of Defense Robert McNamara. There, she tried to persuade the Johnson Administration to support Nationalist troop landings on the mainland as part of a general escalation of the war in Vietnam. Not quite the usual red carpet treatment, nonetheless in 1965 she managed to secure private conversations with members of the Senate and the House of Representatives, and briefly spoke at a luncheon given by the members of the Senate Foreign Relations Committee. And she sipped tea with Lady Bird Johnson in the family quarters of the White House—the last presidential invitation to those historic lodgings. These "soft sell" Washington meetings tested the waters but provoked little action favorable to the Nationalists.

New York, her home away from home, welcomed her with a key to the city and a parade in Chinatown. Speaking in Mandarin, she eschewed her familiar military theme and spoke instead about the pleasure of her "homecoming." And similarly at a dinner of the Sino-American Amity Association, she mentioned her good fortune to visit New York's World's Fair. If not her country's primary envoy in the 1960s, she remained Free China's First Lady and acknowledged that "when one is in public life, it is difficult to say what is public and what is not." *The New York Times*, however, downgraded her to "Mrs. Chiang"; the "Madame" title of distinction no longer applied on its pages. It described her as a relic out of the past, and ran an unflattering photo. "If officials did not rush to greet her with open arms, it was partly because they did not know whether she was coming as friend, or advocate, emissary or tourist."[20]

Emma's acquaintances once more wondered if she had contacted her. Gerard, her apartment building elevator operator, asked if Emma had seen her yet. "If she did come here, she prefers not to be recognized," she replied.

"I wouldn't know her if she did appear," Gerard protested. "I've brought up so many Chinese to your apartment."

A good many residents in Emma's building had long known about her ties to Mayling—some had caught a glimpse of her in the lobby. They usually referred to her as "your friend"—rarely by name.

Thus began the usual round of calls by Mayling, and uptown visits by Emma. T.V. Soong's co-op at 1133 Fifth Avenue served as Mayling's city quarters. A number of old China hands criticized the public relations aspect of her latest visit. Not unexpectedly, David and Jeannette Kung had taken over, blocking access and causing delays in appointments and appearances. Elizabeth Luce Moore asked her to the China Institute and was turned down. "She has now gone to Europe in a huff," recorded Emma, "as has her brother Henry Luce, & said that neither the China Institute or United Services to China [replacing United China Relief] would take part in a large joint Waldorf dinner being considered by the China organizations—and Moore controls both boards. Dr. George Armstrong, recently chosen ABMAC president, had written Mayling & received an unsatisfactory reply from David. A second letter hasn't been answered. Why did she hedge herself in with these two [Kungs]?"[21]

Emma had long observed the low level of efficiency of these family members, and their concern, it seemed, with reflected glory. "With Mayling's emphasis on staying perpetually young, the Kung children can never grow up. The collective sense of humor is cruel, and tears down & ridicules other people. All the fuss over 'hush-hush' is absurd."[22]

Nostalgia for her youthful past brought Mayling back to Macon and the campus of Wesleyan. Accompanied by Georgia senator Richard Russell, Mayling addressed the Fall Convocation. When the auditorium organist played the school's alma mater, she fought unashamedly against tears. After her speech she met a thousand students and reconnected with friends of more than 40 years past, among them, her French teacher Lucy Lester.

A White House invitation for tea from Lady Bird Johnson in 1965 ended with a brief chat with the President on the second-floor balcony. Mayling came to Washington as a "private person" but received a grand welcome on Capitol Hill and from the State Department. (LBJ Library Photograph by Yoichi Okomoto.)

A similar Wellesley homecoming in December 1965 went off without a hitch. Emma rounded up close classmates, who after making housing arrangements at Boston's Ritz-Carlton were switched into the campus College Club at Mayling's expense. As Mayling thought of additional invitees, it was Emma's job to contact each. Finally Emma told her to stop having ideas. "All of which is important only as a concrete example of how badly things are handled for her." Not so with her security measures. In addition to her two personal safety men, the Boston police assigned two detectives to her party from the minute she exited the Massachusetts Turnpike.[23]

President Margaret Clapp had noted that most students knew nothing of China except the views of mainland Communists, so Madame Chiang insisted on giving them a talk on Chinese history since the overthrow of the Qing dynasty and founding of the Republic.

More than 800 students clamored impatiently for seats in Alumnae Hall to hear "Wellesley's most illustrious alumna"—and maybe afterwards shake her hand, even get her autograph, and have something to tell their grandchildren. In a sure and unwavering voice, Mme Chiang satisfied the emotional curiosity of her audience, largely unsympathetic to her political position. She defended her beliefs about China—the Communists were not the legitimate government of China, having taken over the mainland with "gull and gall." Her vest pocket review of the Chinese Republic was specific and factual, albeit slanted, and veiled in philosophical terms, particularly in her abstract, often ambiguous, discussion of the spread of Communist thought. Interspersed with pompous words—recherche, escheated, ineluctably, acoluthic—that elevated talk that annoyed Emma—the presentation, nonetheless, satisfied her audience with the eloquent voice of a respected and powerful world figure, imbued with mutual consideration and personal integrity. She maintained a great sense of who she was.[24]

But elsewhere, a growing bitterness toward Mayling festered. ABMAC's executive assistant Allen Lau lashed out at her and her entourage while at lunch with Emma. "She is doing more harm than good here. Soon stories will appear that she had better go home. But they don't want her in Taiwan." She agreed with much of his outburst. "She certainly is a spoiled brat in many ways, & inconsiderate in her demands, no realization of what it means to the other fellow. She feels free to call upon just about anybody, disregarding their assigned duties."[25]

Mayling's visit stretched well into 1966. That spring she commenced a full agenda of speeches beginning in Washington at the Industrial College of the Armed Forces and National Press Club, and leading on to the Economic Club of Detroit, the nearby School of Government at Grosse Point, and the Executives' Club of Chicago. Her audiences, now less high-level policy-oriented, chiefly were composed of businessmen, congressional wives, ladies "who lunch," and legislative assistants. Mao's cultural revolution swept the mainland by mid–1966. Mayling emphasized its impact in an address at Wesleyan University in Lincoln, Nebraska, stating the Red Guards organization of the Chinese Communist regime was "bent on world enslavement" and "metamorphosing itself into a hot explosion upon gathering momentum in its rampaging destructiveness." During her last weeks in the States on the West Coast that October, she dwelled on the impact of the proletarian cultural revolution in talks at Los Angeles's World Affairs Council and San Francisco's Commonwealth Club.[26]

In New York during the year-long stay, Mayling enjoyed the occasional opportunity to chat and poke around Emma's apartment. Collecting odds and ends, she relished Mills' old dinnerware and silver pieces, and asked Emma's advice on where to find similar items. She remarked on various lamps, tables, paintings, even place mats and paper napkins. A down-to-earth, pleasant and inquisitive Mayling. If only more people could see her like this, if she could only always be like this, concluded Emma.[27] Mayling's New Year's gift that day overwhelmed her hostess: several bottles of Scotch and Bristol Cream, plus a case of bourbon, Emma's favorite hard liquor.

Increasingly, Mayling expressed concern over Emma's financial situation. Did she have enough money to continue not working? Did she need any money? "You can always count on me," she repeated from time to time. Her letters of these years were brief and non-committal to a degree and usually contained a request to do something, chiefly ordering books, renewing magazine subscriptions and buying special articles of clothing.

On an early May afternoon as Emma prepared dinner, Mayling phoned. "I want to show you something. I have moved to a new address."

Emma immediately put aside kitchen chores and headed uptown to an upper East Side apartment at 10 Gracie Square. Mayling had moved into a duplex, taken in the name of her youngest brother, T.A. Soong, now living in San Francisco. The opulent 18-room co-op, overlooking Carl Schurz Park with East River views, would be her last residence. Emma noted that the master bedroom alone seemed big enough to live in; the walk-in closet just off of it held three long bars jammed with dresses. "Isn't it about time you gave some of thoses clothes to the Salvation Army?"

"Nobody would want them; they're Chinese."

Emma asked how she acquired a quaint little rocker in her bedroom. Mayling explained the chair had been a gift from the Brazilian governor of San Paulo and made by prison labor years back. She thought the surface of the wood had broken off on two rough places on the lower part of the back. Emma felt it, and commented that the wood was there, only unfinished and covered with glue.

"The colonels can fix it," referring to her aide, Colonel Sung of the Air Force, and another high-ranking officer.

"He's probably going out of his mind with so little to do," added Emma.[28]

She wanted Emma to look over a speech prepared for the Executives' Club of Chicago to weed out any grammatical errors. Minor changes were suggested, such as giving numbers instead of saying "many" refugees fleeing Red China, and adding a sentence indicating a probable Communist fear of a program of exchange visits by scholars which could lead to defections. Working closely together, Emma noted some perceptible hearing loss by Mayling. And she herself referred to it.

After several visits to the new co-op, the elevator man recognized Emma. Did she know "her" pretty well? "Classmate." Was my husband still in China? "He might be. I hadn't found him yet myself!"

22

Milestones

By the time Mayling began packing her bags for a return to Taiwan, Chiang had already sent word that he wanted her back by his side. Aides found his speech nearly impossible to decipher when his false teeth were removed and misplaced. Only his wife could fully understand him in such situations. Perhaps apocryphal, yet it reinforced the call to Mayling to come home.

By 1967 feelings and reactions over the war in Vietnam arose throughout much of the world. In Hong Kong, Communists were encouraging blatant mischief. At the True Light Middle School, Emma noticed their painted slogans in red on the outside wall of its compound. A bundle of propaganda leaflets, discovered in a toilet in a campus building, was equaling disturbing. Mayling reacted to another war in Asia by setting in motion a "Clothing Drive for Vietnam Refugees," seeking to collect one million garments. A few months later the superintendent of the Hua Hsing Children's Home died. Established by her for the education of homeless orphans of national martyrs, it needed a new director. She would "break in" the person chosen.

In New York more and more sentiment against the Vietnam war grew. "The breakdown in law and order, sense of responsibility, sense of values, makes one wonder," Emma observed. "But I have lived long enough to know nothing remains the same, nothing is final. An optimist by nature. And what is the difference between an optimist and a pessimist? The optimist wakes up and says: 'Good morning, God'; the pessimist wakes up and says: 'Good God, morning.'"[1]

Mayling returned to Taiwan in 1966. But the following year she flew back to New York to attend a memorial service for 86-year-old H.H. Kung, Ailing's husband.

Once again, a death in her family brought Mayling to the States. In 1969 the youngest Soong brother, T.A., chairman of the Bank of Canton, succumbed to a heart attack at age 61.[2] A grief-stricken Mayling flew to California, as did Ailing, from a sickbed in New York. Feverish throughout the service at San Francisco's Grace Cathedral, Ailing afterwards accompanied her sister to Honolulu. There, she rested, but remained ill. She continued on to Taiwan, where

ABMAC executive Allen Lau relaxes with Madame Chiang at an opening of a rehabilitation facility in Taiwan in the 1970s. At the end of that decade, after 35 years with the Bureau, Lau retired as director for programs and field activities. (Courtesy of Shirley Lau Mow.)

with a temperature of 104 degrees and teeth chattering, she required constant nursing care for some ten days. A severe case of pyelitis complicated Ailing's flu-like symptoms. Her convalescence at Sun Moon Lake, a mountain resort, led to a full recovery.

Emma recalled T.A. Soong's youth, remembering her Shanghai days and visits with him and Mayling to the renowned Chocolate Shop for ice cream. And he had never forgotten all the letters received by his sister when she first came home to China. He once remarked that if he saw Emma's handwriting decades later, he'd easily recognize it.

Two years later, in San Francisco, the family's savvy banking whiz died. Called by many the "Alexander Hamilton of China," because of his ability to negotiate multi-million-dollar loans from American and British sources, T.V. Soong choked from food lodged in his windpipe. And in 1973 Ailing became the third Soong to die in four years. Mayling had flown to New York just weeks before her oldest sister's death. She did not linger in the States. Chiang, frail and mentally losing his grip, needed her at his side more than ever. He had made his last public appearance in July 1972; his son, Chiang Ching-kuo, became premier, virtually second in command. Mayling now received important visitors on the Generalissimo's behalf. In spite of strong pockets of opposition and the work of the Committee of a Million for signatures, Communist China would gain membership into the United Nations and be determined to liberate Taiwan. Red China's relations with the United States grew stronger in the administration of President Richard Nixon. Taiwan had prospered mightily with U.S. help, but now stood able to reject all American nonmilitary assistance.

Mayling's role in bringing the Republic of China to the forefront among Asian nations was not overlooked. She received the first Chungshan Medal from the KMT for tremendous achievement in advancing the nation's foreign relations, promoting the women's anti–Communist movement, and leading charity and public welfare programs.

Chiang, in and out of Taipei General Hospital during the winter and spring of 1975, died there of heart failure on April 4. The last of the wartime Allied Big Four, the 87-year-old general's dying wishes were to fulfill Sun Yat-sen's Three Principles, and to recover the mainland, and to restore China's national culture. Most American observers, however, viewed his legacy in a different light. "His traditional Chinese techniques of rule in a modern political philosophy," one of them wrote, "came out sounding so fascist that they had to be disguised for Western audiences."[3]

His son Ching-kuo, more in tune with democratic ways, automatically succeeded him as president. Mayling seems to have harbored the genuine hope of filling her husband's shoes in that capacity. Who was more well-informed, accomplished and experienced, with decades at the side of the Generalissimo, to lead Free China? she thought. But after all, a possible coup by her aging backers never came into focus.

Mayling's detailed account of the outpouring of intense grief by people throughout Taiwan reached Emma in mid–May 1975. "Literally millions of them came out of their homes, many riding buses, bicycles, scooters, motorcycles and their own cars overnight from one end of the island to the other to pay their respects to the President, tearful, kneeling, wailing, prostrate…. My heart went out to them, to these generous, magnificent people whom I must serve as I have always served…. His spirit truly lives on in them, who responded to his call to crusade for freedom really 'with one heart and one mind' as in the lyrics of our National Anthem."[4]

But Mayling after nearly 50 years at the side of the general soon faced the most overwhelming medical crisis in her life. Cancer, discovered in a breast, necessitated immediate attention. She entered a Taiwan hospital for its removal. Doctors voiced pessimism; several indicated only three months to live. Following the operation, Mayling mustered strength to fly to New York for further medical care. Once again, Emma would be on call.

On October 17 she boarded a train to the Kungs' Long Island estate, where her classmate awaited her. "Mayling looks much the same, but has help on steps. Right arm pains her from the breast removal as does her left leg, due to whip lash [from a 1969 auto accident that injured her spinal cord with resultant pain in her right arm and left leg]. Has two Secret Service men, and brought over two of her own, a trained nurse, amah, cook, etc."[5]

There were Kung children in and out of the Locust Valley house left to them by their parents. For greater privacy, Mayling summoned her driver and security guards, and she and Emma went off on an hour's drive in her limo. "It's a '66 model with only 13,000 miles. My nephew wants to trade it in. I said 'no.'"

Months went by without any visits, not even a word from her. Then, in March 1976, Emma's phone rang. A woman asked, with a slight accent, for Miss Mills. Then, another woman came on the line; it was a half a minute or so before Emma realized it was Mayling. "She never identifies herself, & Miss Garvey doesn't name her, either.... Mayling's voice was so changed this time. She said she had been 'very sick' for three and a half months. Skin and nerve condition."[6]

She explained that she was flying off to Taiwan for the first anniversary of her husband's death, and the traditional Chinese "tomb sweeping day."

Meanwhile, Emma's last major involvement with a Chinese benevolent group had occupied countless hours a week, beginning in the mid–1960s. This association stemmed from her long acquaintance with the daughter of Chinatown doctor Farn Chu. Marylin Chu Chou persuaded her to join the board of the Chinatown Planning Council, a volunteer helping-hand community service amalgamation chiefly led by social workers. Her experience in organizational direction, administrative skills and fund-raising soon put the group on track. Besides Marylin, she knew only one other in the group. "They are chiefly concerned about a 500% increase in Chinatown's juvenile delinquency," she wrote after attending her third meeting in the tenement-like rooms of the Community Service Society at 34 Mulberry Street.[7]

Known as the CPC, it faced the influx of Chinese refugees from overseas. Some 500 a month being airlifted to New York needed help to adjust to living in the city. As committees were formed, Emma joined three, charged with everything from drawing specifications for the job of executive director to researching foundations to find which might be persuaded to fund the group. "So far, they are all taking my prodding very well, and one has even said to me I should be president." And, indeed, in 1968 Emma moved into that office, serving as the first non–Chinese and woman. "I am the only one who doesn't have a full-time job, so a lot of the detail work falls on me, but even I have only 24 hours in each day."[8]

As CPC president, Emma conveyed a significant degree of "toughness" to the group with no adverse repercussions among the staff. "She brought a tremendous amount of goodwill to the Board," recalled Allen B. Cohen, executive director at the time. "Emma was a unifying force because of her age, familiarity with China, and ties to Mme. Chiang. She had no personal ax to grind."⁹ Regular meetings ensued as did approved minutes—all basic if an organization sought government and foundation monies. She even donated a modest holding of Lucky Stores, Inc., for a reserve fund.

"Understand less than ever why anybody wants to be president of the U.S. or mayor of N.Y.," she concluded. "We even are mixed up with the teachers' strike, which is basically a fight between unionism and some of the militant ethnic groups who want to take over the management of the schools. We have opened our building for emergency classes, taught largely by striking teachers who are volunteering their services, but have refused to take one side or the other, though pressured to do so. Boy, what I am learning!"[10]

Emma's purely personal social engagements were put on the back burner. When she was not at CPC or on the phone for its behalf, she was exhausted, and often resorted to dusting books or cleaning closets as a sort of at-home occupational therapy to counteract mental fatigue. The Hong Kong True Light School Foundation long since had taken over her apartment's guest room. As treasurer, she housed files and office equipment there, along with guest mailing lists for the bimonthly benefit banquets at local Chinese restaurants—gourmet dining/social outings at a modest price.

Mayling never attended these dinners. While she indicated that New York now would be her home and visits to Taiwan infrequent, she played no visible role in Chinese-American cultural or community activities. ABMAC marked its 40th anniversary in 1977 but she declined to appear at its celebration. Emma helped with her message to be read at its commemorative dinner. Mme Chiang considered herself a private citizen, and Emma at their occasional lunches together found her more relaxed and in better health than for ages. Mayling expressed interest in the study of Western style art, with oil paints on canvas instead of water colors on paper. "And she has done an excellent job on rearranging some of the [co-op apartment] rooms and Chinese art objects."[11]

At her New York quarters or the Long Island country house, food and its preparation was important to Mayling. Usually too much had been cooked and served. When Emma came as a guest, Mayling insisted she take home a shopping bag of leftovers along with one or two Chinese candies and delicacies. "When I'm up to it, I am going to come to your apartment and cook a meal just for you."

Hooked on American TV, Mayling often lay in her bed and tuned in detective series, especially Perry Mason and Ellery Queen. She even enjoyed commercials. If not TV-watching, she'd want to play bridge or Scrabble, or just nap.

When Emma visited, talk often turned to books. Mayling once raised the question of how prolific author Pearl Buck managed to make a literary career for herself. "She graduated from a small college, and had no post-graduate work," Mayling stated, in error.[12] (The daughter of missionaries, Buck grew up in China, and graduated from renowned Randolph-Macon College in Virginia. She also received an M.A. degree from Cornell.)[13]

"Writing ability is in-born," Emma replied, "not the result of formal education." She later thought she might have asked her if Shakespeare had had a Ph.D. Before Emma left for home one afternoon, Mayling asked her to track down in used book stores two copies of the original *Arabian Nights*. She had read from it to her two youngest nephews when they visited in Taiwan, and now wished to read these stories to their children.

Mayling's concern over Emma's well-being increased as they grew older. She worried about her use of the subway and daily walks throughout poor neighborhoods in lower Manhattan. Why not take a cab? Mayling became obsessed with fears of a mugging. And she thought it peculiar that Emma rejected television. Several times she wanted to give her a set but Emma made it clear she'd never bring one into her apartment.

Well into her 80s, Emma maintained a routine of daily marketing, desk work and reading, and walking. New books continued to pile up on her bed table. They, as always, would be put aside to prepare for dinner guests and overnight visitors. Meetings in Chinatown, of course, took priority, but as Emma was experiencing diverticulosis, her trips beyond the city virtually ended. Then, one warm August 1981 evening, upon entering the Museum of Natural History, she fell. Guards called for emergency medical attention. An ambulance rushed her to nearby Roosevelt Hospital where doctors discovered a broken right wrist. She had left home without any identification or money other than carfare. In a state of shock and confusion, Emma could provide no address or next of kin. Hospital staff at first considered her a homeless derelict of some sort. When she began to talk of her close friendship with Mme Chiang, it merely re-enforced their view of a delusionary patient.

Her daily newspapers piled up at her apartment door. Worried neighbor Joseph Kissane remembered she had spoken of going to an event at the museum. He contacted Roosevelt Hospital in that uptown neighborhood and it verified her confinement. Kissane, dean of students at Columbia's School of General Studies, visited her on a number of Sundays. "She didn't really know what happened, and seemed disoriented and not all there."[14]

Although in a cast, the fiercely independent Emma refused outside help, certainly not a nurse's aide. She returned to her time-tested routine, including daily walks of a mile or so on clear days and periodic meetings by subway in Chinatown. She kept in touch by phone with her circle of friends, although the college gang had shrunk in numbers by the 1980s. As always, she waited for Mayling to initiate contact. Apparently, she did not know of Emma's accident. Overnight guests dwindled to Irene Shao, the woman whom she had educated some 30 years earlier, and Chinese ambassador Chen Chi-mai's daughter and granddaughter—Kitty Dean, a college professor, and Cecilia Dean, a future fashion model and journalist. They noticed a decline, physically and mentally, in her determination to keep up to a long-established level of energy and comprehension. She became fixated with "fall" housekeeping all year around, and

Cosmopolitan New Yorker Emma Mills joins the author at a Broadway show opening in 1980, shortly after celebrating her 86th birthday. (Courtesy of Thomas DeLong.)

going through junk mail, piece by piece. The fear of another debilitating fall grew, apparently not in Emma, but in those close by who realized she had failed.

And then it happened. A neighborhood contemporary in early 1984 phoned Emma for several days without getting an answer. She called Joseph Kissane to investigate. With a key from the superintendent, he entered her apartment and found her fully dressed sitting on the living room floor, with one leg under her in a very awkward position. "Let's get you up, and see what we can do." Kissane maneuvered her into the bedroom. Unable to sit up, dehydrated and in pain, she needed immediate medical attention. Emergency medics rushed her to the hospital where doctors operated on a broken hip. She recovered physically to some degree but the fall—and several days of severe dehydration—resulted in advanced senility. For the next three and a half years, she remained in a foggy mental stage, confined to a nursing home wheelchair, recognizing no one. Mayling drove there to Southport, Connecticut, to visit one day in late 1984. But any meaningful communication proved futile. Battling pneumonia, Emma died, age 92, on August 26, 1987.[15] A remembrance gathering followed at the China Institute. Carved on her tombstone at Woodlawn Cemetery in the Bronx were three Chinese characters immortalizing her Sino-American ties.

For Mayling, the Manhattan and Long Island residences provided all the needs and amenities that a former First Lady could wish, or demand. Well staffed and guarded, these spacious dwellings easily accommodated visiting family members—nieces and nephews, and their children and grandchildren. The publication in 1985 of Sterling Seagrave's distorted, acid-tongued biographical *Soong Dynasty* so outraged Chinese historians in Taiwan (and presumably Mayling and her family) with the book's rumors, gossip and conjecture stated as fact and truth—especially the clan's ties to organized crime and theft of U.S. aid—that they placed a full-page detailed protest in *The New York Times*.[16]

Mayling's overseas travel subsided to a mere handful of flights to Taiwan in the 1980s. When sister Chingling Sun, vice chairman of the People's Republic, died of leukemia in Peking in 1981, Mayling ruled out attending her sister's memorial service there, although Communist leaders indicated she would be welcome. The American University Club and American Chamber of Commerce gave a banquet in her honor in Taipei in 1986—her first visit there in 10 years. She spoke on the long relationship of China and America. "We learn from history that we do *not* learn from history. It is also said that history does not repeat itself, yet you and I have seen history definitely repeating itself in this 20th Century."[17]

Several months later, the 100th anniversary of Chiang's birth brought her back. Meetings with senior party officials and old-guard generals led to speculation over whether there might be a role for her as a Nationalist leader. She attended the 1988 convention of the party where, after brief words of a personal greeting, her speech was read by a party official. Chiang's son, Chingkuo, had died in office that year. His designated successor, Lee Teng-hui, a native Taiwanese, added party chairman to his duties. His leadership ended a Chiang family dynasty—and was considered a plus for democracy.[18]

Living in near total seclusion, she turned down requests for interviews. At the North Shore estate, she welcomed the extra surveillance by the local police, and instructed her staff to deny all knowledge of her whereabouts to outsiders. Few ever caught a glimpse of this neighborhood recluse. When she did venture outside her apartment building she insisted that the elevators and lobby be cleared of all other residents and guests. Her family increasingly

Senate Majority Leader Bob Dole (above) called Madame Chiang Kai-shek "the last icon of World War II" when he and Senator Paul Simon welcomed her back to the halls of Congress in 1995. Age 98, and rarely seen in public, she had become tagged as the "Chinese Garbo of New York City." (AP Wide World Photographs.)

surrounded and isolated her. Her nephews and nieces closed the door to the public and outside world. They gave no encouragement to their aunt to compose her memoirs and produce an autobiography.

She surprised Washington and old China hands by accepting a nonpolitical invitation from Senators Bob Dole and Paul Simon to a reception and luncheon on Capitol Hill in 1995. A Congress in session had last seen her 52 years earlier when she addressed both houses and won the acclaim and admiration of the nation. Simon, a son of Lutheran missionaries in China, pointed out that she was the only major figure left from World War II. "This is a gesture of friendship to the Chinese people." Age 98, she had become a World War II icon.[19]

The New York establishment, too, had its moment with Mayling not long after. In a rare appearance she toured an exhibition of Chinese art treasures at the Metropolitan Museum. When photographers annoyed her by constantly taking her picture, she poked her walking stick in their direction and swore, "I'm going to break your cameras."[20]

With no outside to-do, she marked her centennial both by the Chinese calendar in 1996 (which at birth adds a year to a person's age) and by Western calculation in 1997. The New York press made brief notice of her natal milestones of advanced age beyond one hundred. Elsewhere, many newspaper readers wondered if she were still alive, and critics of old re-surfaced with accusations of extravagance and repression of dissidents in her role as First Lady.

Called by the Manhattan media, the Chinese Garbo of New York City, Mayling virtually never stepped out in public, and during the last years restricted her guests to close family members. Her Wellesley godchild Shirley Paxton, daughter of college "big sister" Dickey Lightner, had tea there once a year until Mayling's secretary ruled out visits when it became apparent she failed to recognize people. Hospitalized with flu-like symptoms at the time of her l06th birthday in March 2003, the frail centurion rallied, then returned home to Gracie Square. She had wished never to end her days in a hospital or nursing facility, as did Emma Mills 16 years before. That fall she developed pneumonia and died in her sleep October 24. Her niece, her husband and a step great-grandson were with her. Their protective shield remained in place, even after death. No death certificate would exist in city vital records. One of the world's most admired women 17 times in Gallup polls, Mayling's formidable life touched three centuries. Her exact birth date she never publicly resolved; many accounts of her death subtracted a year. But Emma and Wellesley records got it right: March 20, 1897.

Reports of the passing of old China's voice to the outside world took countless readers by surprise. Her life, so quiet and seclusive, had led many to believe she had died years earlier. Mayling shirked the limelight after leaving Taiwan in the 1970s. Accounts of her formidable role as a charismatic spokesperson and assertive force behind her husband reminded readers of what a powerful global figure she became in the defining events of the 20th century. Nonetheless, the corruption and incompetence of the Chiang era counterbalanced her achievements and humanitarian work.[21]

Deemed a heroic woman of her time, Mayling was memorialized at gatherings in Taipei, London and Washington. In New York streams of mourners at the Frank Campbell chapel included middle-age "orphans" whose fathers died fighting the Japanese. They were "her children," and she, their "mama," had kept in touch with many.[22]

At a memorial service in St. Bartholomew's Church on Park Avenue, former Senator Paul Simon described Mayling "as a person of small physical stature but in every other way, a giant." Mayling wanted to be buried in China, but not in her communist-dominated native land. So her remains were temporarily placed in the Kung family mausoleum in Ferncliff Cemetery, Westchester County, near the body of sister Ailing. The Generalissimo's remains lay half a world away on the grounds of his favorite retreat at Tzuhu near Taipei. Hope for eventual joint burial on the mainland endures, albeit fading.

Epilogue

Mayling and Emma, friends for more than three score years, had seen their lives shift and modulate. Emma, beset with generational hurdles, floundered in trying to utilize her first-rate education—initially in the medical profession, then in journalism and creative writing. It took a war to set her on a course toward a structured and self-fulfilling "re-birth." A signal from far-off China re-connected her with Mayling, and encouraged much-needed Chinese-American friendship, together with tangible aid to sustain a country Emma knew well and loved, and often dreamed of. Emma's role with organizations and groups benefiting the Chinese people continued long past the defeat and withdrawal of Japanese soldiers at the close of World War II.

Mayling had reached the apex of her influence and acclaim when, as China's First Lady, she visited the United States and the Roosevelt White House, toured the country from coast to coast, secured millions of dollars for aid from Washington and private sources, and attended the Cairo Conference with the recognition of China as a major world partner and United Nations founder.

Cessation of hostilities diminished the praise—and U.S. monetary support. Civil war and the loss of the mainland undercut some of her effluence. Yet her clarion call segued into a fervid anti–Communist message and the belief that her husband and Free China one day would return in triumph to Nanking.

From Taiwan Mayling inspired and guided programs to improve public health, child well-being, education and agriculture. Aspects of her legacy from the 1930s—the New Life Movement—thrived in untried and challenging settings.

Yet dark clouds often hung over her. Surrounded by greedy relatives capitalizing on their high-level clout to enrich themselves, Mayling became a willing party to those filling already overflowing private coffers. Their mercenary actions overshadowed the principles of Sun Yat-sen. At home and abroad, the First Lady of China became tarnished by the perceptible graft and corruption of her very own family.

Mayling stayed in the public eye, albeit her influence and magnetism dimmed as did expectation for her government's return to the mainland. Many of the old China hands had left her side by the time the Generalissimo died in 1975, save Emma Mills. Their singular friendship and emotional bond remained strong. And Emma's life, once one of agonized introspection and chronic dissatisfaction, had become richer and fuller by middle age.

Public recognition for Emma came unexpectedly shortly after her 80th birthday in 1974. At a True Light Foundation benefit dinner in New York, friends surprised her with a tribute for her work on Chinese-American causes. Associates from the American Bureau for Medical Aid to China, the China Institute, Chinatown Planning Council, Hong Kong True Light School Foundation and American-Chinese Policy Association, as well as dozens of other friends and acquaintances, saluted her China connections, as did Chinese Consul General in New York Konsin C. Shah, representing the Nationalist government. And from Taipei came special greetings. A cable from Mayling read: "Warmest congratulations to my friend Emma Mills. I only wish I could do it in person. To paraphrase Ecclesiastes, she has rejoiced in her labor. This is the gift of God. Emma is dedicated to people. For herself she asks only the opportunity to serve. Her life has been and is one of the richest and most rewarding to herself and others."[1]

In response, the overwhelmed honoree spoke of their Wellesley ties and her childhood interest in China—beginning with the Chinese scenes with quaint gardens, pond and bridge on the footboard of her mother's lacquered bed. "You remember it?" she asked Mayling in a letter describing the tribute. "I ended up by saying I was a bit disturbed by the presence of True Light and Chinatown Planning representatives, as each group might get the impression I was giving too much time to the other, which brought a laugh. And I couldn't get to sleep that night until after two."[2]

Her thoughts that night whirled around the beginning of their long and endearing friendship, a constant year after year, save the brief hiatus early in Mayling's marriage. The words of Kipling came to mind:

> I have eaten your bread and salt.
> I have drunk your water and wine.
> The deaths ye died I have watched beside
> And the lives ye led were mine.

Chapter Notes

Chapter 1

1. Letter, Mayling Soong to Emma Mills, August 16, 1917.
2. Helen Nicolay, *China's First Lady* (New York: Appleton-Century, 1944), p. 34.
3. Emma Mills, journal, June 4, 1922.
4. Louise Revere Morris, "Tells of Madame Chiang's Stay Here," *Summit Herald*, May 21, 1942. Because Miss Potwin's was co-ed, the community sought a select all-girls' school and in 1894 established Kent Place School.
5. Eunice Thomson, "Soong Sisters of China: Wesleyan's Most Famous Alumnae," *Georgia Magazine-Macon Telegraph*, March 2, 1941.
6. Mary C. Lane, *Centennial History of Piedmont College, 1897–1997* (Demorest, Ga.: N.p., 1997), pp. 58–59.
7. Nicolay, *China's First Lady*, p. 44.
8. The Emma De Long Mills Papers, in possession of author, are chief sources of her early years. They include a taped conversation on October 8, 1976. The author enjoyed a close, personal kinship with Mills from 1959 to her death in 1987. Her recorded book-reading began at age 18 in 1913 with John Fiske's *Discovery of America*. The last recorded entry, in November 1983, was David Graham's *We Must Defend America*. The list totals some 3,500 titles, far short of the ambitious goal of 10,000.
9. Letter, Mayling Soong to Emma Mills, August 16, 1917.
10. *Ibid*.
11. Letter, Mayling Soong to Emma Mills, September 28, 1917.
12. Letter, Mayling Soong to Emma Mills, September 15, 1917.
13. Letter, Mayling Soong to Emma Mills, October 26, 1917.

Chapter 2

1. Letter, Mayling Soong to Emma Mills, January 13, 1918.
2. *Ibid*.
3. *Ibid*.
4. Letter, Mayling Soong to Emma Mills, January 31, 1918.
5. Letter, Mayling Soong to Emma Mills, February 8, 1918. By 1923 there were 8,325 American, British and Canadian missionaries in China, and approximately three million converts to Christianity in a country whose people were fundamentally not religious (Hallett Abend, *My Life in China, 1926–1941* [New York: Harcourt, Brace, 1943], pp. 367–81).
6. Letter, Mayling Soong to Emma Mills, February 8, 1918.
7. Letter, Mayling Soong to Emma Mills, February 13, 1918. A majority of Returned Students studied in American universities on a scholarship fund established in 1908 by money drawn from the Boxer Uprising indemnity paid to the United States. The Boxer Rebellion, an anti–Western attack in 1900–01 by fanatical peasants augmented by Manchu officials, killed some 200 foreigners and Chinese Christians, and damaged their property.
8. Letter, Mayling Soong to Emma Mills, December 7, 1918.
9. Letter, Mayling Soong to Emma Mills, August 24, 1918.
10. Letter, Mayling Soong to Emma Mills, September 21, 1918.
11. Emma Mills, journal, December 13, 1917.
12. Emma Mills, journal, January 17, 1918.
13. Letter, Mayling Soong to Emma Mills, received May 28, 1918.
14. Letter, Mayling Soong to Emma Mills, May 15, 1918.
15. Letter, Mayling Soong to Emma Mills, October 19, 1918.
16. Letter, Mayling Soong to Emma Mills,

August 15, 1918. Mayling refers to British statesman and historian Thomas B. Macauley, noted for immensely popular histories of ancient Greece and Rome.

Chapter 3

1. Professor Katherine Lee Bates (1859–1929) achieved enduring renown as composer of the words to the patriotic song "America the Beautiful" in 1893.
2. Helen Hull, *Mayling Soong Chiang* (New York: Coward-McCann, 1943) and Wellesley College Archives are the major sources on the Soong-Mills undergraduate years 1913–1917.
3. Hull, p. 18.
4. Letter, Emma Mills to Walter Mills, October 7, 1913. The letters from Wellesley by Emma to her father are in the College Archives: reference Class of 1917.
5. Frank P. Ball, "Recalls Wellesley Days with Madame Chiang Kai-shek," *Greenwich (CT) Press*, April 20, 1939.
6. Letter, Emma Mills to Ruth Fowler Oliver (class of '17), May 19, 1959.
7. Emma Wotton De Long, unedited manuscript "Explorer's Wife," author's collection.
8. "Fire Drill Saves 350 at Wellesley," *New York Times*, March 17, 1914; "Fire Hits Wellesley Hard," *New York Times*, March 20, 1914.
9. Emma Mills, journal, April 3, 1917.
10. "Mme. Chiang Tells of Her War Duties," *New York Times*, July 10, 1938.

Chapter 4

1. Between sophomore and junior years at Wellesley (1915), Mayling took a teaching course in education at the University of Vermont.
2. Letter, Mayling Soong to Emma Mills, April 15, 1919.
3. Letter, Mayling Soong to Emma Mills, April 4, 1919.
4. Letter, Mayling Soong to Emma Mills, January 7, 1919.
5. *Ibid.*
6. Letter, Mayling Soong to Emma Mills, June 5, 1919.
7. *Ibid.*; letter, Mayling Soong to Emma Mills, June 15, 1919.
8. *Ibid.*
9. Emma Mills, journal, January 8, 1919.
10. Letter, Mayling Soong to Emma Mills, April 9, 1919.
11. *Ibid.*
12. Emma Mills, journal, April 25, 1919.
13. Letter, Mayling Soong to Emma Mills, May 25, 1919.
14. *Ibid.*
15. Letter, Mayling Soong to Emma Mills, April 9, 1919.
16. Letter, Mayling Soong to Emma Mills, July 9, 1919.
17. Letter, Mayling Soong to Emma Mills, July 24, 1919.
18. *Ibid.*
19. Letter, Mayling Soong to Emma Mills, September 9, 1919.
20. *Ibid.*
21. Letter, Mayling Soong to Emma Mills, November 18, 1919.

Chapter 5

1. Letter, Mayling Soong to Emma Mills, February 11, 1920.
2. Letter, Mayling Soong to Emma Mills, October 11, 1920.
3. Letter, Mayling Soong to Emma Mills, January 24, 1920.
4. *Ibid.*
5. Letter, Mayling Soong to Emma Mills, March 21, 1920.
6. *Ibid.*
7. *Ibid.* Mills' journal from August 31 to November 4, 1919 describes work at Walter Reed Hospital and failed attempts for employment in Washington.
8. Letter, Mayling Soong to Emma Mills, September 5, 1920.
9. *Ibid.*
10. *Ibid.*
11. Letter, Mayling Soong to Emma Mills, October 11, 1920.
12. Letter, Mayling Soong to Emma Mills, February 11, 1920.
13. Letter, Mayling Soong to Emma Mills, October 11, 1920.
14. *Ibid.*

Chapter 6

1. Letter, Mayling Soong to Emma Mills, May 25, 1921.
2. Letter, Mayling Soong to Emma Mills, April 28, 1921.
3. *Ibid.*
4. *Ibid.*
5. *Ibid.*
6. *Ibid.*
7. Letter, Mayling Soong to Emma Mills, July 6, 1921.
8. *Ibid.*
9. Letter, Mayling Soong to Emma Mills, July 25, 1921.
10. Emma Mills, journal, July 21, 1921.
11. Letter, Mayling Soong to Emma Mills, August 10, 1921.
12. *Ibid.*
13. Letter, Emma Mills to Helen McKeag, December 7, 1921.

14. Letter, Emma Mills to Mandy Mandeville, January 22, 1922.

Chapter 7

1. Letter, Emma Mills to Sylvie Mills, April 6, 1922.
2. Letter, Mayling Soong to Walter and Sylvie Mills, March 30, 1922.
3. Emma Mills, journal, March 28, 1922.
4. Emma Mills, journal, April 2, 1922.
5. Emma Mills, journal, April 10, 1922.
6. Emma Mills, journal, July 23, 1922.
7. Letter, Emma Mills to Walter Mills, July 7, 1922.
8. Emma Mills, journal, May 13, 14 and 15, 1922.
9. "New Chinese Alliance Against Wu Pei-fu," *New York Times,* April 18, 1922.
10. H.H. Kung interview, Oral History Research Office, Columbia University, 1958.
11. Emma Mills, journal, May 1, 1922.
12. Emma Mills, journal, June 19, 1922.
13. *Ibid.*
14. Emma Mills, journal, June 29, 1922; "Mrs. Sun Yat-sen's Story of Escape from Canton," *Shanghai Gazette,* ca. July 1922.
15. Emma Mills, journal, June 29, 1922.
16. Emma Mills, journal, May 26, 1922; July 23, 1922.
17. Letter, Emma Mills to Sylvie Mills, July 28, 1922.
18. Letter, Emma Mills to Sylvie Mills, August 11, 1922.

Chapter 8

1. Sterling Seagrave, *The Soong Dynasty* (New York: Harper and Row, 1925), p. 8.
2. Mayling Soong Chiang, "Conversations with Mikhail Borodin," privately printed, 1978, p. 4.
3. Emma Mills, journal, September 3, 1922.
4. Letter, Emma Mills to Sylvie Mills, September 21, 1922.
5. Emma Mills, journal, November 9, 1922.
6. Letter, Emma Mills to Sylvie Mills, May 15, 1923.
7. Letter, Emma Mills to Walter Mills, March 28, 1923.
8. Letter, Emma Mills to Sylvie Mills, August 8, 1923.
9. Letter, Emma Mills to Walter Mills, March 28, 1923.
10. Letter, Emma Mills to Sylvie Mills, July 3, 1923. Pu Chieh later spelled his name "Pu Jie" (Christopher S. Wren, "Imperial China's Offspring Finds New China Noble," *New York Times,* November 21, 1984).
11. Emma Mills, journal, January 13, 1924.
12. Letter, Emma Mills to Emma W. De Long, January 16, 1923.

Chapter 9

1. A job survey in 1929 of the Class of 1917 alumnae placed secretarial and clerical work in first place, followed by teaching and school jobs, social service and medicine (including six MDs), and literary and dramatic employment. Typically, for that generation, the greatest number were housewives.
2. Emma Mills, journal, July 15, 1924.
3. Emma Mills, journal, February 8, 1924.
4. Letter, Emma Mills to Mandy Mandeville, May 4, 1924.
5. Letter, Emma Mills to Emma W. De Long, February 11, 1924.
6. *Ibid.*
7. Letter, Emma Mills to Sylvie Mills, July 2, 1924.
8. Letter, Emma Mills to Walter Mills, October 28, 1924.

Chapter 10

1. Letter, Emma Mills to Sylvie Mills, January 11, 1925.
2. Emma Mills, journal, January 9, 1925.
3. Margaret De Forest Hicks, "China an Odd Paradox of War and Business," *The New York Times,* April 5, 1925.
4. Letter, Dorothy Gould Bess to Emma Mills, October 8, 1925. Eugene Chen (1878–1944), an early supporter of Sun Yat-sen, was often at odds with Chiang. Nonetheless, he served as Nationalist foreign minister in 1931–32, and with several insurgent regimes before and after. With left-leaning tendencies, his allegiances fluctuated. Harbored by the Japanese with whom he earlier had conducted negotiations, Chen died in Shanghai.
5. Letter, Mayling Soong to Emma Mills, January 23, 1926.
6. *Ibid.*
7. Letter, Mayling Soong to Emma Mills, September 9, 1926.
8. Lewis Gannett, "New Strong Man Holds Half of China," *The New York Times,* November 14, 1926.
9. "Mme. Chiang Now in San Francisco," *The New York Times,* September 9, 1927.
10. Henry F. Misselwitz, "Chiang Blames Foes for Talk of 'Wife,'" *The New York Times,* September 25, 1927.
11. "Mayling Says She Will Wed Chiang," *The New York Times,* September 22, 1927.
12. Israel Epstein, *Woman in World History: Life and Times of Soong Ching Ling* (Beijing: New World Press, 1993), p. 209;

Samuel C. Chu, "Madame Chiang Kai-shek Between America and China," in *Madame Chiang Kai-shek and Her China* (Norwalk, Conn.: EastBridge, 2005), pp. 167–68.
13. Letter, Mayling Soong Chiang to Emma Mills, January 24, 1928.
14. *Ibid.*
15. *Ibid.*

Chapter 11

1. Henry F. Misselwitz, "Chiang Blames Foes for Talk of 'Wife,'" *New York Times*, September 25, 1927.
2. Elmer T. Clark, *The Chiangs of China* (New York: Abington-Cokesbury Press, 1943), p. 82.
3. Letter, Mayling Soong Chiang to Emma Mills, January 24, 1928.
4. Emma Mills, journal, January 31, 1929.
5. Emma Mills, journal, December 2, 1932.
6. Ch'en Chieh, *Chiang Kai-shek's Secret Past*, ed. Lloyd E. Eastman (Boulder, Colo.: Westview Press, 1993), p. xxi.
7. Ch'en, p. xxv.
8. Emily Hahn, *The Soong Sisters* (Garden City, N.Y.: Doubleday, Doran, 1941), p. 148. Beyond China, the Chiangs' New Life Movement frowned upon international Chinese-American film actress Anna May Wong's exotic and sinister portrayals of Chinese women—even chided her on the display of bare legs on and off screen.
9. "Six Noted Children at Bier of Mme. Soong; 'Mother-in-Law of the Chinese Revolution,'" *New York Times*, August 18, 1931; Hallett Abend, "Two Likely to Die in Attack on Soong," *New York Times*, July 23, 1931.
10. "24 in Plot To Slay Chinese President," *New York Times*, September 7, 1929.
11. "Chinese President Escapes Gunmen," *New York Times*, July 30, 1931.
12. Madame Chiang Kai-shek, "A Letter from China (August 1928)," *Wellesley Magazine* XV, no. 2 (December 1930). The Legislative Yuan chiefly debated and voted on new legislation. Its 80 or so appointed members had no true backing of elective or popular support. (Jonathan D. Spence, *The Search for Modern China* [New York: Norton, 1990], p. 365).
13. Hull.
14. Hallett Abend, "Chiang's Royal Aims Are Laid to His Wife," *New York Times*, December 9, 1928.
15. Hallett Abend, "Lindberghs Guests of Chiang and Wife," *New York Times*, September 26, 1931.
16. Emma Mills, journal, June 28, 1929.
17. Emma Mills, journal, June 8, 1933.
18. *Ibid.*
19. Emma Mills, journal, November 2, 1934.
20. Emma Mills, journal, June 10, 1935.

Chapter 12

1. "Warns of Tokyo's Plans," *New York Times*, December 31, 1935.
2. Emma Mills, journal, March 9, 1933.
3. Mayling S. Chiang, "Fighting Communists in China," *The Forum*, February 1935.
4. *Ibid.*
5. Robert Berkov, *Strong Man of China: The Story of Chiang Kai-shek* (Boston: Houghton Mifflin, 1938), p. 190.
6. Emma Mills, journal, January 29, 1936.
7. Emma Mills, journal, February 19, 1936.
8. "Big Birthday Fete Honors Gen. Chiang," *New York Times*, November 1, 1936.
9. Mayling S. Chiang, "Fighting Communists in China," *The Forum*, February 1935.
10. Lin Yutang, "A Chinese Gives Us Light on His Nation," *New York Times Magazine*, November 22, 1936.
11. Emma Mills, journal, June 10, 1936.
12. Hahn, *The Soong Sisters*, p. 227.
13. H.B. Elliston, "China's No. 1 White Boy," *Saturday Evening Post*, March 19, 1938, pp. 6–7; Jonathan Fenby, *Chiang Kai-shek* (New York: Carroll and Graf, 2004), pp. 10–11.
14. "China: Dictator Unkidnapped," *Time*, January 4, 1937.
15. W.H. Donald (1875–1946), in 1941, after 39 years in China, left for New Zealand to write his memoirs. But with a Pacific war looming, he soon set out to return to Chiang's headquarters in Chungking. While he was en route, the Japanese attacked Pearl Harbor, and his ship put in at Manila, where the Japanese captured him. As a prisoner, he cleverly hid his identity. Liberated three years later, he returned briefly to China to see the Chiangs, then settled in Australia. Ill health, however, brought him back to Shanghai, where he died and was buried. Donald never got to write his book.
16. Sterling Seagrave, *The Soong Dynasty*, pp. 353–4.

Chapter 13

1. Mayling Soong Chiang, "What Religion Means to Me," *The Forum*, March 1934.
2. Mayling Soong Chiang, *The Sure Victory* (Westwood, N.J.: Fleming H. Revell, 1945), p. 10.
3. Mme. Chiang, *The Forum*, March 1934.
4. "The Chiang Kai-shek Saga," *New York Times*, April 16, 1937.
5. "Mme. Chiang Opens Phone from China," *New York Times*, May 20, 1937.

6. Emma Mills, journal, March 10, 1938.
7. Emma Mills, journal, January 25, 1937.
8. Hanson W. Baldwin, "Lack of Equipment China's Weakness," *New York Times,* July 28, 1937.
9. "Madame Chiang Urges Women of China to Fight Japan, 'According to Their Ability,'" *New York Times,* August 2, 1937.
10. Emma Mills, journal, January 11, 1937.
11. Hahn, *The Soong Sisters,* p. 255.
12. Letter, Mayling Soong Chiang to Wellesley classmates, November 7, 1937.
13. Letter, Mayling Soong Chiang to Emma Mills, January 6, 1938.
14. Agnes Smedley, *Battle Hymn of China* (New York: Alfred A. Knopf, 1943), p. 206.
15. "International: Man & Wife of the Year," *Time,* January 3, 1938.
16. Letter, Emma Mills to Mayling Soong Chiang, December 7, 1937.
17. Letter, Emma Mills to Mayling Soong Chiang, February 1, 1938.
18. Letter, Emma Mills to Mayling Soong Chiang, May 9, 1938.
19. Letter, Mayling Soong Chiang to Emma Mills, April 23, 1938.
20. Letter, Mayling Soong Chiang to Emma Mills, April 26, 1938.
21. Hahn, p. 268.
22. *Ibid.*
23. Mayling Soong Chiang, "Are Treaties Dead?" *China in Peace and War: Selections from the Writings of Mayling Soong Chiang* (Shanghai: Kelly and Walsh, Ltd., 1940), p. 111.
24. "Duty to Husband, Says Mme. Chiang," *New York Times,* March 27, 1938.
25. Letter, Mayling Soong Chiang to Emma Mills, April 26, 1938.
26. *Ibid.*
27. Letter, Mayling Soong Chiang to Emma Mills, June 14, 1938.

Chapter 14

1. "Mme. Chiang Tells of Her War Duties," *New York Times,* July 10, 1938. Six weeks later a *Times* item from Shanghai spoke of Japanese censorship and confiscation of books and periodicals in the mails in the International Settlement. The censors cut the Sunday, July 10, section with the chatty quotes from Mayling's letters, particularly with her reference to "that huge walloping we gave the Japs" at Taierchwang, north of Hsuchow, in May 1938. This, the first great defeat by the Japanese, proved China could not be beaten into the dust.
2. Letter, Mayling Soong Chiang to Class of 1917, June 24, 1938.
3. Letter, Emma Mills to Mayling Soong Chiang, June 28, 1938.
4. *Ibid.*
5. Letter, Emma Mills to Mayling Soong Chiang, July 18, 1938.
6. Emma Mills, journal, August 26, 1938.
7. *Ibid.*
8. Letter, Mayling Soong Chiang to Emma Mills, June 28, 1938.
9. "Mme. Chiang Training New Youth Group: She Joins Girls in Doing Household Tasks," *New York Times,* October 20, 1938.
10. Letter, Mayling Soong Chiang to Emma Mills, September 22, 1938.
11. Letter, Mayling Soong Chiang to Emma Mills, September 26, 1938.
12. Letter, Mayling Soong Chiang to 1917 and other Wellesley friends, September 26, 1938.
13. Letter, Mayling Soong Chiang to Emma Mills, January 14, 1939.
14. *Ibid.*
15. *Ibid.*
16. Letter, Mayling Soong Chiang to Emma Mills, February 8, 1939.
17 Letter, Mayling Soong Chiang to Emma Mills, May 10, 1939; F. Tillman Durdin, "Chungking Is Fighting Vast Fires, Started by Japanese Bombing," *New York Times,* May 6, 1939.
18. *Ibid.*
19. Letter, Emma Mills to Mayling Soong Chiang, July 11, 1939.
20. Hallett Abend, "Chinese Ready for Long War," *New York Times,* May 14, 1939.
21. "Japanese Boycott Favored in Survey," *New York Times,* June 16, 1939.
22. Letter, Emma Mills to 1917er(s), May 15, 1939.
23. Letter, Emma Mills to Mayling Soong Chiang, January 10, 1939.

Chapter 15

1. Letter, Mayling Soong Chiang to Emma Mills, July 14, 1939.
2. Letter, Emma Mills to Mayling Soong Chiang, April 25, 1939.
3. *Ibid.*
4. "Seeks War-Orphan Aid, *New York Times,* October 16, 1939.
5. Letter, Mayling Soong Chiang to Emma Mills, September 10, 1939.
6. *Ibid.* A brief talk to the New York Herald-Tribune radio forum on October 26 did not get through to America—and not even as close as Manila—whether because of a technical mishap or deliberate blocking by the Japanese. "We have ordered a thorough investigation of our local broadcasting system and methods," Mayling explained.
7. Letter, Mayling Soong Chiang to Emma Mills, October 3, 1939.

8. Letter, Mayling Soong Chiang to Emma Mills, November 10, 1939.
9. *Ibid.*
10. Letter, Emma Mills to Mayling Soong Chiang, December 18, 1939.
11. Letter, Mayling Soong Chiang to Emma Mills, March 4, 1940.
12. Hahn, *Soong Sisters,* p. 310.
13. Hahn, p. 323.
14. Hahn, p. 325.
15. Hahn, p. 326.
16. Hahn, p. 328.
17. Hallett Abend, "Soong Riches Kept in Europe, Foe Says," *New York Times,* April 20, 1940.
18. "New Relief Drive for China Started," *New York Times,* November 16, 1940.
19. Donovan Webster, "Blood, Sweat, and Toil Along the Burma Road," *National Geographic,* November 2003.
20. Letter, Mayling Soong Chiang to Emma Mills, June 16, 1940. Wang Ching-wei (1883–1944) had played a significant part as an early backer of Dr. Sun and Chiang, yet was reluctant to yield to the latter's leadership. He urged appeasement and cooperation with Japan. The Nanking Japanese-created "puppet" government brought him notoriety but little autonomy. Wang died before war's end, while in Tokyo for medical treatment.
21. Letter, Emma Mills to Mayling Soong Chiang, May 27, 1940.
22. Letter, Emma Mills to Mayling Soong Chiang, June 10, 1940.
23. Letter, Emma Mills to Mayling Soong Chiang, July 22, 1940.
24. Letter, Emma Mills to Mayling Soong Chiang, October 28, 1940.
25. Letter, Emma Mills to Mayling Soong Chiang, June 10, 1940.
26. *Ibid.*

Chapter 16

1. "$5,000,000 Sought for Chinese Relief," *New York Times,* March 3, 1941.
2. Robert T. Elson, *Time, Inc: The Intimate History of a Publishing Empire 1923–1941* (New York: Atheneum, 1968), p. 471.
3. *Ibid.*
4. "First Lady Sends Gift to Mme Chiang," *New York Times,* May 9, 1941.
5. Letter, Emma Mills to Mayling Soong Chiang, June 30, 1941.
6. "Willkie Urges All to Aid the Chinese," *New York Times,* June 19, 1941.
7. Letter, Emma Mills to Mayling Soong Chiang, June 30, 1941.
8. *Ibid.* By July, however, large corporate and individual gifts boosted the total to some $2 million.

9. Letter, Emma Mills to Mayling Soong Chiang, April 4, 1941.
10. "Mme Chiang Delays Trip," *New York Times,* March 22, 1941.
11. Letter, Mayling Soong Chiang to Emma Mills, April 10, 1941.
12. Ilona Ralf Sues, *Shark's Fins and Millet* (Boston: Little, Brown, 1944), p. 158.
13. Sues, p. 167.
14. F. Tillman Durdin, "Worth Twenty Divisions," *New York Times Magazine,* September 14, 1941.
15. Emma Mills, journal, March 23, 1942.
16. Letter, Mayling Soong Chiang to Emma Mills, April 10, 1941.
17. *Ibid.*
18. Letter, Mayling Soong Chiang to Emma Mills, June 3, 1941.
19. Letter, Mayling Soong Chiang to Emma Mills, July 23, 1941.
20. Ramona and Desmond Morris, *Men and Pandas* (New York: McGraw-Hill, 1966), p. 95.
21. Emma Mills, journal, December 8, 1941. The Japanese captured Hong Kong, turning it into a military base. Residents suspected of opposing them were executed; many civilians spent the rest of the war in disease-ridden camps on the mainland.
22. *Ibid.*; Emma Mills, journal, January 5, 1942.
23. *Ibid.*

Chapter 17

1. Tong, *Dateline: China,* pp. 159–60.
2. Mayling Soong Chiang, "China Emergent," in *We Chinese Women: Speeches and Writings During the First United Nations Year* (New York: John Day Co., 1943), p. 34.
3. Sydney Greenberg, interview, July 7, 2004; "Wartime Rendezvous in China Recalled," *New Canaan (CT) Advertiser,* April 10, 1975.
4. Emma Mills, journal, May 24–28, 1958.
5. Mayling Soong Chiang, "China Emergent," pp. 14–15.
6. Seagrave, *Soong Dynasty,* p. 375.
7. Donovan Webster, *The Burma Road* (New York: Farrar, Straus and Giroud, 2003), p. 130. The improbable cargoes over the Hump included laxatives, chili powder, trash can lids, and live pigs.
8. Mayling Soong Chiang, "China Emergent," pp. 3–5.
9. Jonathan Fenby, *Chiang Kai-shek: China's Generalissimo and the Nation He Lost* (New York: Carroll and Graf, 2003), pp. 372–73.
10. "Chiang Ends Tour of Indian Frontier," *New York Times,* February 16, 1942.

11. Mayling Soong Chiang, "First Lady of the East Speaks to the West," *New York Times Magazine*, April 19, 1942.
12. "Dr. Hu Shih Sees a Better Peace," *New York Times*, June 16, 1942.
13. "Mme. Chiang Asks Equality of Races" *New York Times*, June 14, 1942.
14. Mayling Soong Chiang, "First Lady."
15. Harrison Forman, "Offensive in Asia Urged by Willkie," *New York Times*, October 4, 1942.
16. Harrison Forman, "Willkie To 'Howl' for a Free World," *New York Times*, October 5, 1942.
17. Jonathan Fenby, "The Sorceress," *The Guardian Review*, November 5, 2003.
18. *Ibid.*
19. Steve Neal, *Dark Horse: A Biography of Wendell Willkie* (Garden City, N.Y.: Doubleday, 1984), p. 256.

Chapter 18

1. Sterling Seagrave, *The Soong Dynasty* (New York: Harper and Row, 1985), p. 377.
2. *Ibid.*, p. 379.
3. Bert Andrews, "Mme Chiang Is in U.S. for Treatment," *New York Herald Tribune*, November 28, 1942; "Mme. Chiang Comes to America for Treatment of 1937 Injury," *New York Times*, November 28, 1942.
4. "Meets Mme. Chiang," *New York Times*, December 1, 1942.
5. Eleanor Roosevelt, *This I Remember* (New York: Harper and Row, 1949), p. 287.
6. *Ibid.*, p. 283.
7. *Madame Chiang Kai-shek: Addresses delivered before the Senate of the United States and the House of Representatives on February 18, 1943, together with other addresses delivered during her visit to the United States...* (Washington: U.S. Government Printing Office, 1943), pp. 3–4.
8. *Ibid.*, pp. 5–7.
9. Nancy MacLennan, "China's First Lady Charms Congress," *New York Times*, February 19, 1943.
10. W.H. Lawrence, "President Tells Mme. Chiang More Arms Will Be Rushed," *New York Times*, February 20, 1943.
11. Winifred Mallon, "Mme. Chiang Asks Arms, Not Food; Says Ammunition Is Great Need," *New York Times*, February 25, 1943.
12. Emma Mills, journal, January 23, 1943.
13. "Mme Chiang Hailed by Crowds in Plea for Help to China," *New York Times*, March 2, 1943.
14. "Alma Mater," in *The First Lady of China: The Historic Visit of Mme. Chiang Kai-shek to the United States* (New York: International Business Machines Corp., 1943), pages unnumbered.
15. "The Crossroads of America," in *The First Lady of China*.
16. "Coast Plans Fete for Mme. Chiang: Visitor Sees 'Food Belt,'" *New York Times*, March 24, 1943.
17. "By the Golden Gate," in *The First Lady of China*.
18. "Land of Sun and Flowers," in *The First Lady of China*.
19. Emma Mills, journal, April 18, 1943.
20. Emma Mills, journal, April 19, 1943.
21. *Ibid.*
22. "Mrs. Chiang to Give 14 Jackets to Women as Mementos of Trip," *New York Herald Tribune*, March 2, 1943.
23. Emma Mills, journal, May 3, 1943.
24. Emma Mills, journal, June 20, 1943.
25. Thomas J. Watson, "Madame Chiang Kai-shek," in *The First Lady of China*.
26. Allene Talmay, "May Ling Soong Chiang," *Vogue*, April 15, 1943, pp. 33–38.
27. Hull, p. 20.

Chapter 19

1. Emma Mills, journal, July 8, 1943.
2. Emma Mills, journal, August 31, 1943.
3. Emma Mills, journal, November 5, 1943.
4. Letter, Emma Mills to Mayling Soong Chiang, January 12, 1944.
5. "Mme. Chiang Saved from Foe by Pilot," *New York Times*, July 11, 1943.
6. Ted Morgan, *FDR: A Biography* (New York: Simon and Schuster, 1985), p. 691.
7. Fenby, *Chiang Kai-shek*, p. 409.
8. Seagrave, *Soong Dynasty, passim* pp. 407–16.
9. Tong, p. 199; "Denials by Chiang at Party Related," *New York Times*, December 1, 1944.
10. Letter, Mayling Soong Chiang to Emma Mills, April 6, 1944.
11. Emma Mills, journal, May 8, 1944; Brooks Atkinson, "Political Reform Expected in China," *New York Times*, May 8, 1944.
12. Seagrave is the source of Wallace's quote, p. 400; Keiji Furuya and Chun-Ming Chang, *Chiang Kai-shek: His Life and Times* (New York: St. John's University, 1981), pp. 799–802. A four-star general, Stilwell (1883–1946) returned to Washington to command the army ground forces in the U.S., and in mid-1945, the Tenth Army in the Pacific, and lastly the Sixth Army at the Presidio, San Francisco. When the Ledo Road route to the old Burma Road was completed in January 1945, Chiang renamed it Stilwell Road to honor his contribution to its building.
13. H.H. Kung (1880–1967) left the Bank of China and public service, and the Far East,

as the war came to an end. He chose New York as the base for his investment empire. "H.H. Kung; Chinese Leader," *New York Times,* August 16, 1967.
  14. Emma Mills, journal, *passim* June 21—August 6, 1944.
  15. Emma Mills, journal, June 29, 1944.
  16. Emma Mills, journal, September 20, 1944; Dave Charnay and Neal Patterson, "Mme. Chiang, Convalescing, Plans China Social Security," *Daily News (NY),* July 19, 1945.
  17. Emma Mills, journal, September 20, 1944.
  18. Emma Mills, journal, October 1, 1944.
  19. Letter, Emma Mills to Lt. Cmdr. De Long Mills, February 11, 1945.
  20. Emma Mills, journal, August 2, 1945.
  21. *Ibid.*; Mme. Chiang's article, "Public Opinion and World Peace," ran in the *Herald Tribune,* September 9, 1945.
  22. *Ibid.*
  23. *Ibid.*
  24. Emma Mills, journal, August 3, 1945.
  25. Emma Mills, journal, August 12, 1945.
  26. Nancy MacLennan, "Mme. Chiang Opens Peace Campaign," *New York Times,* August 15, 1945.
  27. Emma Mills, journal, August 12, 1945.

Chapter 20

  1. Henry R. Lieberman, "Chiang Talks of His Hopes for China," *New York Times Magazine,* October 14, 1945.
  2. Emma Mills, journal, December 1, 1945.
  3. Emma Mills, journal, November 30, 1945; letter, Emma Mills to Mayling Soong Chiang, January 7, 1946.
  4. Diarist Mangle Minthorne Thompson in 1862 married Sylvie Wotton, sister of Emma Wotton De Long. He died at sea during the Civil War. Their only child, Wotton, who lived most of his life with Emma De Long, left his estate to her in 1938. The edited diary has never been published.
  5. "Chiang Thanks Russians," *New York Times,* January 26, 1946.
  6. Letter, Emma Mills to Mayling Soong Chiang, November 11, 1945.
  7. Emma Mills, journal, June 26, 1946.
  8. Emma Mills, journal, February 18, 1947.
  9. Emma Mills, journal, January 8, 1947.
  10. Letter, Mayling Soong Chiang to Emma Mills, June 12, 1946.
  11. Emma Mills, journal, February 18, 1946.
  12. Letter, Emma Mills to Mayling Soong Chiang, August 16, 1946. Randall Gould, an American newspaperman in China as early as the 1920s, perceptively observed in 1946: "China's internal unity and development are dependent upon the achievement of fundamental and sweeping reforms entailing an unprecedented acceptance by Chinese leaders of democratic procedures. Unless the Chinese unite permanently, solidly, and in a way which will bring benefit to the people as a whole, they face tragedies beyond anything they have so far experienced. An early, obvious consequence would be unprecedentedly furious and destructive civil war." Gould, *China in the Sun* (Garden City, N.Y.: Doubleday, 1946), p. 370.
  13. Henry Lieberman, "Mme. Sun—China's 'Conscience,'" *New York Times Magazine,* August 11, 1946; "Sun Fo Urges Coalition," *New York Times,* January 11, 1947.
  14. Emma Mills, journal, June 27, 1947. Robert Lim, an eminent scientist and surgeon, founded the Chinese Red Cross Medical Corps and organized much-needed mobile field units.
  15. "Capital Awaits Madame Chiang, Due Tomorrow," *New York Herald Tribune,* November 20, 1948.
  16. Carl Levin, "Mme. Chiang Sees Marshall, Is 'Encouraged,'" *New York Herald Tribune,* December 4, 1948.
  17. Mary Hornaday, "Mme. Chiang and Americans: Applause Fades in Five Years," *New York Herald Tribune,* December 2, 1948.
  18. Letter, Mayling Soong Chiang to Emma Mills, December 14, 1948.
  19. Emma Mills, journal, July 25, 1949.
  20. Harold B. Hinton, "U.S. Puts Sole Blame on Chiang Regime for Collapse, Holds More Aid Futile," *New York Times,* August 6, 1949.
  21. Emma Mills, journal, August 10, 1949.
  22. Note, Mayling Soong Chiang to Emma Mills, August 9, 1949.
  23. Emma Mills, journal, August 20, 1949. The public affairs program "On Trial" debaters also included Garrad W. Glenn and Samuel M. Lane. Born in Hong Kong, Allen Lau (1912–1995) joined ABMAC in 1945 as an assistant to the executive director. A graduate of Lignan Middle School in Kwangtung and of the University of Chicago, he began his long career at the Bureau in charge of purchasing and transporting vital medical supplies for post-war China. Later, his responsibilities included coordinating programs for the training of Chinese doctors in medical research.
  24. Chiang's other son, the adopted Chiang Wei-kuo, played a very inconspicuous part in China history. Dai Jitao, a KMT comrade during Chiang's early stay in Japan, "fathered" this child with a Japanese. She later begged Chiang to adopt him when Dai, who had married, did not wish to acknowledge him. Rumors persist that Wei-kuo was Chiang's own

offspring. In the 1930s he trained with the German Third Reich army, in the civil war led a Nationalist armored unit, and later as a lieutenant general commanded the Taiwanese Military Staff College. See Jonathan Fenby, *Chiang Kai-shek: China's Generalissimo and the Nation He Lost* (New York: Carroll and Graf, 2003).
 25. David Sentner, "Mme. Chiang Plans Return," *New York Journal-American,* September 7, 1949.
 26. Mayling S. Chiang, "The Text of Mme. Chiang's Farewell," *New York Times,* January 9, 1950.
 27. "Mme. Chiang Asks Advisers from U.S.," *New York Times,* January 21, 1950.
 28. Emma Mills, "Executive Secretary Reports on Visit to Taiwan (Formosa)," *ABMAC Bulletin,* 2nd and 3rd quarters, 1950.
 29. Letter, Emma Mills to Mayling Soong Chiang, May 25, 1950.
 30. Letter, Emma Mills to Mayling Soong Chiang, June 22, 1950.

Chapter 21

 1. Marguerite Higgins, "Miss Higgins Interviews Chiang," *New York Herald Tribune,* October 15, 1951.
 2. Conversation between Mayling Soong Chiang and Thomas A. De Long, Shinlin, Taiwan, September 8, 1972.
 3. "Speaking of Pictures ... Madame Chiang, far from home, paints lovely landscapes of her native land," *Life,* October 13, 1952; Madame Chiang Kai-shek, *Paintings,* volume 1 (Taipei: Shih-ling Studio, 1958).
 4. Emma Mills, journal, March 17, 1953.
 5. Emma Mills, journal, March 21, 1953.
 6. *Ibid.*
 7. Emma Mills, journal, February 3, 1955.
 8. Mayling Soong Chiang, *Selected Speeches: 1958–1959* (Taipei: Office of the President, 1959).
 9. Emma Mills, journal, February 2, 1959.
 10. Emma Mills, journal, March 31, 1959.
 11. Emma Mills, journal, August 14, 1958.
 12. Emma Mills, journal, September 17, 1958.
 13. Emma Mills, journal, September 25, 1958.
 14. Emma Mills, journal, December 15, 1958.
 15. Emma Mills, journal, December 28, 1958.
 16. Emma Mills, journal, May 18, 1959.
 17. Emma Mills, journal, October 9, 1959.
 18. Emma Mills, journal, March 15, 1960.
 19. Emma Mills, journal, June 16, 1962.
 20. John W. Finney, "Out of the Past—Mrs. Chiang," *New York Times,* September 12, 1965;

Alfred Friendly, Jr., "Mystery Shrouds Mrs. Chiang Here," *New York Times,* April 17, 1966.
 21. Emma Mills, journal, October 16, 1965.
 22. Emma Mills, journal, March 15, 1959.
 23. Emma Mills, journal, November 24, 1965.
 24. Gail Migdal, "Mme. Chiang Creates Image of Gentility During Speech," *Wellesley College News,* December 10, 1965; Madame Chiang Kai-shek, *Selected Speeches: 1965–1966* (Taipei: China Publishing Co., 1968), pp. 22–33.
 25. Emma Mills, journal, December 2, 1965.
 26. Madame Chiang Kai-shek, *Selected Speeches,* p. 174.
 27. Emma Mills, journal, January 1, 1966.
 28. Emma Mills, journal, May 8, 1966.

Chapter 22

 1. Letter, Emma Mills to Mayling Soong Chiang, March 10, 1968.
 2. "300 at Services for T.A. Soong," *San Francisco Chronicle,* March 15, 1969.
 3. Henry S. Bradsher, "Chiang, Last of Big Four Allied Leaders, Dies at 87," *Washington Star,* April 6, 1975.
 4. Letter, Mayling Soong Chiang to Emma Mills, May 13, 1975.
 5. Emma Mills, journal, October 19, 1975.
 6. Emma Mills, journal, April 13, 1976.
 7. Emma Mills, journal, May 4, 1966.
 8. Letter, Emma Mills to Mayling Soong Chiang, March 10, 1968.
 9. Interview, Allen B. Cohen, April 4, 2006. CPC is now called the Chinese-American Planning Council to reflect a widespread Chinese population beyond Manhattan's Chinatown.
 10. Letter, Emma Mills to Mayling Soong Chiang, November 2, 1968.
 11. Letter, Emma Mills to Thomas De Long, April 20, 1979.
 12. Emma Mills, journal, July 30, 1977.
 13. Pearl Buck (1892–1973) received a Pulitzer Prize for *The Good Earth,* a novel of flood, famine and pestilence in rural China that had little or no appeal for Mayling. Buck's words, "There are no experts on China, only varying degrees of ignorance," perhaps alienated her, too.
 14. Interview, Joseph Kissane, March 23, 2005.
 15. "Emma D. Mills Is Dead; Headed Chinese Panels," *New York Times,* August 28, 1987; "Emma De Long Mills; aided China," *Chicago Tribune,* August 28, 1987. Her brother, De Long Mills (1897–1972) retired from the U.S. Navy at the close of World War II and settled in Virginia Beach. He died without issue.

16. Jonathan Spence, "The Clan That Changed China," *New York Times Book Review* (*The Soong Dynasty*), March 17, 1985; Advertisement, "A Solemn Statement Refuting Distortions of Modern Chinese History in THE SOONG DYNASTY," *New York Times,* May 1, 1985; Donald G. Gillin, *Falsifying China's History: The Case of Sterling Seagrave's "The Soong Dynasty"* (Stanford, Cal.: Hoover Institution, 1986).

17. "Madame Chiang Says: 'See Ye to It' Risky Policy for Statesmen," *Free China Journal,* December 15, 1986.

18. Susan Chira, "Taiwan President Will Also Head Party," *New York Times,* July 9, 1988.

19. Francis X. Clines, "Latest Taiwan Uproar Brings Back Old Hand," *New York Times,* July 24, 1995.

20. Nadine Brozan, "Chronicle: Madame Chiang Kai-shek, nearing 99, visits the Metropolitan Museum," *New York Times,* March 12, 1996.

21. Mark Feeney, "Madame Chiang Kai-shek, 106, at center of China's tumult," *Boston Globe,* October 24, 2003; "'Brains of China' dies in New York," *Calcutta Telegraph,* October 25, 2003. Mme. Chiang at 106 was not the last surviving member of the class of 1917. Eleanor Russell Reycroft, a championship golfer into her 90s, died in Lexington, Mass., at 109 (*Boston Globe,* November 7, 2004).

22. Joseph Berger, "An Epitaph for Madame Chiang Kai-shek: 'Mama.'" *New York Times,* October 30, 2003.

Epilogue

1. Telegram, Mayling Soong Chiang to Emma Mills (c/o Thomas De Long), December 1974.

2. Letter, Emma Mills to Mayling Soong Chiang, December 15, 1974.

Bibliography

Papers

The Emma De Long Mills papers are in the possession of the author.

Books

Acheson, Dean. *Present at the Creation: My Years in the State Department.* New York: Norton, 1969.
Berkov, Robert. *Strong Man of China: The Story of Chiang Kai-shek.* Boston: Houghton Mifflin, 1938.
Byrd, Martha. *Chennault: Giving Wings to the Tiger.* Tuscaloosa: University of Alabama Press, 1987.
Chang, Iris. *The Rape of Nanking: The Forgotten Holocaust of World War II.* New York: Basic Books, 1997.
Chang, Jung. *Wild Swans: Three Daughters of China.* New York: Anchor Books, 1991.
_____, and Jon Halliday. *Mao: The Unknown Story.* New York: Alfred A. Knopf, 2005.
Chennault, Anna. *The Education of Anna.* New York: Times Books, 1980.
Chiang Kai-shek, Madame. *China in Peace and War: Selections from the Writings of May-ling Soong Chiang.* Shanghai: Kelly and Walsh, Ltd., 1940.
_____. *China Shall Rise Again.* New York: Harper Bros., 1941.
_____. *Conversations with Mikhail Borodin.* Privately printed. Undated.
_____. *Selected Speeches: 1958–1959.* Taipei: Office of the President, 1959.
_____. *Selected Speeches: 1965–1966.* Taipei: China Publishing Co., 1968.
_____. *The Sure Victory.* Westwood, N.J.: Fleming H. Revell, 1955.
_____. *We Chinese Women: Speeches and Writings During the First United Nations Year (February 12, 1942–November 16, 1942).* New York: John Day, 1943.
Chu, Samuel C., ed. *Madame Chiang Kai-shek and Her China.* Norwalk, Conn.: EastBridge, 2005
Clark, Elmer T. *The Chiangs of China.* New York: Abingdon-Cokesbury, 1943.
Cray, Ed. *General of the Army: George C. Marshall, Soldier and Statesman.* New York: Norton, 1970.

Crozier, Brian, with Eric Chou. *The Man Who Lost China: The First Full Biography of Chiang Kai-shek.* New York: Charles Scribner's Sons, 1976.
De Long, Emma Wotton. *Explorer's Wife.* New York: Dodd, Mead, 1938.
DeLong, Thomas A. *The De Longs of New York and Brooklyn: A Huguenot Family Portrait.* Southport, Conn.: Sasco Associates, 1972.
Eastman, Lloyd E., ed. *Chiang Kai-shek's Secret Past: The Memoir of Ch'en Chiej-ju, His Second Wife.* Boulder, Colo.: Westview Press, 1993.
Edwards, Lee. *Missionary for Freedom: The Life and Times of Walter Judd.* New York: Paragon House, 1990.
Elson, Robert T. *Time Inc.: The Intimate History of a Publishing Enterprise 1923–1941.* New York: Atheneum, 1968.
Epstein, Israel. *Woman in World History: Life and Times of Soong Ching Ling (Mme. Sun Yatsen).* Beijing: New World Press, 1993.
Fenby, Jonathan. *Chiang Kai-shek: China's Generalissimo and the Nation He Lost.* New York: Carroll and Graf, 2003.
Furuya, Keiji. *Chiang Kai-shek: His Life and Times.* New York: St. John's University, 1981.
Glasscock, Jean, gen. ed. *Wellesley College 1875–1975: A Century of Women.* Wellesley, Mass.: Wellesley College, 1975.
Gould, Randall. *China in the Sun.* Garden City, N.Y.: Doubleday, 1946.
Gunther, John. *Inside Asia.* New York: Harper, 1939.
Hahn, Emily. *China to Me: A Partial Autobiography.* Philadelphia: Blakiston Co., 1944.
_____. *The Soong Sisters.* Garden City, N.Y.: Doubleday Doran, 1941.
Hauser, Ernest O. *Shanghai: City for Sale.* New York: Harcourt, Brace, 1940.
Hodges, Graham Russell Gao. *Anna May Wong: From Laundryman's Daughter to Hollywood Legend.* New York: Palgrave Macmillan, 2004.
Hull, Helen. *Mayling Soong Chiang.* New York: Coward-McCann, 1943.
Hutchings, Graham. *Modern China: A Guide to a Century of Change.* Cambridge: Harvard University Press, 2001.
Jessup, John K. (ed). *The Ideas of Henry Luce.* New York: Atheneum, 1969.
Larrabbe, Eric. *Commander in Chief: Franklin Delano Roosevelt, His Lieutenants, and Their War.* New York: Harper and Row, 1987.
MacMillan, Margaret. *Paris 1919.* New York: Random House, 2002.
Meng, Chih. *Chinese American Understanding: A Sixty-Year Search.* New York: China Institute, 1981.
Morris, Ramona, and Desmond Morris. *Men and Pandas.* New York: McGraw-Hill, 1966.
Morris, Sylvia Jukes. *Rage for Fame: The Ascent of Clare Boothe Luce.* New York: Random House, 1997.
Neal, Steve. *Dark Horse: A Biography of Wendell Willkie.* Garden City, N.Y.: 1984.
Nicolay, Helen. *China's First Lady.* New York: Appleton-Century, 1944.
Peters, Charles. *Five Days in Philadelphia: The Amazing "We Want Willkie!" Convention of 1940 and How It Freed FDR to Save the Western World.* New York: Public Affairs, 2005.
Phillips, Cabell. *The Truman Presidency: The History of a Triumphant Succession.* New York: MacMillan, 1966.
Pu Yi, Henry. *The Last Manchu.* New York: Putnam's Sons, 1967.

Robottom, John. *Twentieth Century China*. New York: Putnam's Sons: New York, 1971.
The Rookie: 1917–1942. (25th Reunion Book of the Class of 1917). Wellesley, Mass.: Wellesley College, 1942.
Roosevelt, Eleanor. *This I Remember*. New York: Harper, 1949.
Samson, Jack. *Chennault*. New York: Doubleday, 1987.
Schurmann, Franz and Orville Schell. *Republican China: Nationalism, War, and the Rise of Communism, 1911–1949*. New York: Vintage Books, 1967.
Seagrave, Sterling. *The Soong Dynasty*. New York: Harper and Row, 1985.
Smedley, Agnes. *Battle Hymn of China*. New York: Alfred A. Knopf, 1943.
Spence, Jonathan. *The Search for Modern China*. New York: Norton, 1990.
Spencer, Cornelia. *Three Sisters: The Story of the Soong Family of China*. New York: Junior Literary Guild and John Day Co., 1939.
Sues, Ilona Ralf. *Shark's Fins and Millet*. Boston: Little Brown, 1944.
Swanberg, W.A. *Luce and His Empire*. New York: Scribner, 1972.
Tong, Wellington, ed. *Chiang Kai-shek: Soldier and Statesman*. Shanghai: China Publishing Co., 1937.
_____. *China Handbook: 1937–1945* (with 1946 supplement). New York: Macmillan, 1947.
_____. *Dateline: China—The Beginning of China's Press Relations with the World*. New York: Rockport Press, 1950.
Tong, Wellington, with Sun Fo. *President Chiang Kai-shek: His Life Story in Pictures*. Taipei: Government Information Office, Republic of China, 1972.
Tuchman, Barbara W. *Stilwell and the American Experience in China, 1911–45*. New York: Macmillan, 1971.
Watt, John R. *A Friend in Deed: ABMAC and the Republic of China, 1937–1987*. New York: American Bureau for Medical Aid to China, 1992.
Webster, Donovan. *The Burma Road*. New York: Farrar, Straus and Giroux, 2003.
Whelan, Russell. *The Flying Tigers: The Story of the American Volunteer Group*. New York: Viking Press, 1942.
Willkie, Wendell. *One World*. New York: Simon and Schuster, 1943.

Periodicals

Amsden, Roger. "Madame Chiang Had Long-time Ties to NH Lakes Region." *New Hampshire Union Leader* (Manchester), October 25, 2003.
Bennett, James W. "Modern Chiang Kai-shek and Old Chang Tso-lin." *New York Times*, June 10, 1928.
Billingham, A.J. "Rearing China's Orphans." *New York Times*, August 2, 1936.
Bullitt, William C. "A Report to the American People on China." *Life*, October 13, 1947.
Chiang, Mayling Soong. "An Open Letter to My Alma Mater." *Wellesley Magazine*, June 1938.
_____. "Democracy Reaps the Whirlwind." *Liberty*, December 21, 1940.
_____. "Fighting Communists in China." *The Forum*, February 1935.
_____. "Public Opinion and World Peace." *New York Herald Tribune*, September 9, 1945.
_____. "What Religion Means to Me." *The Forum*, March 1934.

Cohen, Paul A. "Between China and America: The Career of Madame Chiang Kai-shek." *Wellesley Magazine* 88, no. 2 (winter 2004).
De Long, Thomas A. "What One Has to Do." *Carson McCullers Society Newsletter* no. 4 (2001).
Denson, John. "Madame Chiang's New Role in the Orient." *Colliers,* June 2, 1951.
Durdin, F. Tillman. "Worth Twenty Divisions." *New York Times Magazine.* September 14, 1941.
Elliston, H.B. "China's No.1 White Boy." *Saturday Evening Post,* March 19, 1938.
Gibbons, Herbert Adams. "Strong Chinese Forces Arrayed Against Unity." *New York Times,* June 8, 1930.
Hahn, Emily. "Notes on Madame Chiang." *American Mercury,* September 1944.
Harrington, Jean. "Madame Chiang Kai-shek (Meil-ling Soong) '17." *Wellesley Magazine,* February 1938.
Hauser, Ernest O. "China's Soong: Mysterious Brother-in-Law Finds Funds to Keep China Fighting." *Life,* March 24, 1941.
Hu, Susan. "Mayling Soong and Emma De Long Mills: A Chinese-American Friendship." *Geneasia* (Wellesley College Asian/Asian American Magazine) 8, no. 2 (winter 2004).
Kuhn, Irene Corbally. "Shanghai: The Way It Was." *Los Angeles Times Magazine*, part 2, October 19, 1986.
Lieberman, Henry. "Chiang Talks of His Hopes for China." *New York Times Magazine,* October 14, 1945.
_____. "Madame Sun—China's 'Conscience.'" *New York Times Magazine,* August 11, 1946.
Luce, Henry. "China: To the Mountains." *Life,* June 30, 1941.
"Madame Chiang, far from home, paints lovely landscapes of her native land." *Life,* October 13, 1952.
"Man and Wife of the Year." *Time,* January 3, 1938.
McNaughton, Frank. "Mme. Chiang in the U.S. Capitol." *Life,* March 8, 1943.
Migdal, Gail. "Mme. Chiang Creates Image of Gentility During Speech." *Wellesley College News,* December 10, 1965.
"Mme Chiang Tells of Her War Duties." *New York Times*, July 10, 1938.
Mills, Emma De Long. "Inconclusive Dialogue." *Asia Magazine,* May 1935.
Peffer, Nathaniel. "Threats of Japan Find China Divided." *New York Times,* November 24, 1935.
Porter, Thurston. "The Chiangs and China's Intricate Family Life." *New York Daily News,* August 27, 1944.
Senter, David. "Mme. Chiang Plans Return." *New York Journal-American.* September 7, 1949.
Sokolsky, George E. "China's Warrior-President Outwits His Foes By Speed." *New York Times,* June 28, 1932.

Index

Abend, Hallett 125
Acheson, Alice 200–201, 215
Acheson, Dean 200
Adams, Ruth 174
Ainsworth, Eloise 8
Ainsworth, Malcolm 162
Ainsworth, W.N. 174
Aldrich, Lucy 58
American Bureau for Medical Aid to China (ABMAC) 3, 106, 109, 111, 125, 126, 128, 130, 133, 135, 139, 142, 147, 152, 172, 194–196, 198, 200, 202, 204, 205, 209, 210, 215, 216, 218, 225, 233
American-China Policy Association 196, 233
American Committee for Non-participation in Japanese Aggression 121
Armstrong, George 216
Atkinson, Brooks 182

Baldwin, Hanson 104
Balzac 184
Baruch, Bernard 174
Bates, Katherine Lee 23, 236
Bates, Sylvia Chatfield 100
Benchley, Robert 171
Bernstein, Leo 215
Bess, Dorothy Gould 70, 79
Blaine, James G. 139
Borodin, Mikhail 56, 71
Bowron, Fletcher 171
Brown, Florence Pomeroy 79
Buck, Pearl 33, 159, 225, 243
Burke, Margie 7
Burma Road 133, 134–136, 138, 150
Byrnes, Reno Reynolds 109

Cagney, James 171
Calkins, Mary Whiton 23, 24
Calpin, Eunice Higgins 109, 137
Calpin, Raymond 137
Carr, Julian 9
Chang Hsueh-liang 88, 92, 96
Chang Tso-lin 51, 52, 66, 67, 70, 87

Charlton, Ruth 173
Ch'en Chieh-ju (Jennie) 74, 75, 80, 158, 183
Chen, Eugene 49, 51, 53, 70, 74, 237
Chen, Lilyan Chao Foo 210
Chen, Pearl 143, 159
Chen Chih-mai 210, 226
Chen Chiung-ming 52, 55
Cheng Pao-nan 106, 107, 141
Chennault, Claire 101, 102, 144, 201
Chiang, Mayling Soong (Mme): acknowledges value of Mills letters 3; acquires New York co-op 219; appears in early sound newsreel 84; assassination attempt 82; attends Cairo Conference 179–180; attends 1988 Nationalist Party convention 228; auto accident 106–107; becomes permanent resident of New York 223; birth 5, 230; books published 56, 113, 121; to Brazil and New York (1944–45) 183–192; brings Flying Tigers into place 102; to Burma 151; to Canada 174; in Canton with Suns 40, 41; Capitol Hill reunion (1995) 230; celebrates holidays in Shanghai 13, 14; Chungking bombings 123–125, 134; clothes 12, 48, 139, 176; death and tributes 230–231; death of father 19, 20; death of mother 82; dismay over U.S. isolationism, neutrality 113, 127; earliest education 5, 34; early illnesses and ailments 14, 20, 21, 36, 56; early writings 21, 22, 97, 98, 99; Eleanor Roosevelt as role model 99, 100; engagement announced 25; enjoyment of books 22, 28; 50th birthday of Gen. Chiang 91; as First Lady in Nanking 78–82; forms Officers' Moral Endeavor Association 80; gift of pandas to Bronx Zoo 145, 146; "homesick" for America 15, 16, 23; importance of religion in life 42, 80, 97, 98; to India 150; invites Emma Mills to China 44, 45; journey home from college 5, 9, 10; lauds Mills' life 233; learns to drive a car 188; legacy summarized 232; at Macon, GA's Wesleyan College for Women 7–9, 174, 216; magazine

subscriptions 12; marital rumors, gossip 157–158, 181–182; marriage ceremonies 75–77; medical regimen in New York (1952–53) 208; member of Legislative Yuan 82; at Nationalist stronghold, Taiwan (Formosa) 204; organizes women's New Life Corps 119, 120; profile of father 1–2; promotes air travel 91; promotes New Life Movement 80, 81, 105; proposal of marriage by Chiang 72, 73; purchases furnishings for Kungs' estate 211–212; radio broadcasts 112, 125, 126, 132, 133, 148, 153, 203; relations with Wendell Willkie 154–156, 173; reunion gifts at Wellesley 114, 115, 215; Roosevelt White House guest (1943) 159–161; as Secretary of Air Force 101, 104; seeks a profession 38, 39; seeks aide from American friends 107, 110–111; seeks postwar aid in U.S. (1948–50) 199–204; Shanghai community activities 13, 15, 17, 18, 29, 30, 34, 35, 42; Sian kidnapping of Chiang 92–96; Soong residences in Shanghai 12, 20; starts Children of the Revolution school 80, 98; studies Chinese language and literature 37; suitors 10, 12, 33, 41, 58, 72; thoughts and outlook on marriage 15, 16, 17, 31, 32, 33, 54, 58, 72, 77; Time-Life coverage 108, 117, 139; travel to trouble spots 89, 90; U.S. "homecoming" (1942–43) 158–176; U.S. lecture tour (1958–59) 211; war orphans project 111, 112, 117, 126, 128, 129, 221; wartime reunion with sisters 131; to Washington and Johnson White House (1965) 215; as Wellesley student 23–27; Y.W.C.A. leadership role 13, 15, 17, 34
Chiang Ching-kuo 203, 222, 223
Chiang Kai-shek 2, 3, 71–223*passim*
Chiang Wei-kuo 242
China Institute 184, 200, 209, 216, 228, 233
Chinatown Planning Council 3, 224, 233, 243
Chou, Marylin Chu 224
Chou En-lai 92, 154
Chu, Farn B. 106, 109, 224
Chu, Mary 106
Churchill, Sarah 179
Churchill, Winston 171, 173, 178–180, 188, 193, 215
Clapp, Margaret 208, 218
Clark, Elmer T. 78
Clark, Grover 63
Clarke, Amelia 211
Co Tui, Frank 109, 126, 195
Cohen, Allen B. 224, 225
Committee of One Million 210, 223
Connally, John 163
Coolidge, Calvin 63
Cowles, Gardner 155, 156
Croke, Vicki C. 146
Crosby, Bing 171

Dai Jitao 242
Davies, Joseph E. 197
Davis, John W. 63, 197
Dean, Cecilia 226
Dean, Kitty 226
De Long, Emma Wotton (Ma) 1, 2, 26, 31, 45, 56, 59, 64, 69, 116, 117, 137, 140
De Long, George Washington 1, 116
Dewey, Thomas E. 135, 166, 183, 199
Dole, Bob 230
Donald, William H. 90, 93–96, 106, 107, 190, 238
Doolittle, James 171
Douglas, Paul 205
Durdin, F. Tillman 143

Elizabeth, Queen 186
Ellsberg, Edward 116
Ensign, Loring 8
Erickson, Helen 209

Farley, Miriam 194
Fenby, Jonathan 155
Feng Yu-hsiang 66, 67, 70, 71, 88
Ferris, Gil 84, 137
Ferris, Mandy *see* Manderville, Agnes
Ferris, Mary 84
Ferris, Rita 84
Fiske, John 235
Fontaine, Joan 188

Gannett, Lewis 72
Garside, B.A. 140
Garvey, Dorothy 185, 190, 202, 211, 213, 224
Geist, Rebecca 106
Goodman, Benny 118
Gould, Randall 242
Graham, David 235
Green, Mildred Smith 109, 208
Greenberg, Syd 149
Gregersen, Magnus 202
Gugel, Marjorie 8

Hahn, Emily 81, 113
Harkness, Ruth 146
Harrington, Frank 183
Hart, Sophie C. 109
Hicks, Margaret De Forest 69
Higgins, Marguerite 207
Hirohito 146
Hitler, Adolf 130
Hoskins, Carrie Bowbeer 109
Howard, Roy 87
Hsu Shih-chang 51
Hu Shih 152, 153
Hull, Cordell 100, 102, 128, 147
Hull, Helen 24, 82
Humphreys, George 215
Huston, Walter 171
Hutchins, Robert 169

Index

James, Henry 32
Johnson, Lady Bird 215
Johnson, Lyndon B. 215
Johnson, Nelson 108, 140
Johnston, Anne Fellows 36
Johnstone, William C. 194
Judd, Walter 205

Kelly, Edward 167
Kennedy, Joseph 185, 186
Kiem Wen Yu 121
Kipling, Rudyard 233
Kirkham, Alice DeLisle 26
Kissane, Joseph 226, 227
Knowland, William F. 205
Kohlberg, Alfred 186, 194, 196, 210
Koo, Wellington 68, 171, 199
Kuang, Z. 81
Kuhn, Irene 212, 231
Kung, Ailing 7, 21, 29, 34, 37, 42, 45, 52, 55, 58, 59, 67, 70, 74, 75, 100, 105, 112, 131–133, 174, 183, 184, 186, 221, 222
Kung, David 21, 189, 213, 216
Kung, Debra Paget 7
Kung, H.H. 21, 51, 52, 55, 58, 59, 67, 68, 70, 74, 75, 93, 132, 138, 155, 157, 181, 186, 189, 190, 208, 221, 241
Kung, Jeannette 34, 158–160, 184, 216
Kung, Louis 7, 159, 171, 183, 184, 186, 189
Kung, Pauline 21, 52

La Guardia, Fiorello 139, 165
Landis, Kenesaw Mountain 169
Lattimore, Owen 144
Lau, Allen 202, 218, 242
Lee Teng-hui 91
Lehman, Herbert 140
Lester, Lucy 216
Li, Peter 10
Li Yuan-hong 58
Lightner, Margaret Griffin (Dickey) 19, 119, 129, 188, 201, 230
Lightner, Milton 119
Lim, Robert 184, 198, 242
Lin Sen 179
Lin Yutang 104, 105
Lindbergh, Anne 83
Lindbergh, Charles 83
Liu Chi-wen 72
Loeb, John 200
Lovett, Robert A. 200
Luce, Clare Boothe 2, 139, 140, 151, 163, 185
Luce, Henry 2, 108, 109, 174, 184–186, 200

MacArthur, Douglas 152
Macaulay, Thomas B. 22, 236
Magruder, John 144
Mandeville, Agnes (Mandy) 18, 44, 45, 56–58, 63, 84, 137
Mao Fu-mei 72, 74

Mao Tse-tung 88, 179, 193, 194, 198, 200, 202, 218
Marshall, George C. 198, 200, 201
May Fourth movement 29
Mayling Soong Foundation 153, 178, 194
McAfee, Mildred 117, 167, 176, 189
McCandless, Marian Jones 82
McCormick, Cyrus 169
McCullers, Carson 100, 137
McCullers, Reeves 137
McKeag, Helen 45
McNarmara, Robert 215
McTyeire, Holland 9
Meyer, Sophie 109
Mills, De Long 10, 44, 85, 140, 147, 243
Mills, Sylvie De Long 10, 37, 48, 69, 85
Mills, Walter 10, 37, 38, 48, 66, 85
Moore, Elizabeth Luce 186, 216
Morgan, Ted 180
Moses, Harriet 7
Mountbatten, Louis 179
Mydans, Carl 139
Mydans, Shelley 139

Nehru, Pandit 150, 178
Nicholson, Betty 24
Nixon, Richard 223
North China Language School 59, 62, 63

Oka, Kenneth 213

Pandit, Chandralehka 178
Paxton, Shirley Lightner 230
Peebles, Harry 137
Peffer, Nathaniel 202
Pendleton, Ellen 27, 36, 37
Peron, Eva 109
Petrillo, James C. 169
Petrov, Appolio 193
Pickford, Mary 171
Porter, Caroline J. 109
Pretzfelder, Rosella Peck 109, 209
Pu Chieh 59–61
Pu Yi 59, 83, 88

Rainer, Luise 133
Rayburn, Sam 162–163
Reycroft, Eleanor Russell 244
Rice, Isaac 10
Rinden, Arthur 8
Robinson, James Hervey 43
Rockefeller, John D., Jr. 58
Rogers, Edith Nourse 163–164
Roosevelt, Eleanor 2, 99, 125, 133, 140, 149, 158–161, 164, 179, 188, 189, 200
Roosevelt, Elliott 190
Roosevelt, Franklin D. 2, 121, 123, 129, 135, 136, 138, 146, 148, 153–155, 159–161, 164–165, 171, 172, 179–183, 188, 193, 200
Roosevelt, James 140

Rosinger, Lawrence 194
Rossi, Angelo 170
Rubinstein, Artur 146
Rusk, Dean 205
Russell, Richard 216

Saltonstall, Leverett 166, 167
Schurman, Jacob Gould 58
Seagrave, Sterling 228
Selznick, David O. 171
Sentner, David 203
Shah, Konsin C. 233
Shao, Irene 209, 210, 226
Sheldon, Harriet 115
Sheldon, Polly 115
Shelton, Cornell 158, 178
Shepherd, George W. 120
Sian kidnapping 92–96, 98
Simon, Paul 230, 231
Smith, Alexander H. 205
Smith, Alfred E. 145
Soong, Ailing *see* Kung, Ailing
Soong, Charlie 1, 9, 14, 19, 81
Soong, Chingling *see* Sun, Mme. Yat-sen
Soong, Ni Kwei-tseng 9, 12, 13, 14, 17, 19, 20, 21, 38, 39, 41, 46–48, 73–75, 81, 82, 97, 98, 100
Soong, T.A. 12, 21, 70, 170, 181, 219, 221, 222
Soong, T.L. 12, 132, 181
Soong, T.V. 5, 9, 26, 37, 47, 52, 53, 70–72, 74, 76, 81, 82, 93, 94, 112, 132, 150, 156, 157, 175, 181, 197, 198, 200, 216, 222
Stalin, Joseph 195
Stevens, Helen 184, 195, 204
Stilwell, Joseph 151, 179, 180–182, 201, 241
Stimson, Henry 88
Storer, George B. 213
Sues, Ilona Ralf 142, 143
Sun Fo 197
Sun Yat-sen 2, 13, 29, 40, 47, 51, 53, 55, 56, 64, 65, 67, 68, 71, 72, 74, 75, 78, 127, 170, 193
Sun Yat-sen, Mme. 7, 9, 13, 29, 34, 40, 45, 52, 53, 55, 64, 67, 68, 69, 72, 74, 110, 112, 131, 132, 174, 181, 197, 202. 228

Taft, Robert 135
Taylor, Myron C. 133
Tee-Van, John 146
Temple, Shirley 171
Thompson, Mangle Minthorne 242
Thompson, Wotton (aka Wotton Minthorne) 242
Tobin, Maurice 167
Tompkins, Daniel D. 154
Tong, Annabel 59, 61
Tong, Hollington 181
Toscanini, Arturo 183

True, Clarence 10
True Light Middle School of Hong Kong 210, 221, 225, 233
Truman, Harry S. 188, 198, 199, 200, 206, 207, 215
Tsao Kun 58
Tuck, Joseph 126
Tufts, Edith 23
Tuthill, Ruth 39
Tzu Hsi, Dowager Empress 5, 77

United China Relief 109, 139, 140, 147, 152, 166, 182, 184, 216
United Nations organization 154, 162, 170, 172, 191

Van Arnam, Cornelia 209
Van Nest, Ruth Peel 135
Vandenberg, Arthur 109

Wagenaar, Bernard 137
Wagner, Augusta 109
Wallace, DeWitt 133
Wallace, Henry 182
Walter, James 8
Wan Bing Chung 5
Wang, C.T. 84, 102
Wang Ching-wei 125, 127, 130, 131, 134, 240
Warren, Earl 170
Washington, George 165
Washington, Martha 165
Watson, Thomas J. 133, 175
Wavell, Archibald 151
Wayne, John 155
Wedemeyer, Albert 201
Wegenaar, Irene 137
Wei, Joseph 109
Wei Li-huang 149
Wellesley College 2, 19, 23–27, 28, 36, 37, 41, 62, 66, 83, 84, 97, 106, 109, 110, 114–117, 176, 201, 208, 213, 215, 218
Wesleyan College for Women 7, 8, 9, 70, 71, 174, 216
White, William Allen 169
Wilhelmina, Queen 161
William, Maurice 194
Willkie, Wendell 2, 135, 136, 140, 153–158, 166, 172, 173, 183, 200
Wong, Anna May 238
Wotton, James Avery 31
Wotton, Marguerite 117
Wotton, Sylvie 242
Wright, Frank Lloyd 57
Wu Pei-fu 52, 66, 88

Yang Hu-cheng 92, 94, 96
Yen, W.W. 51
Yu Tsune-chi 29
Yuan Shih-kai 166

www.ingramcontent.com/pod-product-compliance
Lightning Source LLC
Chambersburg PA
CBHW051215300426
44116CB00006B/586